To Kim

Best Rogards

[signature]

Kim,

Best Wishes

[signature]

50

PHABULOUS
PHILLIES

by Skip Clayton
and Jeff Moeller

Sports Publishing Inc.
www.SportsPublishingInc.com

Layout and design: Erin J. Sands
Dust jacket design: Julie L. Denzer
Coordinating editor: Claudia Mitroi
Copy editor: David Hamburg

Photos courtesy of Larry Shenk, Philadelphia Phillies, Ed Dolan, Rich Detwiler, Jerry
Stark, Liz Ennis, Ruly Carpenter, Baseball Hall of Fame, and AP/Wide World Photos

ISBN: 1-58261-224-2
Library of Congress Number: 00-00-100027

Sports Publishing Inc.
www.SportsPublishingInc.com

To the memory of my dad, who I still miss and took me in 1948 to see the Phillies for the first, but not the last, time, and to my mother, who still follows the Phillies.

My parents were there for me when I was growing up and always taught me the difference between right and wrong, and to my wife, Joanne, who is a tower of strength and is always there for me when I need her, especially during the hours that it took to write this book. I love them all.

— Skip Clayton

This book is dedicated to the memory of my father, Carl Moeller, who supported me through all of my ventures and continues to be my primary inspiration, and to my daughter, Brooke, who keeps my world bright.

— Jeff Moeller

Table

of contents

Acknowledgments

Thanks to all the people who were interviewed and who helped make this book possible. Thanks to Larry Shenk and the Phillies, who helped set up interviews and provided photos for the book. Thanks go to Ed Dolan of Ed Dolan Jr.'s Baseball Fanatic in Gloucester, New Jersey. I would also like to thank Rich Detwiler of Pennridge Sportscards in Sellersville, Pennsylvania; Jerry Stark of Philadelphia; Liz Ennis of Huntington Valley; and Ruly Carpenter, each of whom supplied photos for the book. Special thanks to Bob Vetrone for reading the stories and giving his input.

— *S k i p C l a y t o n*

Acknowledgments

This book was also made possible through the support of my mother, Helen, who supports me in family and business; Danielle, who always is there; Danny and Marie Romano, who always make me feel at home; Rob Heffelfinger, Chuck Hixson and Jim Lyons, who are good friends and business associates; Randy Miller, who always provides the proper perspective; Jack Scheuer, Bob Vetrone Sr. and Dan Baker, who have guided me through the years; Don Bostrom, who gave me direction and provided boundless enthusiasm; Rosemary Rahn, who has provided me with numerous photos over the years and great support; and Traci Cyr, Jerry Gross, Joe Kramer, Tony Koury and the Notre Dame girls' basketball team, who have taught me how sports and life can intertwine and result in success and joy.

Special thanks to Rob Roth for his tireless and excellent work in all our ventures.

—Jeff Moeller

Foreword

by Harry Kalas

T his book, *50 Phabulous Phillies* is a treasure, a keepsake for
any Phillies fan of any age. We call Skip Clayton "Memory
Lane" because of his uncanny recollection of Phillies teams
and heroes of the past, especially the 1950 Whiz Kid team. Jeff Moeller's
love of baseball and the Phillies has been
with him since childhood. Together, they
have interviewed those who have embla-
zoned their names in Phillies baseball history. This book brings to life those men
who have shaped and continue to shape
the history of Phillies baseball. If you are
a Phillies fan—or simply a baseball fan—
I'm sure you will find it a fascinating read.

1980 World Series Champions

50

PHABULOUS
PHILLIES

One

Grover Cleveland Alexander

Last Phillies 30-Game Winner

by Jeff Moeller

He is one of the greatest Phillies pitchers of all time, as well as one of the most liberated.

Grover Cleveland Alexander won 190 games in his eight-year Phillies career, a mark even more remarkable considering he didn't win any games at all during his final tour in 1930, which featured nine starts.

He garnered the nickname "Ol' Pete" in recognition of his known alcohol indulgence during the prohibition years, when his mound game shined.

Ironically, Alexander's exploits were prominently displayed in the film *The Winning Team*, which starred Ronald Reagan and depicted how Alexander was awakened from a drunken nap during the 1926 World Series as a member of the St. Louis Cardinals and struck out the Yankees' Tony Lazzeri with the game on the line.

Later, Alexander would refute the claim of his drunkenness to a writer and boast of being sober when he fanned Lazzeri with two outs and the bases loaded.

"I don't want to spoil anyone's story," Alexander was quoted as saying. "But I was cold sober. There were plenty of other nights before."

Alexander did most of his damage at the famed Baker Bowl, known better as a hitter's paradise. He was discovered by Patsy O'Rourke, a scout for then-owner Horace Fogel in the summer of 1910. O'Rourke was a manager at Albany, and Alexander was a player for Syracuse, both in the New York-Penn League.

O'Rourke persuaded Fogel to draft Alexander at the end of the season, and he reportedly signed for $750.

Alexander led the league as a rookie in 1911 with 28 victories, 31 complete games, and seven shutouts, including four consecutive whitewashings. He went on to win 19, 22, and 27 games in succeeding years.

But Alexander shined during the Phillies' pennant run of 1915 when he won 31 games and lost just 10, had a minuscule ERA of 1.22 and struck out 241 batters in 376 innings. He threw four one-hitters during the season and was the winning pitcher in the lone World Series game won by the Phillies.

He won 33 games during the 1916 season, when he recorded an amazing 16 shutouts that set the National League record for most in a season; his record has yet to be broken. After his 1.22 ERA in 1915, Alexander would keep that marker below 2.00 in his remaining two years as a Phillie.

Alexander was traded after the 1917 season to the Chicago Cubs in a cost-cutting move by the Phillies. He later pitched for St. Louis, where he helped the Cardinals to a World Series title in 1926 and won 21 games the following year.

The Nebraska native won his 373rd game as a Cardinal in 1929, tying the National League mark set by Christy Mathewson. But Alexander's social life would get the best of him, and his failure to meet several team curfews would eventually send him back to the Phillies in 1930. In his final year as a Phillie, he was 0-3 with a 9.00 ERA.

Alexander quit the team at age 43 and began working vaudeville shows. In 1938, he was voted into the Hall of Fame.

In 1940, Alexander was spotted working in a flea circus around the Times Square area in New York and was quoted as saying, "It's better living off the fleas than having them live off you."

His final 20 years were a dichotomy from what he had achieved on the mound. Alexander would spend the majority of his time drifting from job to job, suffering from alcoholism and cancer. He reportedly lived off $25 a week in the late 1940s, which came from the estate of St. Louis owner Sam Breadon.

In a 1939 interview with the *Evening Bulletin*, Alexander said he "had control of everything but myself. Control with bats, but none with dollars."

Alexander was to be a guest of Phillies owner Bob Carpenter at the 1950 World Series, but he fouled up his travel plans from his Nebraska home and never made it there.

He died at the age of 63 in 1950 in a hotel room in Nebraska, a month after the Phillies had been in the World Series.

Grover Cleveland Alexander Phillies Statistics

Year	W	L	SV	PCT	G	GS	CG	SH	IP	H	BB	SO	ERA
1911	28	13	3	.683	48	37	31	7	367.0	285	129	227	2.57
1912	19	17	3	.528	46	34	25	3	310.1	289	105	195	2.81
1913	22	8	2	.733	47	36	23	9	306.1	288	75	159	2.79
1914	27	15	1	.643	46	39	32	6	355.0	327	76	214	2.38
1915	31	10	3	.756	49	42	36	12	376.1	253	64	241	1.22
1916	33	12	3	.733	48	45	38	16	389.0	323	50	167	1.55
1917	30	13	0	.698	45	44	34	8	388.0	336	56	200	1.83
1930	0	3	0	.000	9	3	0	0	21.2	40	8	6	9.14
Totals	**190**	**91**	**15**	**.676**	**338**	**280**	**219**	**61**	**2513.2**	**2,141**	**563**	**1,409**	**2.18**

Two

Dick Allen

Hit the Longest Home Runs

by Jeff Moeller

He was known as "Crash," and his home runs were often compared to moon shots.

Richard Anthony Allen will certainly go down in the annals of Phillies baseball as one of the most colorful and controversial players ever to wear red-and-white pinstripes. His nine-year career as a Phillie included 204 of his 351 career homers and a Rookie of the Year award in 1964.

His 1964 season included 29 homers, 91 RBIs, 38 doubles, 13 triples, 201 total hits, and a .318 batting average through 162 games. His numbers should have been good enough to merit an MVP award, the one captured by Ken Boyer. The runner-up spot went to Allen's teammate Johnny Callison.

But Allen would always have controversy follow hand in hand with his hitting exploits.

In 1965, Allen engaged in an ongoing battle with first baseman Frank Thomas, and the two would eventually brawl. During batting practice, Thomas was needling Allen. Finally, Allen had enough, he took a swing at Thomas, Thomas swung back with his bat and hit Allen on the shoulder. After the game, Thomas was released.

Allen responded with his finest season in 1966, collecting 40 homers, 110 RBIs, and hitting .317. In 1967, Allen again became the target of fans, this time for his tardiness. On Aug. 24 he suffered a cut hand, stating that he punched a headlight on an old car he was pushing. The injury ended his season, and the rumors of his exit began to surface.

Yet Allen remained a fixture with the Phillies, this time moving to left field due to the hand injury, which affected his throwing. Though his average dipped to .263, Allen still clubbed 33 homers.

In 1969, Allen continued his productivity on the field, slamming 32 homers, but his popularity in the clubhouse also continued to diminish. Interim manager George Myatt was quoted as saying that "God almighty himself" couldn't handle Allen.

Allen would be traded in the off-season to the St. Louis Cardinals for Curt Flood in the move that would signal the beginning of the battle over the reserve clause.

The slugger with the 40-ounce bat would return to the Phillies in a trade with the Atlanta Braves, with the club knocking on the door of a championship. But, Allen failed to exhibit the skills so prominent in his younger days, as he hit a combined 27 homers in the next two years.

Handling managers was one of the more colorful traits of Allen's Phillies career, as well as dealing with the everyday pressures surrounding the club and the era in which he played. Allen would later make peace with Thomas, and the two played in several Old-Timers games.

"The first time I played here, it wasn't so pleasant until I got between the lines," Allen said. "What happened in the past is now behind me.

"But once I was able to get a good read on things back when I played in Philadelphia, I was able to have as much fun as anybody. I had my share of tough moments, but I also found out that I had a lot of friends in Philadelphia."

Allen shared a love-hate relationship with former manager Gene Mauch, who left during the 1968 season. Mauch said he never enjoyed a player more than Allen during the 1964 season, but the relationship spiraled downward after that.

"Dick was certainly a talent in the game," said Mauch. "He showed everyone a lot during the 1964 season. But he was always a very independent player. He did things his way."

Allen would later have confrontations with manager Danny Ozark, one in which Ozark erupted into a trash can-kicking episode after a Sunday home game when Allen didn't play.

Allen moved on to St. Louis and Los Angeles before he spent three seasons with the Chicago White Sox and longtime friend and manager Chuck Tanner. He was voted MVP of the American League in 1972 during his time in Chicago. He ended his career with Oakland in 1977.

Since 1994, Allen has been involved with the Phillies as a marketing representative. He also periodically roams the minor leagues as fielding and hitting instructor and performs various public-speaking duties.

Dick Allen Phillies Statistics

Year	G	AB	R	H	2B	3B	HR	RBI	AVG	OBP	SLGP
1963	10	24	6	7	2	1	0	2	.292	.280	.458
1964	162	632	125	201	38	13	29	91	.318	.382	.557
1965	161	619	93	187	31	14	20	85	.302	.375	.494
1966	141	524	112	166	25	10	40	110	.317	.396	.632
1967	122	463	89	142	31	10	23	77	.307	.404	.566
1968	152	521	87	137	17	9	33	90	.263	.352	.520
1969	118	438	79	126	23	3	32	89	.288	.375	.573
1975	119	416	54	97	21	3	12	62	.233	.327	.385
1976	85	298	52	80	16	1	15	49	.268	.346	.480
Totals	1,070	3,935	697	1,143	204	64	204	655	.290	.371	.530

Three

Sparky Anderson

Phillies' Second Baseman in 1959

by Skip Clayton

Ordinarily, the man who plays just one year in the major leagues leaves few marks on baseball history.

A notable exception is George "Sparky" Anderson, whose entire major league playing career consisted of the 1959 season with the Phillies.

Anderson had played in the minors before 1959 and again afterward. But his claim to fame came not as a player but as a manager years later. On Dec. 23, 1958, Roy Hamey made his final deal as the Phils' general manager when he acquired Anderson from the Dodgers.

"I'll always remember opening night with the Phillies," said Anderson. "We opposed Cincinnati, and Don Newcombe was pitching for them. I got a base hit in the eighth inning, driving in Chico Fernandez, and that put us up, 2-0. They got one in the ninth as [Robin] Roberts went all the way."

Although Anderson had problems with the bat, his fielding was outstanding. He was easily the Phils' best defensive second baseman since the days of Emil Verban.

Anderson had spent six years in the minors. He was a shortstop his first year and then moved over to second. His batting averages ranged from .260 to .298.

"One thing I remember, especially in Connie Mack Stadium," Anderson said, "were two fans. One would sit on the first-base side, and the other was on the third-base side. They had a megaphone or a microphone and they would yell things through them and make fun of guys who weren't doing good. They used to give me a pretty good going over."

Sparky hit only .218 in 152 games. He was back with the Phillies in spring training in 1960. "The day we left Miami to go to Cincinnati for the season opener was when I left the Phillies," Anderson said. "Eddie Sawyer told me Toronto bought me."

Anderson spent four years playing second for Toronto in the International League. In 1964, he took over as manager of Toronto and brought the club home in fifth place. The call to return to the majors as a player never came.

"I never thought about managing until 1962," Anderson said. "Charlie Dressen was our manager, and he said to me, 'You're going to be a manager someday.'

"I told him I had never thought about managing, but from then on I started to. This guy here knows baseball, and if he thinks I can manage, I'm going to think along those lines."

Anderson spent five years managing in the minors. In those years, his clubs won two championships. After a year with San Diego as a coach in 1969, his next stop was Cincinnati, where Sparky put together a dynasty starting in 1970.

Anderson managed Cincinnati for nine years. He won the World Series in 1975 and 1976, won two other pennants in 1970 and 1972, and only once lost a playoff—to the Mets in 1973.

After the 1978 season, Anderson was let go as the Reds' manager, but he didn't stay out of work long. In June 1979, he took over the Tigers and won the World Series in 1984.

He retired after the 1995 season as the third-winningest manager, with a record of 2,194-1,834, behind Connie Mack (3,731- 3,948) and John McGraw (2,763-1,948). Anderson, who lives in Thousand Oaks, Calif. then spent three seasons broadcasting for the Anaheim Angels on television.

Anderson won seven division titles, five pennants, and three World Series. He is one of four managers to win pennants in both leagues, but nobody else has won a World Series in each league. Anderson was voted iinto the Hall of Fame in 2000.

Sparky Anderson Phillies Statistics

Year	G	AB	R	H	2B	3B	HR	RBI	AVG	OBP	SLGP
1959	152	477	42	104	9	3	0	34	.218	.282	.249

Four

Richie Ashburn

Hall of Fame Center Fielder and Broadcaster

by Skip Clayton

Richie Ashburn played 12 years with the Phillies and received just about every honor imaginable. In 1969 and 1983, he was voted the all-time best center fielder in Phillies history. If a vote were taken today, he would still be voted the best. In 1979, he was voted into the Philadelphia Baseball Hall of Fame and the Phillies retired his number (1). Then came his long overdue selection to the Baseball Hall of Fame in Cooperstown, N.Y., in 1995.

There has never been a more popular person in the history of Philadelphia sports than Richie. In fact, when you think of Philadelphia, you think of the Liberty Bell, Billy Penn on top of City Hall, and Richie Ashburn.

He died on Sept. 9, 1997, in New York, and a city was in mourning. He had been a part of Phillies baseball as a player (12 years) and as a broadcaster (35 years) and was in the game for 54 years.

Ashburn signed with the Phils in 1944, shortly after Bob Carpenter bought the club. He joined Utica of the Eastern League and hit .312 in 1945. Signed as a catcher, he saw action behind the plate in 17 games, but manager Eddie Sawyer saw his great speed.

"It was Eddie's idea to move me from catcher to the outfield," said Ashburn. "I thought I was a pretty good catcher, but I had great speed, and Eddie felt it could be used much better in the outfield."

Ashburn spent the 1946 season in the Army, but the next year was back at Utica and hit .362 (second highest in the Eastern League) and had his biggest day, going 6-for-6 with a grand slam.

In 1948 he was in Clearwater for spring training.

"I didn't have a Phillies contract," he said, "but Harry Walker, the center fielder who had won the batting title in 1947, was a holdout. Another center fielder, Charlie Gilbert, got hurt in spring training and the club didn't have anyone to play center.

"I was with Robin Roberts and a few of the younger prospects in kind of a rookie camp, and they called me over to the big club. I had a great spring—probably the best I ever had—and they kept me."

He was in the lineup opening day, leading off against the Boston Braves at Shibe Park, and got his first hit, a single off Johnny Sain. Three days later at Brooklyn in the first inning, he stole his first base, and it was a steal of home.

Ashburn hit .333 in his rookie year, second to Stan Musial's .376. He led the league in stolen bases with 32. He tied the club rookie record for consecutive games with a hit (23) and was voted the starting center fielder for the National League All-Star team (He went 2-for-4 and stole a base). *The Sporting News* named him Rookie of the Year, even though he missed the final six weeks with a broken finger.

In 1949, Ashburn suffered the sophomore jinx, and his average dropped to .284 as the Phillies finished third.

"The last thing Eddie Sawyer said to us on the last day of the season," Ashburn recalled, "was, 'Boys, come back in 1950, we're going to win it.'"

They did just that in 1950. The club known as the Whiz Kids took over first place for good from the St. Louis Cardinals on July 25, when they shut out the Chicago Cubs twice at Shibe Park. Ashburn singled home the winning run in the ninth inning of the second game.

Going into the last game of the '50 season at Ebbets Field, the Phils led Brooklyn by one game. Win the finale, and the pennant was theirs. Lose it, and the two clubs would meet in a best-of-three playoff.

With the game tied, 1-1, in the bottom of the ninth, Brooklyn had two on and nobody out. "Duke Snider came up," Ashburn said, "and I was thinking one thing with the winning run on second. I knew he couldn't bunt, but I did shorten up a step or two.

"Duke hit a sharp one-hop single to me. It came right to me, and it was a routine play for an outfielder at a crucial time."

"The Dodgers used bad judgment sending Abrams home. I was never known to have a strong arm, but I had an accurate arm. I got rid of the ball quickly and threw Abrams out by 20 feet."

In the bottom of the 10th, Dick Sisler hit a home run—the Phillies' version of the "shot heard round the world." It was on to the World Series against the New York Yankees after Roberts retired Brooklyn in order in the bottom of the inning.

"Winning that pennant didn't sink in for two days," said Ashburn. "It was a big thrill to win the pennant, but a big disappointment to lose the World Series in four to the Yankees."

After hitting .303 in 1950 and leading the league in triples (14), Ashburn hit .344 in 1951, but once again finished second to Musial at .355. Ashburn had 538 putouts, still the second highest for an outfielder in a season.

He was voted the starting center fielder on the All-Star team. He had two hits in four trips, and made the outstanding defensive play of the game, robbing Vic Wertz of a homer.

Despite a fifth-place finish for the 1951 Phillies, Ashburn led the league in hits with 221, and tied the club record for most singles in a season with 181. He dropped to .282 in 1952 but was back strong in 1953 with a .330 average. His 205 hits led the league, and he got his 1,000th career hit on July 1, when he singled off Billy Loes in Brooklyn.

He made the All-Star team and got into the game in the bottom of the fifth as a pinch hitter. With the game scoreless, he singled off Allie Reynolds to drive in Eddie Mathews, and the National League went on to a 5-1 victory.

In 1954, he came back to hit .313. He led the league in on-base percentage (.442) and became the first Phillies player since Chuck Klein to be on base 300 or more times in a season (304). Ashburn led the league in walks with 125.

At the end of the year, Ashburn had played in 731 consecutive games. The National League record (since broken) was held by Gus Suhr, who had played in 822 straight. An outfield collision with Del Ennis in an exhibition game in Wilmington, Del., right before the season broke Ashburn's streak.

In 1955, Ashburn batted .338 and won his first batting title. He led the league again in on-base percentage (.449).

"That title was important to me," Ashburn said. "I had flirted with several, and when I got it, it didn't seem that hard to come by. It was just one of those years."

The next year, Ashburn hit .303 with 190 hits. Between games of a double-header with Pittsburgh, he was honored at Connie Mack Stadium. Over 32,000 jammed the park. "It was a very sentimental night, and I was given a lot of nice gifts," he said. "That night we took two from the Pirates, and I had four hits."

In 1957, Ashburn's average dropped to .297, but he tied for the league lead in walks with 94.

In 1958, he came back to win the batting title with a .350 average. He also became only the second player in National League history to lead the league in hits (215) and walks (97) in the same year. He was on base 316 times and led the league in on-base percentage (.441) and triples (13).

The batting race came down to the last weekend of the season. Willie Mays was hitting .346 with three games left in St. Louis while Ashburn had an average of .344. The Phillies' final three games were in Pittsburgh, and Richie tore into Pirates pitching, going 8-for-13. Mays was 5-for-13 in St. Louis.

Ashburn barely won the batting crown.

"I had to beat out Mays for the second batting title," Ashburn said. "Aaron and Musial were in it, but slumped toward the end. Mays and I kept hitting."

During the season, he was picked for the All-Star Game but didn't play. He picked up his 2,000th career hit when he singled off Carlton Willey of the Braves in Milwaukee.

The 1959 season saw Ashburn's average drop to .266. Before the 1960 season, he was traded to the Cubs for Alvin Dark, Jim Woods, and John Buzhardt.

It wasn't a good trade for the Phillies. Ashburn hit .291 for the Cubs and led the league in on-base percentage (.416) and walks (116).

Today, Ashburn is second on the club in games played (1,794), at-bats (7,122), hits (2,217), and walks (946). Mike Schmidt passed him in all those categories.

Ashburn remains third in runs scored, (1,114) eighth in batting (.311), and second in on-base percentage (.394).

After two seasons in Chicago, Ashburn spent the 1962 season with the Mets. He was chosen to the All-Star team and got a pinch single, giving him a .600 average in All-Star Games, still the highest lifetime average in these dream games.

Ashburn became the Mets' first .300 hitter, batting .306. He is the last National League regular to hit .300 in his final season.

Ashburn retired after 1962 with a lifetime batting average of .308 and 2,574 hits.

"My only regret in not continuing to play was not being able to go for 3,000 hits," said Ashburn. "I had a chance and I had a good career, but I was with the Mets, and they weren't going to win many games."

When Ashburn retired, he had set outfielders' records that will stand a long time: most years with 400 or more putouts (nine) and most years with 500 or more putouts (four). No other outfielder ever had more than 500 putouts in a season twice. In fact, six of the top 10 seasons in putouts belong to Richie who is tied with Max Carey for most years (9) leading outfielders in putouts.

Although Ashburn didn't have the greatest arm, it was better than he was ever given credit for. He led the league in assists twice and tied for the lead a third time. Ashburn also made the most important throw in Phillies history in 1950 to save the pennant.

After he retired, he became a part of the Phillies' broadcasting team. Ashburn took to the booth, and the fans fell in love with him as a broadcaster, just as they had as a player.

Over the years, people were not wondering when he would make the Hall of Fame, but if he would even make it to begin with. It was ridiculous that he hadn't been voted in sooner, but the day finally came when he got the great news in 1995.

Over 25,000 were at Cooperstown on July 30 when Ashburn and Schmidt were inducted. At the time, the turnout was the biggest ever seen at an induction ceremony. Ashburn's family was there, along with some of his former teammates and his former manager, Eddie Sawyer.

He talked for about 20 minutes and got as big an ovation as anyone who has ever been inducted, telling everyone how happy he was to be there. Everyone was wearing red, and the fans didn't seem to mind the heat as they watched two of Philadelphia's greatest ever take their place along with some of the greats of the game.

After Ashburn died, the radio booth where he spent so much of his life was named after him. Ashburn was not only one of the greatest players in Phillies history, but also the most popular player ever in Philadelphia sports.

Richie Ashburn Phillies Statistics

Year	G	AB	R	H	2B	3B	HR	RBI	AVG	OBP	SLGP
1948	117	463	78	154	17	4	2	40	.333	.410	.400
1949	154	662	84	188	18	11	1	37	.284	.343	.349
1950	151	594	84	180	25	14	2	41	.303	.372	.402
1951	154	643	92	221	31	5	4	63	.344	.393	.426
1952	154	613	93	173	31	6	1	42	.282	.362	.357
1953	156	622	110	205	25	9	2	57	.330	.394	.408
1954	153	559	111	175	16	8	1	41	.313	.441	.376
1955	140	533	91	180	32	9	3	42	.338	.449	.448
1956	154	628	94	190	26	8	3	50	.303	.384	.384
1957	156	626	93	186	26	8	0	33	.297	.390	.364
1958	152	615	98	215	24	13	2	33	.350	.440	.441
1959	153	564	86	150	16	2	1	20	.266	.360	.307
Totals	1,794	7,122	1,114	2,217	287	97	22	499	.311	.394	.388

Five

Dave Bancroft

Hall of Fame Shortstop

by Jeff Moeller

H e was known as "beauty," apparently because of those pitches he let pass while at bat. Yet Dave Bancroft should have been referred to by his nickname for being the prototype shortstop of his time.

Phillies fans came to Baker Bowl in the early 1900s to witness the fine fielding exploits of Bancroft, who would set the trend for the club's All-Star shortstops to come.

In those days, a shortstop wasn't expected to hit for power as he is today. It was the only flaw in the 5-foot-9, 160-pound package composed of quickness, agility, range, a strong arm, and natural leadership abilities many would later equate with Larry Bowa.

While at bat, the switch-hitting Hall of Famer would play textbook baseball —making contact, hitting behind runners, and drawing walks.

Also referred to as "Banny," Bancroft began his Phillies career in 1915 and was a key contributor on the club's first National League championship that year. He hit .254 with 85 runs scored, 18 doubles, 15 stolen bases, and a then-high seven homers. The following season, an ankle injury slowed his progress as well as the team's, as his club fell just two and a half games short of the New York Giants.

Bancroft was born in Sioux City, Iowa, in 1891 and became a professional ballplayer at the age of 17.

He spent three years with Portland of the Wisconsin-Minnesota League. Bancroft took some time to get adjusted and hit just .213, which played a huge part in his demotion to his city's Class B Northwestern League, where he raised his mark to .244. He returned to the Pacific Coast League in 1914 and hit .277, recording a league-leading 435 putouts.

At the time, the Phillies had a shortstop named Mickey Doolan. In a preview of what was to engulf the game in the forms of high payrolls and free agency, a battle had ensued between the established league and the upstart Federal League, which was formed by wealthy businessmen.

Among the starters lured away was Doolan, and the Phillies couldn't afford to lose a player of his stature. Doolan was never known for his hitting, but he could field with the best of them at the time.

Manager Pat Moran made the call to give Bancroft a shot in 1915, and the 24-year-old didn't disappoint. His debut was overshadowed by stars Grover Cleveland Alexander and Gavvy Cravath.

In the field that season, Bancroft committed 64 errors, but he still drew comparisons to Doolan. Yet Moran praised his rookie as being the key to the club's rise to the pennant.

During the World Series, the Phillies' bats went silent, as they hit just .182 against Red Sox pitching. Bancroft, however, hit .294, second behind teammate Fred Luderus, who hit .438. No other Phillie hit above .200, and Bancroft notched 13 putouts, 10 assists, and an error.

The following season, Bancroft slumped miserably, as he hit just .212 and topped the National League with 60 errors. He rebounded to hit .243 with 22 doubles in 1917.

During the war-shortened 1918 season, Bancroft hit .265 and led the league with 371 putouts. But he also committed 64 errors.

As the war ended and the 1919 season began, few players were left from the Phillies' 1915 championship run. Moran moved on to Cincinnati, Alexander pitched for the Cubs, and Cravath was a part-time player.

On the other hand, Bancroft continued to pick up his game. Limited by injuries, he hit a then-career high .272 in 92 games.

Bancroft was traded in 1920 to the Giants for shortstop Art Fletcher, pitcher Bill Hubbell, and $100,000. Upon his arrival in New York, Bancroft was named team captain by manager John McGraw.

Ironically, the Phillies entered a period during which they became basement dwellers, while the Giants became perennial contenders. Bancroft would blossom into the shortstop the Phillies always expected, as he hit better than .300 in his four seasons with the Giants. He also scored 100 or more runs during his first three years in New York and reached career highs in RBIs (67 in 1921) and hits (209 in 1922). Bancroft set a major league record for most chances (984) in 1922.

He struggled with his bat in the postseason, but he was excellent in the field. It did help matters that from 1921 to 1923, the World Series was an all-New York contest that showcased the likes of Babe Ruth.

In November of 1923, Bancroft was traded to the Boston Braves, and the 31-year-old also assumed the role of manager.

Bancroft hit .319 in 1925 and .311 in 1926. He slumped to .243 in 1927 and was released at the end of the season. Bancroft made a deal with the Brooklyn Dodgers in 1928 and shrewdly became the highest-paid player at the time.

His stay was short, however, as he spent two rather mediocre seasons with the Dodgers before he returned to the Giants as a coach in 1930.

Bancroft later spent some time managing in the American Association before he officially retired in 1947.

He was named to Baseball's Hall of Fame in 1971. "I never worried about making errors," he was quoted as saying at the time.

In his six seasons with the Phillies, Bancroft hit .251 with 14 homers and 331 runs scored in 681 games. In his 16-year career, Bancroft hit .279 with 32 homers and 1,048 runs scored in 1,913 games. He finished with a .944 fielding percentage.

Bancroft died on Oct. 9, 1972, in Superior, Wis., at the age of 80.

Dave Bancroft Phillies Statistics

Year	G	AB	R	H	2B	3B	HR	RBI	AVG	OBP	SLGP
1915	153	563	85	143	18	2	7	30	.254	.346	.330
1916	142	477	53	101	10	0	3	33	.212	.323	.252
1917	127	478	56	116	22	5	4	43	.243	.307	.335
1918	125	499	69	132	19	4	0	26	.265	.338	.319
1919	92	335	45	91	13	7	0	25	.272	.333	.352
1920	42	171	23	51	7	2	0	5	.298	.337	.363
Totals	681	2,523	331	634	89	20	14	162	.251	.330	.319

Six

Dick Bartell

National League's First All-Star Shortstop

by Skip Clayton

Whenever the great shortstops in Phillies history are listed, there are always a few who are certain to appear.

One of them is Dick Bartell, a fiery performer who gave the Phillies four sparkling years in the early 1930s.

Bartell was an excellent hitter, an equally excellent fielder, and the spark plug and, ultimately, captain of the Phillies. Playing with the club from 1931 through 1934, Bartell twice batted over .300 while he was here. In 587 games as a Phillie, he compiled an overall batting average of .295.

Often called "Rowdy Richard" because of his fiercely competitive ways, the native of Chicago, Ill., put in 18 seasons altogether in the big leagues. In addition to the Phillies, he played for the Pittsburgh Pirates, New York Giants, Chicago Cubs, and Detroit Tigers, compiling 2,165 hits and a lifetime batting average of .284 with 1,130 runs, 710 RBIs, and 79 homers.

Twice he was selected as the starting shortstop for the National League All-Stars, including 1933, the year that the first game was played.

"It was a great thrill to be selected to the first All-Star Game," said Bartell, who went 0-for-2. "The game itself was a tremendous thrill," he added. "It was an experience that nobody can ever take away from me."

Bartell had vivid memories of his days playing in Baker Bowl for the Phillies, especially in 1932, when the club reached fourth place, its only first-division finish between 1918 and 1948.

"Finishing fourth was the highlight of my four years with the club," he recalled. "After the season, each of us got an extra $343 (in World Series shares) for finishing fourth."

Dick came to the club on Nov. 6, 1930, in a trade with the Pittsburgh Pirates. The Phillies gave up pitcher Claude Willoughby and shortstop Tommy Thevenow.

"I wasn't upset about coming to the Phillies," Bartell said. "I had a job to do, and that's all I was interested in."

As soon as he arrived in Philadelphia, Bartell got a taste of another local institution—the Philadelphia A's. The A's and the Phillies always met in a City Series right before the regular season began.

"It was quite an experience," he said, "especially seeing their pitchers, George Earnshaw, Lefty Grove, and Rube Walberg. We were looking at as good pitching as you could could ever see."

In his first season with the Phillies, Bartell's average was .289. Defensively, he led the league's shortstops in double plays and errors.

The following year, Bartell was the league leader at his position in putouts and assists. His batting average jumped to 308 and he hit 48 doubles to establish a still-standing modern club record for a right-handed batter.

Bartell's average dropped to .271 in 1933, but his glove remained as good as ever. He led all shortstops in putouts and double plays. Doubles were Bartell's specialty, and in 1933 he etched his name in the record books for another two-bagger spree. On April 25, Dick slammed four consecutive doubles against the Boston Braves at Baker Bowl to tie a major league record.

The following season, Bartell hit .310, the highest average ever compiled by a Phillies shortstop. He also led National League shortstops in putouts, assists, and double plays.

After the season, Bartell was traded to the New York Giants for shortstop Blondy Ryan, third baseman Johnny Vergez, outfielder George Watkins, pitcher Pretzels Pezzullo, plus cash.

In 1936, a year after Bartell had joined them, the Giants won the National League pennant. Dick hit .298 and led NL shortstops in assists with 589, just 12 short of the league record set in 1924 by Glenn Wright (who played in 153 games to Dick's 144).

That fall, the Giants met the Yankees in the World Series. The Yankees had a streak of 12 straight Series wins. But in the opener at the Polo Grounds. Bartell laced a home run in the fifth inning off Red Ruffing that snapped a 1-1 tie, and the Giants went on to capture a 6-1 win.

Although the Giants eventually lost the Series, 4-2, the homer provided Bartell with one of the highlights of his career.

"It was a tremendous thrill just to be in the World Series, but it was a bigger thrill to hit the home run that put us ahead," Bartell said.

"A lot of people don't know this, but when I hit that homer, I had one thought on my mind, believe it or not. I almost missed first base. In fact, I had to go back and tag it. I kept thinking all the way around the bases that my dad had an enlarged heart, and he was at the World Series when the doctor had told him he couldn't go. But my dad said his son was in the World Series and he was going. He told the doctor he was flying. The doctor said, 'That's even worse.'

"The only thing that I had on my mind when I hit that home run was, 'My God, my dad is going to have a heart attack,'" Bartell continued. "I couldn't wait to get to home plate to see if he was all right. And there he was. He was jumping up and down, waving his hat and yelling, 'That's my son, Dick Bartell.' What a relief it was to see him whooping it up."

Bartell hit .381 in the Series, the highest among Giant regulars. The following year, he was chosen for the second time as the starting shortstop for the National League in the All-Star Game.

Again, the Giants won the pennant, again they met the Yankees in the World Series, and again they lost, this time 4-1. Dick was named the major leagues' All-Star shortstop in 1937 by *The Sporting News.*

In 1938, Bartell batted .262 and accomplished the rare feat of hitting two grand slams in one game.

That winter, he was traded to the Chicago Cubs. He put in one year with the Cubs, then moved to Detroit, where in 1940 he played in his third World Series.

Early in the 1941 season, the Tigers released Bartell. Four days later, he joined the Giants and stayed three seasons, then went into the service for the 1944 and 1945 campaigns.

"I came back in 1946 and played in just five games under Mel Ott," he added. "I was primarily his third-base coach. The next season, I was supposed to stay on as a player-coach, but they decided to get rid of me. I spent three years in the minors as a manager, coached six years in the majors, and then retired.

"After I was through with baseball, I looked hard for a job, and I finally went to work for Berkley Farms Creamery," Bartell said. "I worked for them for six and a half years. Then an opportunity came along for me to get what was supposed to have been a great job promotion in a liquor store. I went into it with a friend of mine for 10 years. After that, I retired."

Bartell died on Aug. 4, 1995, in Alameda, Calif. He was 87. Dick also wrote a book on his career, *Rowdy Richard,* which came out in 1987.

Dick Bartell Phillies Statistics

Year	G	AB	R	H	2B	3B	HR	RBI	AVG	OBP	SLGP
1931	135	554	88	160	43	7	0	34	.289	.325	.392
1932	154	614	118	189	48	7	1	53	.308	.379	.414
1933	152	587	78	159	25	5	1	37	.271	.340	.336
1934	146	604	102	187	30	4	0	37	.310	.384	.373
Totals	**587**	**2359**	**386**	**695**	**146**	**23**	**2**	**161**	**.295**	**.358**	**.379**

Seven

Bob Boone

Gold Glove Catcher

by Jeff Moeller

Bob Boone had his share of highlights and disappointments during his 10-year Phillies career.

The main highlight, of course, was being a part of the 1980 world championship team. Even though he was signed as a third baseman in the sixth round of the 1969 June draft, Boone finished his career catching more games than any other player in major league history (2,225) until Carlton Fisk broke it by one game.

Boone won seven Gold Gloves and had his best hitting years with marks of .286 (1979), .284 (1977), and .283 (1978) during a five-year span in which Boone was chosen to the National League All-Star team four times.

But he was also part of some of the most disappointing moments in Phillies history. It was during the same time that "Boonie" experienced some of his best years behind the plate.

In fact, Boone believed the Phillies could have won three or four titles during the late 1970s into the '80s.

"In 1976, the Cincinnati Reds were a better team," Boone said. "But I really believe that we were the best team in baseball during the 1977 season. Things just didn't go our way. Funny things can happen in a short series, and we experienced our share."

Manny Mota, Vic Davalillo, and Greg Luzinski were all part of the nightmarish mix that saw the Phillies surrender a ninth-inning lead to the Dodgers in Game 3. Game 4 was the famous "Hurricane Feeney" game that began and continued through a driving rainstorm.

"That was a travesty and a farce," Boone seethed. "For a game of that magnitude to have been played in those conditions is unconscionable. We might have well just flipped a coin to see who won. It certainly was no test of skill."

But time would eventually be on Boone and the Phillies' side. The catcher is still shaken by the epic five-game playoff battle with Houston in the 1980 NLCS, and he still hasn't watched the tape. He referred to the entire magical run as a swirling kaleidoscope in his mind.

He took out his years of frustration in a scintillating World Series performance. Batting ninth for the first time in his career (as the designated hitter was used in the World Series), Boone hit a sizzling .412. He was behind the plate and called for a duster from Dickie Noles that knocked George Brett down and altered the complexion of the Series.

And he was a major part of an unorthodox play that has been a hallmark of the Series.

That was Frank White's foul pop fly in the ninth inning of Game 6 that popped out of Boone's mitt and into Pete Rose's glove.

"It could have been a real calamity. If the ball falls in, they rally and I am Bill Buckner before Bill Buckner," Boone said.

He would then catch the Series-clinching strike from Tug McGraw. Boone raised both arms in the air and slowly meandered to the mound to join in the celebration.

"That was running full speed for me," said Boone, who gutted out the final 10 days of the quest on a badly bruised leg and foot, courtesy of a collision with Houston's Jose Cruz.

"What a relief it was," Boone said. "I could finally relax. I had to keep a tremendous amount of focus on every pitch and I was physically beat up, too. I was not coming out of there. We were on a mission. We all knew that this was going to be it."

Boone viewed the championship as a climax to a long-term goal.

"When you look back at the glory days, you a see a team that grew up together. Mike Schmidt, Greg Luzinski, Larry Bowa, Larry Christenson, Dick Ruthven, and myself all started in the farm system. We all took some knocks along the way, but we became a real power.

"We were a family and Danny Ozark was a big part of it. He was there with us every step of the way. We just had too much talent, and we were not going to be denied every time. We were going to win it sooner or later.

"And with a little more luck, we could have been a real dynasty. We could have won four or five championships."

Boone also finally gained the trust of Steve Carlton, who used Tim McCarver as his personal catcher through the years. He got his chance in 1980, and "Lefty" posted the second most productive year of his career with a 24-9 record and a couple of World Series wins.

"A catcher has to earn a pitcher's trust and Steve finally trusted me," Boone said. "When I was in doubt, I would call for his slider down and in. Steve was able to put every pitch where he wanted it. It was one of the most amazing things I ever saw."

Bob Boone Phillies Statistics

Year	G	AB	R	H	2B	3B	HR	RBI	AVG	OBP	SLGP
1972	16	51	4	14	1	0	1	4	.275	.333	.353
1973	145	521	42	136	20	2	10	61	.261	.311	.365
1974	146	488	41	118	24	3	3	52	.242	.295	.322
1975	97	289	28	71	14	2	2	20	.246	.322	.329
1976	121	361	40	98	18	2	4	54	.271	.348	.366
1977	132	440	55	125	26	4	11	66	.284	.343	.436
1978	132	435	48	123	18	4	12	62	.283	.347	.425
1979	119	398	38	114	21	3	9	58	.286	.367	.422
1980	141	480	34	110	23	1	9	55	.229	.299	.338
1981	76	227	19	48	7	0	4	24	.211	.279	.295
Totals	1,125	3,690	349	957	172	21	65	456	.259	.325	.370

Eight

Larry Bowa

Baseball's Top-Fielding Shortstop

by Jeff Moeller

For Larry Bowa, the moment captured his baseball career.
It was the final swing from Kansas City's Willie Wilson off a Tug McGraw pitch in the 1980 World Series, and Bowa's baseball career flashed before his eyes.

"That still stands out," said Bowa, who was a coach with the Anaheim Angels during the 1999 season, when he recalled his Phillies career. "It topped everything."

"But I'll never forget those standing ovations for my play in the field. You rarely see something like that."

He was the consummate underdog. A scrawny, 155-pound California kid who broke in with the Phillies in 1970, Bowa was billed, along with second baseman Denny Doyle, as the next great Phillies' double-play combination under manager Frank Lucchesi.

"I owe a lot to a guy like Frank Lucchesi," Bowa said. "He was a guy that stuck by me and gave me a chance. I probably would have never made it to the big leagues if it wasn't for him."

The double-play combination never quite emerged as an impact on the game, but Bowa certainly did.

He went on to lead National League shortstops in fielding five times, winning two Gold Gloves, and he established a major league fielding percentage mark of .991 in 1979, a season in which he committed just six errors. In the 1980 World Series, he helped turn seven double plays.

Listed at 5-foot-8, Bowa was never short on desire. He took his shots at the fans in print and had an ongoing battle with sportswriters, who took their shots at his swings and slumps.

"It bothered me then, but I realized a lot of them never took a swing in organized baseball. But if I knew that I busted my tail, it was what I needed to satisfy the people who paid my salary and my peers," Bowa said.

"I had my moments with Phillies fans, too. I taunted them and said some things I shouldn't have. I just got caught up in the heat of the moment and my own anger and frustrations when I was younger. They had their right to boo me at times."

The 1980 season was a roller-coaster ride for Bowa, whose World Series ring was as satisfying as any moment in his 34-year-old life at the time.

He spouted off in spring training about his reported $325,000 salary, apparently miffed that other shortstops with lesser credentials were making more than he was. He later issued an apology.

Later, he refused to speak to the press and became withdrawn. Life had been crumbling around him. His career, along with his drive toward a championship, was saved by a talk from then-owner Ruly Carpenter, with whom Bowa enjoyed a close relationship.

"He called me up to his office in September to see what was was wrong," Bowa recalled. "He told me he wasn't seeing the real Larry Bowa out there, and I didn't appear to be ready to play.

"We talked for a few hours, and a lot of things hit home. He called me on the road trip we then went on, and I seemed to get out of my funk.

"When we won the World Series, he was the first guy to come up to me and told me how proud he was how I responded down the stretch."

Aside from Carpenter, one of his most rooted relationships in baseball is with Dallas Green.

In 1972, Green had just become the Phillies' farm director and Bowa was in his third season with the Phillies. Green had made his intentions clear that he was high on No. 1 draft pick Craig Robinson to become the parent club's next short-stop.

It was the first stage of an ongoing simmering relationship between the two, which ironically would play itself out over Bowa's remaining baseball career with the Phillies, and later the Chicago Cubs.

Bowa withstood the test of baseball time, and Green took over a team composed of Bowa and other veterans late in the 1979 season. It was a matter of who would blink first.

"When Danny [Ozark] got fired in 1979, I knew Dallas was the right guy to come in here and take over the ship," recalled broadcaster Chris Wheeler. "Guys like Bowa and the other veterans here knew that Dallas could take charge.

"It was a matter of who was going to give in," Bowa said. "Each of us started to give a little bit, and we started playing like we were capable of playing. It wasn't the best of times, and we never seemed to do things easy.

"Winning the World Series was the ultimate. Our title might have been a little tarnished because of the relationships some of us had with Dallas at the time, but we overcame a lot of adversity to do it.

"I remember one day when Pete Rose reminded a bunch of us that we should be playing for ourselves and take pride in our game. We just had to put all of the little things aside and take charge out there.

"We did."

Along with his World Series highlight, Bowa can bask in the moment of a July game of the 1983 season when he gained his 2,000th major league hit, a mark most wouldn't have ever dreamed about for Bowa.

He lined a single to right to score a run, and the 50,000-plus crowd at Dodger Stadium saluted one of the game's hardest-working shortstops with a standing ovation.

What made the milestone even more appealing was that Bowa hit .300 or better only once in his 16-year career, batting .305 in 1975. He had 192 hits during the 1978 season and collected 184 in 1974, the two high-season marks for him. Bowa finished his career with 2,191 hits.

"That was still unbelievable," he said. "I really never thought I would reach that many hits. I never really was a consient hitter like Pete Rose."

Bowa became embroiled in a contract dispute with the Phillies after the 1981 season and was sent to the Chicago Cubs, along with top farmhand Ryne Sandberg, for Ivan DeJesus.

Then in the twilight of his career, Bowa was reunited with Green, who then took over the reins of running the daily operations of the franchise.

"We overcame a lot during that time," Bowa said of his relationship with Green. "We had a lot of respect for each other. That was a big key for all of us on that '80 team. We didn't always get along, but we respected each other.

"Whatever happened, we can always say that we were the best team for that year."

Larry Bowa Phillies Statistics

Year	G	AB	R	H	2B	3B	HR	RBI	AVG	OBP	SLGP
1970	145	547	50	137	17	6	0	34	.250	.277	.303
1971	159	650	74	162	18	5	0	25	.249	.293	.292
1972	152	579	67	145	11	13	1	31	.250	.291	.320
1973	122	446	42	94	11	3	0	23	.211	.252	.249
1974	162	669	97	184	19	10	1	36	.275	.298	.338
1975	136	583	79	178	18	9	2	38	.305	.334	.377
1976	156	624	71	155	15	9	0	49	.248	.283	.301
1977	154	624	93	175	19	3	4	41	.280	.313	.340
1978	156	654	78	192	31	5	3	43	.294	.319	.370
1979	147	539	74	130	17	11	0	31	.241	.316	.314
1980	147	540	57	144	16	4	2	39	.267	.300	.322
1981	103	360	34	102	14	3	0	31	.283	.331	.339
Totals	1,739	6,815	816	1798	206	81	13	421	.264	.301	.324

Nine

Jim Bunning

Hall of Fame Pitcher

by Skip Clayton

O n Dec. 4, 1963, the Eagles were closing out a 2-10-2 season and the club was in the process of being sold to Jerry Wolman. Pro basketball was back in town and the 76ers were playing their first season—a losing one—in Philadelphia.

It took Phillies general manager John Quinn to give the fans something to cheer about. Quinn swung a trade with the Detroit Tigers, picking up pitcher Jim Bunning and catcher Gus Triandos in exchange for pitcher Jack Hamilton and outfielder Don Demeter.

The 1963 Phillies had won 87 games, their highest total since 1952, and their fourth-place finish was the best showing since 1955. Adding Bunning gave the Phillies high hopes for 1964.

Jim had pitched for the Tigers for parts of the 1955 and 1956 seasons. He came up to stay in 1957, when he won 20 games, tying for the league lead. He led the American League in innings pitched (267.1), and was second in strikeouts with 182. Bunning was the starter and winner in the All-Star game. He pitched three innings and retired nine straight.

In 1958, he threw a no-hitter against the Boston Red Sox in Fenway Park. In the ninth with two out, Bunning got Ted Williams on a fly ball to Al Kaline in right field. He struck out 12 and allowed two walks.

"I thought about Williams in the eighth inning, and if I didn't walk or hit anybody, that he would be the last out," said Bunning. "I had good luck with him with pitches off the plate inside. He doesn't swing at a ball, but sometimes, and Ted tells me this 37 years later that they knew every pitch I was throwing in that game. Del Wilber, the first-base coach, was signaling by mouth whether it was going to be a fastball or a curveball, but the problem was, when I threw my fastball, it looked like my slider, and I had been getting Williams out with sliders in on his hands, nice fly balls to right field, all day. I wasn't concerned about it. You make a mistake and boom, it is over. It is one of the few times that Williams swung at the first pitch and he said, 'The reason that I did that was the people were screaming so loud that I couldn't hear Wilber's signs.' Yes, he gave some concerns, as great as a hitter as he was. He hit as well as anybody I know against me in all of the time I played in the major leagues."

Bunning won 118 and lost 87 with Detroit before heading to Philadelphia. He had pitched in six All-Star Games and had given up only two earned runs in 14 innings. He started the second game in 1961 at Fenway and started the 1962 game in Washington, D.C., with President John F. Kennedy on hand.

Bunning got off to a great start in 1964. He pitched a one-hitter against Houston, yielding only a fifth-inning single to Jim Wynn.

He was 6-2 by the time the Phillies went on to Shea Stadium on June 21 to play the New York Mets in a double-header. Starting the opener, Bunning pitched the first perfect game since Don Larsen of the Yankees set down 27 Brooklyn Dodgers in the fifth game of the 1956 World Series.

"The only change-up I threw all day was the one that Jesse Gonder almost got a hit on when Tony Taylor made a great play," said Bunning. "I didn't have very good control in the first three innings, but all of a sudden I got good control. I had a very good breaking ball the last three innings."

Bunning says he was aware of what was going on, although silence is supposed to be the policy during a no-hitter. "Usually there isn't too much said on the bench during a no-hit game," he said. "I had been through one and I wanted to make sure that if I blew it, I wasn't going to have a big letdown. So I talked about it a lot on the bench, told them how many outs we had left to go. When we went out for the ninth, I said, 'If it is close, dive for the ball.' I think the team was more relaxed going into that inning than they normally would have been had I not spoken about it."

Charlie Smith led off the ninth and popped out to Bobby Wine in foul territory back of third base. Then Jim struck out pinch hitters George Altman and John Stephenson.

Jim threw 90 pitches, 69 of which were strikes. He struck out 10. Bunning also doubled and drove in two runs.

Despite Bunning's perfect game, the Phillies went on to blow a 6 1/2-game lead with 12 games left in the season. The Phillies lost 10 straight and finished the season in a tie for second with Cincinnati, and St. Louis took the pennant for the first time in 18 years.

Bunning had a great year for the Phillies. His record was 19-8 with an earned run average of 2.63. He also hurled two scoreless innings in the All-Star Game.

"My biggest disappointment was never pitching in the World Series," said Bunning. "We had our chance in 1964, and didn't make it."

One of the things that hurt the Phillies down the stretch was not having a day off in September, and another was the injury to Frank Thomas in early September. One day off would have helped the whole pitching staff.

Jim had another super year in 1965, posting a 19-9 record and setting a club record (which was later broken) for most strikeouts in a season (268). He struck out 10 or more in a game nine times during that season. That year, Bunning also became the first Phillies pitcher to win a 1-0 shutout and also hit a homer, as he connected off Warren Spahn in the sixth inning at Shea Stadium. Jim also pitched seven shutouts, the most in a season by a Phillies pitcher since Grover Cleveland Alexander tossed eight in 1917.

In 1966, Jim won 19 games for the third straight year. But he lost 14. He also posted his 2,000th career strikeout when he fanned Jesse Gonder, then with the Pirates, at Connie Mack Stadium. He pitched 314 innings, second in the league to

Sandy Koufax (323), and was second in strikeouts with 252 to Koufax (317). And his five shutouts tied him for the league lead with five other pitchers.

In 1967, Jim posted a 17-14 record, but in the process he tied a National League record for most 1-0 games lost in a season with five. He led the league in shutouts with six, innings pitched (302.1), and strikeouts (253) and was second in earned run average (2.29) to Atlanta's Phil Niekro (1.87).

After posting 76 wins in four years with the Phillies, Bunning was traded to Pittsburgh in December 1967, for Woodie Fryman, Bill Laxton, Harold Clem, and Don Money. The news wasn't too popular with Phillies fans.

Jim lasted a year and a half in Pittsburgh. He finished the 1969 season in Los Angeles, then rejoined Philadelphia in 1970. Bunning posted a 10-15 record in the club's final season in Connie Mack Stadium. That year, Bunning registered a 6-5 win over the Astros in the Astrodome for his 100th career National League victory. He thus became only the second pitcher ever to win 100 games in each league.

With the Phillies moving into Veterans Stadium in 1971, Bunning started the first game and beat Montreal. After the season, he retired.

Bunning finished with a 224-184 career record and an earned run average of 3.27. He struck out 2,855 batters, which at the time, was second best in major league history.

Jim's record with the Phillies was 89-73, but in the six years he was in Philadelphia, the club had only two finishes in the top four.

After retiring as a player, Jim spent the next five years managing in the Phillies farm system at Reading, Eugene, Toledo, and Oklahoma City.

He then left baseball and returned to his home in Fort Thomas, Ky., where he got involved in representing ballplayers and also worked in the brokerage business.

Later, Bunning got into politics. "They asked me to run for city council," he said. "I ran and was successful. Then they asked me to run for state legislature. Again, I ran and was successful."

Jim stayed in politics, was elected to the U.S. Congress, and later became senator from Kentucky.

One thing everyone was wondering was when Jim Bunning will be elected into the Hall of Fame. It took until1996, when the Veterans Committee voted him in along with Earl Weaver. There is no doubt that Jim Bunning was one of the greatest pitchers the Phillies ever had. It would have been greater for the team had he come to the club sooner, rather than later.

Jim Bunning Phillies Statistics

Year	W	L	SV	PCT	G	GS	CG	SH	IP	H	BB	SO	ERA
1964	19	8	2	.704	41	39	13	5	284.1	248	46	219	2.63
1965	19	9	0	.679	39	39	15	7	291.0	253	62	268	2.60
1966	19	14	1	.576	43	41	16	5	314.0	260	55	252	2.41
1967	17	15	0	.531	40	40	16	6	302.1	241	73	253	2.29
1970	10	15	0	.400	34	33	4	0	219.0	233	56	147	4.11
1971	5	12	1	.294	29	16	1	0	110.0	126	37	58	5.48
Totals	89	73	4	.549	226	208	65	23	1520.2	1361	329	1197	2.93

Ten

Johnny Callison

Phillies' All-Star Outfielder

by Skip Clayton

The outlook for the Phillies was rather bleak as they finished the 1959 season in last place for the second straight year. John Quinn had been hired as the general manager before the start of the season, and what he saw that year convinced him that a lot of changes had to be made. There were still a lot of strong arms on the pitching staff, but the remainder of the team wasn't much to cheer about.

Quinn had built the Boston-Milwaukee Braves into a strong contender, winning three pennants and one World Series. With the Phils, he started wheeling and dealing. After the season, Quinn swung into action. He acquired Johnny Callison from the Chicago White Sox for Gene Freese. After a series of trades, Quinn had built up a solid club that would have its first winning season in 1962 and would almost win the 1964 pennant.

"I felt lousy when I was traded to the Phillies," Callison said. "The White Sox had just won the 1959 pennant and I had been learning my way around the American League. The Phillies had finished in last place two years in a row."

Callison, who was born in Qualls, Okla., on March 12, 1939, played in 1,886 total games. He hit .264 with 226 home runs and had 840 runs batted in. In his 10 years with the Phillies, he hit 185 home runs, seventh most in Phillies history.

Signed by the White Sox right after high school, Callison started his career when he was 18 years old with Bakersfield in the California League and hit .340 in 1957. The next year, he moved up to Indianapolis of the American Association, the White Sox' top farm team, and led the league in home runs with 29, while driving in 93 runs and hitting .283. The White Sox brought him up toward the end of the season and he hit .297 and clouted his first major league home run.

Callison played in 49 games with the White Sox in 1959 and batted only .179. He started the season with Chicago, but in late June, he was sent back to Indianapolis, where he hit .299.

"My first year with the Phillies, my knee was still bothering me," Callison recalled. "I had been injured playing winter ball. And I also injured the knee again during my first year with the Phillies, towards the end of May."

Callison hit only .266 in 1960 and .260 in 1961, as the Phillies finished in last place both years. In 1961, the club had a record 23-game losing streak.

"That season and the losing streak was a nightmare," Callison said. "I was being platooned in left field. At times, you were wondering whether you could play.

"When we came back from Milwaukee after snapping that 23-game losing streak, there were about 5,000 fans waiting for us at the airport. We were a little worried about what they would do, but they were good fans, and they cheered us."

Things really looked up in 1962, when the Phillies posted an 81-80 record for their first winning season in nine years. Callison, who had moved to right field for good, had a strong year, hitting .300 with 23 homers and 83 runs batted in. He became the first Phillies player since Chuck Klein to reach figures in doubles (26), triples (10), home runs (23), and stolen bases (10) in the same season. He made the All-Star team for the first time.

He also showed that season that he was a clutch hitter. On consecutive days, he hit game-winning homers in the bottom of the ninth. The first was off Warren Spahn of the Milwaukee Braves, and the second was off Lindy McDaniel of the St. Louis Cardinals. The Phillies won both games by the score of 2-1.

The Phillies moved up to fourth in 1963, and Callison had another solid season with 26 home runs, 78 runs batted in, and a .284 average. He hit for the cycle in Pittsburgh on June 27, the last time a Phillies' player accomplished this feat until Gregg Jefferies matched it in 1995.

"We had Richie Allen up for good in 1964 and picked up Jim Bunning and we thought we had a good team," Callison said. "We took off and had that 6 1/2-game lead with 12 to go. We lost that lead in a week because Cincinnati and St. Louis, who were chasing us, went on winning streaks.

"We won together and we lost together that year. We were officially eliminated on the last day, when St. Louis beat the Mets.

Callison had his biggest moment that season when he hit a game-winning homer in the All-Star Game. The National League beat the American League, 7-4, at Shea Stadium.

"I had flied deep to Mantle the first time I faced Dick Radatz. Next time, I decided, I would swing a little earlier and as hard as I could," Callison recalled. "Once I hit it, I knew it was gone. It was the hardest-hit ball I had all year. Rocky Colavito got the ball back and gave it to Bunning, and he gave it to me. I still have it."

Callison was voted the Most Valuable Player of the All-Star Game. Had the Phillies won the pennant, Callison probably would have been MVP of the National League. He hit 31 homers, drove home 104 runs, and batted .274, but Ken Boyer of the pennant-winning St. Louis Cardinals got the award and Callison finished second.

Callison was solid in 1965 in what would be his last big year with the Phillies. He slammed 32 homers, drove in 101 runs, and hit .262. Callison had three homers in one game against the Cubs in Wrigley Field, becoming the first Phillies player to have a pair of three-home run games in a career. His first was a year earlier against Milwaukee at Connie Mack Stadium during the 10-game losing streak. He also led all outfielders in assists for the fourth straight year.

Gene Mauch managed the All-Star team in 1965 and selected Callison as a reserve outfielder. They didn't use him in the game in Minnesota.

"Leading the league in assists didn't help much in the contract talks," said Callison. "All John Quinn wanted to talk about was offense."

In 1966, his average jumped up 14 points to .276, but his RBI total dropped to 55, and his home run total tailed off to 11. He led the league in doubles with 40, but his slugging percentage dropped from .509 to .418.

"I had to get glasses that year," Callison said. "That was the year that injuries started to set in."

Callison's average for the rest of his career with the Phillies wavered between .244 and .265, and his high in home runs in his final four years was 16 in 1969.

After the 1969 season, he was traded to the Cubs for pitcher Dick Selma and outfielder Oscar Gamble. "I wasn't shocked when I was traded by the Phillies," Callison said. "I wanted to be traded."

After the 1971 season, Callison was traded to the New York Yankees for pitcher Jack Aker. In his last full year in the majors, Callison hit .258. During his 1973 season with the Yankees, he was released after hitting .176.

Callison's lifetime batting average with the Phillies was .271. His 185 home runs are still the seventh most in the team's history. He hit 86 of those home runs in Connie Mack Stadium, the most ever hit there by a left-handed batter.

After he retired, Callison worked at selling cars and was a bartender. He has been retired for several years and still lives in Glenside, right outside Philadelphia.

Callison had a fine career with the Phillies and will always be remembered as a top outfielder for his team and for his game-winning homer in the 1964 All-Star Game.

Johnny Callison Phillies Statistics

Year	G	AB	R	H	2B	3B	HR	RBI	AVG	OBP	SLGP
1960	99	288	36	75	11	5	9	30	.260	.360	.427
1961	138	455	74	121	20	11	9	47	.266	.363	.418
1962	157	603	107	181	26	10	23	83	.300	.363	.491
1963	157	626	96	178	36	11	26	78	.284	.339	.502
1964	162	654	101	179	30	10	31	104	.274	.316	.492
1965	160	619	93	162	25	16	32	101	.262	.328	.509
1966	155	612	93	169	40	7	11	55	.276	.338	.418
1967	149	556	62	145	30	5	14	64	.261	.329	.408
1968	121	398	46	97	18	4	14	40	.244	.319	.415
1969	134	495	66	131	29	5	16	64	.265	.332	.440
Totals	1,432	5,306	774	1,438	265	84	185	666	.271	.338	.457

Eleven

Dolf Camilli

Ace First Baseman of the 1930s

by Skip Clayton

Mention the best and worst trades in Phillies history, and Dolf Camilli is certain to be named in not only the former but also the latter. The 5-10, 185-pound left-handed first baseman came to the Phillies in 1934 from the Chicago Cubs in what was one of the best swaps the Phillies ever made. And he was dealt away from the club to the Brooklyn Dodgers in 1938 in one of the worst Phillies trades of all time.

In between, Camilli gave the Phillies four outstanding seasons during which he led the team in home runs each year, slamming 92 over that period, while batting .295 in 540 games.

The Phillies traded him at the peak of his career, and Camilli went on to become a standout with the Dodgers, even winning the National League's Most Valuable Player award in 1941, when he led the circuit in home runs (34) and RBIs (120).

Camilli, who is credited with 12 years of service in the big leagues (having broken in in 1933 and finished in 1945 with the Boston Red Sox), had a lifetime batting average of .277. In 1,490 games, he had 1,482 hits, including 239 home runs. He collected 950 RBIs and scored 936 times.

The San Francisco native was also an outstanding fielder, generally regarded as one of the best defensive first basemen in Phillies history. In 1937, he led National League first sackers in fielding with a .994 percentage.

Camilli was 26 when he came to the majors, having spent eight years in the minors. He joined the Chicago Cubs in 1933 and was traded to the Phils for first baseman Don Hurst on June 11, 1934.

"My reaction about coming to the Phillies was pretty poor," Camilli said. "I was going from a possible pennant contender and a real good club to a second-division team. The Phillies didn't draw well and they didn't pay well.

"I was going to quit. I was going to return home and not report. But the Phillies came to town right after the trade, and their manager, Jimmie Wilson, talked to me and told me that I would play every day. Naturally, that was what I wanted."

Dolf went on to lead the Phillies in home runs with 12 while batting .265. Camilli had particular success against the New York Giants. "I had some pretty good games against the Giants," Camilli remembered. "They always had great pitching, one of the best pitching staffs around, with guys who could throw the ball and knew what to do with it. Percentage-wise, I didn't know what I hit off Carl Hubbell, but power-wise, I hit quite a few homers off him. He got me out a lot of times, but when I got hold of one, it didn't matter who I was batting against.

"Hubbell and Dizzy Dean were two of the best pitchers I saw," Camilli added. "Diz could throw the ball by anybody.

"The first time I faced him as a Phillie was in 1934, when he won 30 games. I had beaten Lon Warneke, who was one of the best pitchers in the league, with a homer in Chicago. Next day, we played the Cardinals, and Dean was pitching. I hit two homers and we beat him, 14-4. The next day, we beat Paul Dean, and my triple was instrumental in winning that game.

"I had a few good days against Dizzy, but not many. He shut the door in your face real quickly." In 1935, Camilli increased his home run total to 25, including seven against the Giants, while batting .261. The following year, he raised his totals to 28 and .315, while driving in 102 runs. His home run total was second in the league behind Mel Ott (33), and his RBI total tied for fifth.

"The Phillies always had a good-hitting club," Camilli said. "We never had the pitching, although we had some good young players like Claude Passeau and Bucky Walters who proved themselves later with other clubs.

"As hitters, we held our own with most of the clubs, especially in Baker Bowl. Sometimes, I wonder if that park was that much of an advantage to me. I liked big parks better, because the line drives I hit at Baker Bowl were singles, while they would be homers in some of the bigger parks. But I guess it all averaged out."

Camilli had some other recollections of his days at Baker Bowl.

"We always faced tough pitching in that park," he said. "Other teams knew we had good hitting, and they didn't pitch any humpty dumpties against us. They threw their four best at us, and often they were left-handers. As a result, I think I hit them better then right-handers. I hit the left-handers good, and the more I saw them, the better I hit them."

Tough pitching didn't stop Camilli in 1937. He hit a career-high .339, setting a Phillies record for the highest batting average for a first baseman in the 20th century. He also smacked 27 home runs and drove in 80 runs.

One thing Camilli did argue frequently about was his Phillies salary. He had held out in the spring of 1937, and he did it again in 1938. It paved the way for his departure from the Phillies.

"No matter what kind of a year you had, all they wanted to do was give you about a $1,000 raise," Camilli said. "So I held out in 1937. I didn't report to spring training and didn't report for two weeks of the season. I got into shape on my own. When I came back, I had one of the best years I ever had. They offered me another $1,000 raise and I returned it. That's when they made the deal with Brooklyn."

The Phillies shipped Camilli to the Dodgers for the mere sum of $50,000 and an unknown outfielder Eddie Morgan, who had played 39 games in the majors and never played a single game for the Phillies. The swap ranked as one of the worst the Phillies ever made.

Camilli went on to have a glittering career with the Dodgers. From 1938 to 1942, his home run totals were 24, 26, 23, 34, 26. Four times he drove in more than 100 runs, and four times he scored more than 90. His highest average was .290 in 1939.

In 1941, the Dodgers won their first pennant in 21 years with Camilli having a banner season that led to his MVP award.

The Dodgers, however, lost the World Series in five games to the Yankees.

Two seasons later, Camilli was sold by the Dodgers to the New York Giants. But he refused to report and sat out the rest of the season at home. The next year (1944), Camilli was a player-manager for Oakland of the Pacific Coast League. Then in 1945, he joined the Red Sox for his final year as a player.

Over the next 25 years, Camilli spent most of his time in baseball as a scout, working for the Yankees, A's, and Angels. He retired in 1971.

Camilli had a son, Doug who spent nine years in the majors during the 1960s with the Los Angeles Dodgers and the Washington Senators.

Camilli died on Oct. 21, 1990, at the age of 90. He was easily one of the best Phillies first basemen ever—both with the bat and with the glove.

Dolf Camilli Phillies Statistics

Year	G	AB	R	H	2B	3B	HR	RBI	AVG	OBP	SLGP
1934	102	378	52	100	20	3	12	68	.265	.350	.429
1935	156	602	88	157	23	5	25	83	.261	.336	.440
1936	151	530	106	167	29	13	28	102	.315	.441	.577
1937	131	475	101	161	23	7	27	80	.339	.446	.587
Totals	540	1,985	347	585	95	28	92	333	.295	.395	.510

Twelve

Steve Carlton

Four-Time Cy Young Award Winner

by Jeff Moeller

S teve Carlton was the Phillies' proof that silence is golden. The southpaw Hall of Famer let his pitching arm do most of his talking.

Carlton had a running feud with the media in Philadelphia and refused to talk with them, mainly due to alleged unfair treatment from one of the members of the local media. His public comments were already few and far between in his second season in Philadelphia in 1973, and he had stopped granting interviews totally in 1978.

There were, however, isolated instances when he did speak to the media, generally those involved in television, as his feud was with the print media. Even when the Phillies retired his number during a ceremony in 1989, Carlton spoke briefly with former teammate Tug McGraw, who had been working for a local television station at the time.

The Colorado native prided himself on an unprecedented daily stern work ethic, one in which he would do 1,000 sit-ups with 15-pound weights around each ankle and wrist. He would rarely speak to his teammates on days he pitched, and he stuffed cotton in his ears in order to achieve total concentration.

"That [cotton] really helped me," he said during a 1989 interview. "I started with that either in Shea Stadium with those jets flying over or in Houston in the Astrodome. It was loud at those places.

"It was piercing and it hurt. I have sensitive ears and I damaged them from pistol shooting when I was young."

So Carlton used every procedure possible to stay focused.

"It was all about being mentally strong out there," said Carlton during a televison interview upon his return to Philadelphia in a 1999 ceremony to honor the team's all-century team. "I knew what I had to do to succeed.

"The media was, in many ways, a negative influence. But my relationship with them was more related to strengthening my own game."

Carlton reportedly gained most of his inner strength from reading books on psychology, Taoism, and Buddhism.

"It was about taking a positive approach in life," he said. "It had worked for me. I always tried to stay on an even keel when it came to talking about wins and losses."

"I never had a problem with concentration or knowing what I had to do. I wasn't as focused when I was younger, but I realized it was something that I had to do."

Even though Carlton presented an image of a loner, he was far from it. He involved himself in charity work, especially work pertaining to children.

"Away from the ballpark, you would never know he was the same guy," said the late Richie Ashburn in1989 during the ceremony retiring Carlton's number. "He was very outgoing and very friendly. He loved to have a good time.

"But on the day he pitched, no one got near him, even his good friend Tim McCarver. And if any of his visits ever got back to the media, he would never go to that place again."

Carlton's 329 career wins rank him second among left-handers behind Warren Spahn (363) and his 4,136 career strikeouts put him ahead of Spahn (2,583) in that category.

The late Tom Ferrick, a former player and advance scout for the Kansas City Royals in Philadelphia during the late 1980s and early 1990s, once compared Carlton and Spahn.

"Spahnie was a finesse pitcher who didn't throw real hard, but he was cute out there. He had that screwball and slider and really kept the hitters off guard with his deceptive moves.

"Steve, on the other hand, was totally a power pitcher. He had that 90-mile-per-hour-plus fastball and that great slider of his, and he had excellent command of his pitches."

Carlton's pitching record with the Phillies will be one to marvel at. It began, ironically, when former general manager John Quinn traded the popular Rick Wise for Carlton following the 1971 season.

Carlton came to Philadelphia as a relatively unknown pitcher, despite coming off a 20-9 season with St. Louis. Before that, he had a 57-53 career mark.

But he quickly won over the fans with an incredible 27-10 record and a 1.98 ERA and a league-leading 310 strikeouts. He also won 15 straight games, a club record. Carlton hurled eight shutouts, pitched a career-high 346.1 innings and completed 30 of the 41 games he started.

He walked off with the first of his four Cy Young Awards (1972, 1977, 1980, and 1982), five 20-win seasons, and a National League-record six one-hitters.

Former Pittsburgh Pirates slugger Willie Stargell paid one of the greatest compliments to Carlton when he once described trying to hit him as "drinking coffee with a fork."

In the postseason, Carlton lost games in the 1976 and 1977 National League Championship Series and won games in the 1978, 1980, and 1983 NLCS.

In the 1980 World Series, Carlton was the winning pitcher in the second and sixth games. He was the losing pitcher in the third game of the 1983 World Series.

During 1984, Carlton posted a 13-7 record and won his 235th game as a Phillie, a club record. Injuries would hamper him through the next two seasons, and he won his final game as a Phillie on June 1, 1986. He pitched his final game against his ex-team in St. Louis on June 21 and was later released by the club.

After brief stints with the Giants, White Sox, Indians, and Twins over the next two seasons, a 44-year-old Carlton came to spring training with the Phillies in 1989, but he realized his career was finally over.

But five years later, Carlton was elected to the Hall of Fame, as he received 436 of 455 total ballots cast, or 95 percent.

He spoke to the media during a lengthy press conference in New York City and recalled some of the special moments during his career.

He described his silent posture with the media as "something I thought about for a long time.

"I was afraid that I was cheating the fans, and I concluded that performance on the field is a player's first responsibility. So, rather than have the media quote me, I would rather have them write how I performed on the field."

Carlton is admittedly proud of his four Cy Young Awards, but he likes to put that accomplishment in its proper perspective.

"A lot of it was luck," Carlton said. "Sometimes it had to do with what other pitchers in the league were doing or didn't do. In 1976, Randy Jones and I had both had good records. They happened to choose him for the Cy Young. Sometimes when I won, other pitchers deserved consideration."

He also had his own feeling about his approach toward the 1980 World Series.

"I approached the Royals as just another game of catch," he said about a Series in which he had a 2-0 record and allowed four earned runs over 17 innings.

One of the long-standing fixtures in his career was Tim McCarver, who was his personal catcher during the 1972 season and also from 1975 to 1979.

"Lefty was far ahead of his time," McCarver said. "His training and fitness techniques were orginally met with scorn. The establishment couldn't see it.

"Here was a man who firmly convinced himself that he was a man who took great pride in his hitting, in every aspect of his game. His only weakness, albeit a minor one, was poorly covering first base. But his follow-through, which was such a big part of his effectiveness, was so powerful that he'd be a little off balance toward first base.

"Some people said that he should have gotten out of the game earlier because he embarrassed himself. A man has to keep chasing his dream. If a major league team wanted to sign him, he shouldn't have retired."

Steve Carlton Phillies Statistics

Year	W	L	SV	PCT	G	GS	CG	SH	IP	H	BB	SO	ERA
1972	27	10	0	.730	41	41	30	8	346.1	257	87	310	1.97
1973	13	20	0	.394	40	40	18	3	293.1	293	113	223	3.90
1974	16	13	0	.552	39	39	17	1	291.0	249	136	240	3.22
1975	15	14	0	.517	37	37	14	3	255.1	217	104	192	3.56
1976	20	7	0	.741	35	35	13	2	252.2	224	72	195	3.13
1977	23	10	0	.697	36	36	17	2	283.0	229	89	198	2.64
1978	16	13	0	.552	34	34	12	3	247.1	228	63	161	2.84
1979	18	11	0	.621	35	35	13	4	251.0	202	89	213	3.62
1980	24	9	0	.727	38	38	13	3	304.0	243	90	286	2.34
1981	13	4	0	.765	24	24	10	1	190.0	152	62	179	2.42
1982	23	11	0	.676	38	38	19	6	295.2	253	86	286	3.10
1983	15	16	0	.484	37	37	8	3	283.2	277	84	275	3.11
1984	13	7	0	.650	33	33	1	0	229.0	214	79	163	3.58
1985	1	8	0	.111	16	16	0	0	92.0	84	53	48	3.33
1986	4	8	0	.333	16	16	0	0	83.0	102	45	62	6.18
Totals	**241**	**161**	**0**	**.600**	**499**	**499**	**185**	**39**	**3,697.1**	**3,224**	**1,252**	**3,031**	**3.09**

Thirteen

Bob Carpenter

Rescuer of the Phillies' Franchise

by Skip Clayton

In 1943, the Carpenter family shelled out $400,000 to purchase a down-trodden Phillies team that hadn't won a pennant in 28 years, that hadn't even finished in the first division in 11 years, and that had few players of major league caliber, no farm system, and no ballpark of its own.

The Carpenters' 26-year-old son, Robert R.M. Carpenter Jr., was installed as president of the club, thereby becoming the youngest team president in major league history.

In the year after that late 1943 purchase, Bob Carpenter became a pillar among major league chief executives, and his team became one of the top franchises in the National League.

Carpenter presided over the Phillies for 29 years. In that period, he not only put the franchise back on its feet, he saved it from possible extinction. He also built one of baseball's most productive farm systems and was the driving force behind the erection of Veterans Stadium.

"Our interest in baseball started before we bought the Phillies," said Carpenter. "My father [Robert R.M. Carpenter Sr.] was a great friend and a great fan of Connie Mack. Mr. Mack asked him if he would be interested in running a minor league team in Wilmington in the Inter-State League for the A's. My father said he was. So Mr. Mack put a team down there and my father built a park. It sat about 4,000 people.

"Another dear friend of my father's was Herb Pennock, who lived in Kennett Square. After we'd run the team in Wilmington for a few years, Herb came to my father and told him the Phillies were for sale. 'You have so much fun with this minor league team, why don't you buy the Phillies?' he said.

"We got the club, and Pennock, who was the farm director for the Boston Red Sox, was our first choice as general manager and he took the job."

The job facing Carpenter and Pennock was a tough one. With a bad ball club and no minor league players to speak of, it would take time and money to build a respectable team.

"It was probably the worst major league team I have ever seen, including the old St. Louis Browns," recalled Carpenter. "It was a terrible team. Herb tried to improve it with little deals here and there, but he didn't have anything to deal.

"I went into the Army, and when I came back in time for the 1946 season, we finished fifth, which was then a great thing. We packed Shibe Park. It was quite a success."

Soon afterward, though, tragedy struck. At a winter meeting in New York in 1948, Pennock dropped dead from a heart attack.

"It was a severe blow to the Phillies when we lost Herb, because he had the team and the farm system well under way," said Carpenter. "Herb was very active in the free agent market. In those days, you could sign anybody. There wasn't a draft then, and we were one of the active clubs in signing players.

"We had good scouts. That's how we got the basis of the team that won the 1950 pennant."

In the 1940s, the Phillies spent more than $2 million to sign players. In the process, the Carpenters gained a reputation for their generosity and good treatment of their players.

After a sixth-place finish in 1948, the Phillies moved up to third in 1949, their highest finish since 1917.

"In 1949, with the spirit and the way [Eddie] Sawyer was managing, you could see the ability coming," Carpenter said. "By the middle of the 1950 season, I thought we had a chance to win the pennant against the great Brooklyn Dodgers club, which I would say had the finest arms, legs, and physical ball club I ever saw, except for pitching. And that includes the Yankees of the late 1940s and early 1950s."

On July 25, 1950, the Phillies moved into first for the rest of the season. After stretching their lead to seven games in early September, the Phillies almost blew the pennant, taking only a two-game lead into the final two-game series at Ebbets Field against Brooklyn. They clinched it on the final day of the season behind the five-hit pitching of Roberts and Dick Sisler's three-run homer to beat the Dodgers, 4-1, in 10 innings.

"I couldn't believe what happened that last week," Carpenter said. "It was a good enough lead with our pitching. We should have never gotten into the position where Roberts had to pitch with two days' rest on the last day. It was a horrible experience until Sisler hit the fastball into the stands.

"We had a disaster the final month. Bubba Church was hit under the eye by a line drive off the bat of Ted Kluszewski, which was the worst accident I ever saw in baseball. We lost Bubba. Bob Miller had a bad arm and then Curt Simmons was in the National Guard and his unit was activated."

Despite the ecstasy of winning the pennant, the Phillies lost to the New York Yankees in the World Series in four straight, 1-0, 2-1 in 10, 3-2, and 5-2.

"I always felt that if we had our regular pitching staff—and I am not saying we would've beaten the Yankees—but it wouldn't have been like that," said Carpenter. "We were only out of one of those four games and that was when we started Miller."

Although they came close to winning the pennant in the next decade, the Phillies remained a solid club through 1957, finishing in the first division four times and with a record of .500 or better four times.

"We had good solid clubs after 1950," Carpenter said. "But I felt I should have done a better job with the farm system, because ownership's influence goes down from top to bottom. All I said was, 'Be sure you guys show up with pitchers or there is going to be trouble,' but we sort of got overbalanced. I always felt that was my fault. We would show up with fine pitching material, but little else."

Roy Hamey was the general manager from 1954 to 1958. Then John Quinn took over and remained until he was succeeded by Paul Owens in 1972. The Phillies came close to winning a pennant in 1964, but lost a 6 1/2-game lead with 12 games to go.

"I didn't know who to feel sorry for, John Quinn or myself," said Carpenter. "That lead was impossible to lose. But if you are in the big leagues, you are going to get hurt once in a while."

Carpenter made two big moves during the 1960s. He brought in his oldest son, Ruly, to work for the club, and in 1965, Owens was put in charge of the farm system, which by then, hadn't been sending many top players to the big leagues.

By then, though, Carpenter was tiring of the everyday duties of running the club. In 1972, the time had arrived for him to turn the club over to Ruly.

"When Ruly moved over, I moved out," said Bob, "because I didn't think it was right for the old man to lean over somebody's shoulder and tell him what to do. I wouldn't have put him there if I thought I had to do that."

When Bob Carpenter was president, the one thing the fans didn't have to worry about was seeing a Robin Roberts or Richie Ashburn sold to another team to meet a payroll.

When the Carpenter family sold the Phillies in 1981 to a group headed by Bill Giles, the Phillies were in a lot better shape than they were when the Carpenters bought the team in 1943.

On July 8, 1990, Bob Carpenter died at the age of 74. Later, the new field house at the University of Delaware was named after Bob.

Bob Carpenter saved Phillies baseball—no ifs, ands, or buts about it.

Fourteen

Ruly Carpenter

President of 1980 Phillies' World Series Champs

by Skip Clayton

On Nov. 22, 1972, Bob Carpenter stepped down as president of the Phillies after 29 years. Nobody had ever been president of the club that long. He turned over the job to his son Ruly, who had been working for the club for nine years.

During his tenure as president of the Phillies, Ruly saw the club win the East Division championship four times, the club's third pennant in 1980, and the team's only World Series that same year. Seventeen months later, the Carpenter family put the club up for sale.

"I toyed with the idea in my last year at Yale of going to law school, but the Phillies were so bad in 1960 and 1961, I just decided maybe there was something I could do," Ruly said. "I took a couple business courses at Delaware and helped Tubby Raymond coach the baseball team, which was in the spring of 1963.

"In the fall of 1963, I started working for the team in the treasurer's office with George Harrison. I spent a year with him.

"I went into the farm system because that is where I wanted to be," said Carpenter. "That is where you start. My first assignment was camp administrator at Leesburg, Fla., in 1965, and that was a blessing in disguise. That is where I met Paul Owens, who was camp coordinator.

"I knew the farm system was bad and I knew what our problems were. Paul and I talked many times about it. We knew we had a long ways to go if we were going to be competitive. In 1965, the first year of the free agent amateur draft, Paul became the farm director, and his first official function representing the Phillies was the June draft.

"I had recommended Paul to my dad and Mr. [John] Quinn to be the farm director to replace Clay Dennis," he said. "It started then, but it wasn't until about 1973 that we could see what we had accomplished. That is when things started to turn at the major league level, and that was because of what we had developed in the farm system."

Before the club could turn the corner, every scout, no matter how long he had been with the club, was evaluated by Ruly. It wasn't a pretty picture. The farm system, for the most part, had stopped producing since the Whiz Kids won it in 1950.

"I put together a little book which turned out to be a big book and we took every player that our scouts had signed and looked to see where they ended up," said Carpenter. "A lot of changes were made based on that study."

Meanwhile, the Phillies were going backwards, beginning in 1967, when they finished fifth. It would be their last winning season until 1975. Slowly but surely, the farm system started to send players up to the majors, beginning in 1970.

There were some big changes in 1972. Owens took over as the general manager, replacing John Quinn. Dallas Green, who had been the assistant farm director, took over for Owens. In the middle of July, Frank Lucchesi was let go as manager. Owens took over and decided to see firsthand what was happening with the club. Before the year was over, Danny Ozark was named the new manager and Bob Carpenter resigned as president and moved up to chairman of the board. At the age of 32, Ruly became the president. Bob had been only 28 when he assumed those same duties back in 1944.

"At the end of the 1972 season, my dad told me he was stepping down and that I had some exposure with the team," recalled Ruly. "I had been in the farm system since 1965 and that is what I always liked, anyway. I tried to talk him out of it. I told him I thought we were going to get better real soon. I told him he had some tough years, why don't you stick around and enjoy it?"

The Phillies started to improve in 1973, and in 1976, the Phillies won their first National League East Division title with 101 wins, the most ever by a Phillies team. The Phillies won another 101 games in 1977 in what many think might have been the Phillies' greatest team. The Phillies made it three straight first-place finishes in 1978, but in all three seasons, they lost in the playoffs.

"In 1976, we lost to Cincinnati," said Carpenter. "They swept us and followed up by sweeping the Yankees in the World Series. Then came those frustrating losses to the Dodgers in 1977 and 1978."

After losing the 1978 playoffs to the Dodgers, the Phillies picked up Pete Rose and everyone thought getting Rose was the missing link. As it turned out, he was, but not until 1980.

"The first time we got together with Rose, we couldn't sign him," recalled Carpenter. "Bill Giles drove Pete back to the airport. Bill opened up another avenue. He was convinced that there was something else that we could do to sweeten the pot. Then we worked out something with WPHL-TV where they kicked in some additional money, and thanks to that added effort, we were able to work out a deal.

"We always kept my dad informed on what was going on, on the money end, and I had told him that we could finally sign Rose but it will be major money, and if you think it will be too much, we won't sign him. He said, 'If it helps, make the deal.'"

With Rose taking over at first, the Phillies looked like they should have no problem winning the division for the fourth straight year. Instead, they finished fourth. Danny Ozark was let go as the manager near the end of August after losing eight of nine at the Vet. Green took over as the manager.

It all came together in 1980. The Phillies clinched the East Division crown on the next-to-last day of the season. Then they beat the Houston Astros in the five-game championship series, with four games going extra innings. The World Series was easier, as the Phillies took the Kansas City Royals in six games.

"After all of the years of frustration, especially for my father, it was the highlight of all of the years of the Carpenter family ownership to win the World Series. I know my dad was real happy."

Many observers thought the Phillies could make it two straight in1981, but before the season began, the Carpenter family decided to sell the club.

"It was my idea," said Ruly. "I thought about it. In the winter of 1980, there had been settlement with the Players Association on every issue with the exception of the free agency issue. That was held in advance and was going to be negotiated out and we had the strike of 1981.

"During the winter, my philosophy was, that because we were negotiating this free agency thing, most of the owners would take a hard-nosed approach with their negotiations on free agents and possibly send a little message. Something will happen and it will be meaningful, and Mr. Ted Turner signed Claudell Washington to a five-year deal at $750,000 a year, and when I read that in the paper in November, under the circumstances, I just couldn't believe this was happening. I thought it was not going to get any better. Maybe we better start thinking about making a move. I talked to my father several times about it and to my brother, Keith, and we just decided that this was about it. We made the announcement in spring training that the club was for sale. Of course, we were pleased that it was Bill's group that ended up buying it.

Ruly still keeps busy today. He is involved in other business interests outside baseball. He is also on the Board of Trustees for the University of Delaware. Ruly was an excellent executive for the Phillies in whatever capacity he was in and still is the only club president who had a world champion.

Fifteen

Gavvy Cravath

Early Baseball Home Run King

by Jeff Moeller

When it comes to the Phillies' home run kings, Mike Schmidt stands out in bold relief. In fact, Schmidt is on an esteemed list of five players who have led their league in homers six or more times.

Another former Phillie home run king, however, remains obscure among Phillies fans, mainly because he played ball before World War I.

Clifford Carlton Cravath, better known as "Gavvy" or "Cactus," played nine seasons for the Phillies, between 1912 and 1920. Cravath won or tied for the National League home run title six times, finished second once, and also tied for third. He was the regular right fielder on the Phillies' 1915 championship team.

A well-carved and solid 5-foot-10 1/2 and 186 pounds, Cravath was baseball's all-time home run leader until Babe Ruth passed him in 1921 with his 120th homer. Cravath hit as high as .341 and led National League outfielders in assists three times.

According to published reports, Cravath, a native of San Diego, left school at age 15 to make his way in the world, and he held numerous odd jobs before he landed a position as a telegraph operator for the Santa Fe Railroad.

He began playing semipro baseball as a catcher. Cravath was given the nickname "Gavvy" when he hit a seagull while at bat, and a fan yelled, "Gaviota," the Hispanic word for bird. Hence, his name was shortened to "Gavvy."

His play eventually attracted more than a few major league scouts, and he joined Los Angeles of the Pacific Coast League.

"Catchers were a drag on the market," Cravath was quoted as saying. "But they [Los Angeles] needed outfielders really bad. They told me that any catcher could play the outfield, so I did."

Cravath played as many as 200 games during a Pacific Coast League season, and he became proficient at stealing bases, swiping as many as 50 in one season, a trait that didn't follow him to the majors.

Boston purchased his contract in 1908, but Cravath's playing time was cut short due to a surplus of outfielders and a sore arm. In 94 games, he hit .256 with just one homer, and his time was reduced due to the emergence of future stars named Tris Speaker, Duffy Lewis, and Harry Hooper.

But Cravath soon found his mark. Then nicknamed "Cactus" by his Boston teammates, Cravath hit 14 homers for the Minneapolis Millers in 1910.

The following year, Cravath exploded onto the scene in the American Association when he rolled up an amazing 387 total bases on 221 hits. Among those were 53 doubles, 13 triples, 29 homers, and a league-leading .363 average.

A number of big-league clubs showed interest, and the Phillies were one of the more interested ones. They won the bid for Cravath, paying as much as a reported $9,000, a large sum in those days.

The Phillies opened 1912 with a space in their outfield when incumbent John Titus was traded to the Boston Braves during the off-season.

Cravath batted .284, below his minor league marks, but hit 11 homers for a third-place spot among the National League leaders. His bat added some needed punch and formed one of the league's most formidable outfields.

The following year, Cravath hiked his average 57 points and captured his first home run crown with 19 homers. He also led his team in hits (179), RBIs (128), and slugging percentage (.568), as he was a key to the club' second-place finish.

Putting together a season worthy of MVP honors, Cravath was deprived of the honor by Brooklyn's Jake Daubert, the league's batting champion. In an interview, Cravath referred to the honor as an "absurd system which gives a man as much credit for hitting scratch singles as home runs."

He defended his home run title with 19 in 1914, but his average dipped to .299, and he lost the RBI title to teammate Sherry Magee, who topped him, 103 to 100.

But Cravath took his club to its first pennant in 1915 when he blasted 24 homers, knocked in 115 runs, scored 89 runs, and posted a .510 slugging percentage. He also led all outfielders in assists with 28 from his right-field position.

Cravath couldn't carry the magic over to the World Series, however, as he managed just two hits in 16 at-bats, and his club fell to the Red Sox in five games.

The following year, he lost his grip on the home run title, falling four short (with his 12 overall) to Cy Williams of the Chicago Cubs. In 1917, he shared the crown with Dave Robertson of the New York Giants. During the war-shortened season of 1918, Cravath's production fell to eight, but that total still managed to lead the league.

When manager Pat Moran left for Cincinnati in 1919, Jack Coombs took over the reins. But Coombs proved to be a disaster, as the club sank to last place. With the team floundering with an 18-44 mark, the 38-year-old Cravath was named manager.

He shared time in right field with Leo Callahan that season, and he accumulated just 214 at-bats. Cravath still managed to sock 12 homers, the lowest total by any major league home run leader in the 20th century. He did hit .341 and had a .640 slugging percentage.

In 1920, Cravath began the season as manager and implemented a youth movement. He assigned 29-year-old Casey Stengel to right field. Cravath's role was basically reduced to that of a pinch hitter, but he still managed 12 homers.

The club finished eighth for the second consecutive season and Cravath was released. He retreated to his home state of California and signed on as a player-manager with Salt Lake City of the Pacific Coast League. The following season he finished his career batting .277 for Minneapolis.

Never one to mince words, Cravath will also be remembered for some of his more popular sayings, such as "Short singles are like left-handed jabs in the boxing ring. A home run is like a knockout punch"; "There is no advice that I can give in batting except to hammer the ball"; "Some players steal bases with hook slides and speed, but I steal bases with my bat"; "There is nothing that takes the backbone out of a pitcher like a home run"; and "Four singles in succession may not score a run, but a four-base hit always does."

Cravath dabbled in real estate and later began a flamboyant 36-year career as a justice of the peace in Long Beach, Calif. He remained active in his later years until he died at age 82 in 1963.

Gavvy Cravath Phillies Statistics

Year	G	AB	R	H	2B	3B	HR	RBI	AVG	OBP	SLGP
1912	130	436	63	124	30	9	11	70	.284	.358	.470
1913	147	525	78	179	34	14	19	128	.341	.407	.568
1914	149	499	76	149	27	8	19	100	.299	.402	.499
1915	150	522	89	149	31	7	24	115	.285	.393	.510
1916	137	448	70	127	21	8	11	70	.283	.379	.440
1917	140	503	70	141	29	16	12	83	.280	.369	.473
1918	121	426	43	99	27	5	8	54	.232	.320	.376
1919	83	214	34	73	18	5	12	45	.341	.438	.640
1920	46	45	2	13	5	0	1	11	.289	.407	.467
Totals	**1,103**	**3,618**	**525**	**1,054**	**222**	**72**	**117**	**676**	**.291**	**.381**	**.489**

Sixteen

Darren Daulton

The Ultimate Leader

by Jeff Moeller

Darren Daulton will never be recognized for his overall statistics with the Phillies, but he will be forever remembered for his leadership abilities.

"Dutch" was the captain and the heart and soul of the 1993 pennant-winning club that captivated the city.

He was a 25th-round draft pick in 1980, hailing from Arkansas City High School in Kansas. In two-plus minor league seasons, Daulton worked his way to becoming a Double-A All-Star at Reading before he was a late-season recall on the "Wheez Kids" squad of 1983, when he appeared in two games.

Despite being labeled "too small" because of his roughly 185-pound frame, Daulton began to open some eyes with a solid season at Portland in 1984, where he hit a solid .298 in 80 games, despite being nagged half of the season with right shoulder problems.

Two seasons later, Daulton was one of the team's young upstart catchers, along with John Russell, but it would be Daulton who would officially begin a 13-year run that would later cause his name to be mentioned in the same breath with Andy Seminick and Bob Boone.

Yet, just over two months later, he would endure the first of nine knee surgeries. Some of those he played through with his enduring courage and dedication; others would eventually lead to his retirement after the 1997 season. When he went down in late June 1986, Daulton was among the league leaders in walks and home runs per at-bat. Dutch had hit eight homers in 49 games—a pace for 25 for a full season.

He made a miraculous, quick comeback, as he appeared in a May 1987 game, but his mobility limited him to just 53 games, and his average dipped to .194.

In 1988, the Phillies still had free-agent signee Lance Parrish under contract, but they realized his stay would be short. Still, Parrish's presence cut into Daulton's playing time, as Parrish earned an All-Star Game selection.

But Parrish's play went south after the All-Star break. Daulton figured he would get a shot to play more down the stretch, but manager Lee Elia stayed mostly with Parrish.

Dutch hit .208 in 56 games, and he missed the final month of the season due to a broken right hand he suffered after punching the wall in the team video room.

Daulton was seemingly at the crossroads of his young career, and at age 26, he wondered about his future with the Phillies. General manager Lee Thomas apparently had enough of Parrish and wasn't willing to re-sign him. Instead, he dealt Parrish to California in a deal for minor leaguers.

Rumblings rolled through the organization that Thomas was searching for a starting catcher and that, apparently, Daulton wasn't the answer. Thomas acquired veteran backup Steve Lake, but Lake was viewed as an everyday catcher.

After some discussion with the front office, Thomas decided to give Daulton the opportunity to win the job, but he didn't want Daulton to approach the situation as a do-or-die one. Daulton welcomed the chance and was ready to establish himself.

Daulton took the first steps. He hit .201 in 131 games, with Lake serving as his backup. Apparently, Thomas wasn't enamored of Daulton's performance, as he hunted after former Cardinal free agent Tony Pena to solve the team's catching problems. Thomas had an agreement with Pena, but Boston outbid him at the last minute for Pena's services.

Again, Daulton was given another chance. This time, though, he responded in full. He hit 12 homers and drove in 57 runs, and the Phillies had committed to Daulton by signing him to a three-year, $6 million contract.

But life was not quite ready to be fulfilling for Daulton. He was involved in an in-season auto accident with Lenny Dykstra that nearly took his life. He missed 63 games.

As a final, unfitting blow, Daulton played his last game in early September, as he would have to undergo knee surgery to remove bone chips. He still hit 12 homers, but his .196 batting average and 66 strikeouts in 285 at-bats didn't sit well with the fans.

"It was a tough year to go through," Daulton recalled. "But I couldn't control how the fans felt. I can understand their frustration on how the team was going bad, but it's not like we wanted to be in that accident."

But Daulton would again reach back and revive his career. This time he would respond with a blockbuster season, one that would establish himself as one of the top receivers in the game.

Daulton hit a career-high 27 homers and he led the league in RBIs with 109, he was also the fourth catcher to lead the league in RBIs and was the first NL player to win the RBI title with fewer than 500 at-bats—others in the AL, Babe Ruth (3 times) and Roger Maris (1 time). He launched a three-run homer in his first at-bat at home, and he also quickly gained back the confidence of the fans. Daulton received a curtain call.

"That was a great feeling," he recalled. "We didn't win that game, but it beat being booed. I've grown up with the fans here, and I realized that they were behind me."

Bill Giles was also pleased with Daulton, as he signed the 31-year-old catcher to a four-year extension at the end of spring training with a club option for 1998.

Needless to say, it proved to be one of numerous moves that resulted in positive results for the 1993 club. Daulton's average dipped a bit, from .270 to .257, but his overall production remained on schedule as he hit 24 homers and drove in 105 runs. His offensive numbers, however, were of little interest.

"It [1993] was my most enjoyable year," said Daulton. " We began to experience a certain feeling from the first day of spring training.

"We just started to jell from the first day of spring right on through. There were a bunch of great individual players here, but we were more of a team."

Daulton was firmly entrenched as the clubhouse leader, as witnessed by the large lounge chair that sat in front of his locker. Just as his career hit an emotional and physical high, it took another downward spiral the following season, as a broken clavicle ended his season in mid-June.

In 1995, Daulton had to endure the spoils of the game both on and off the field, as a bitter divorce battle and baseball labor problems compounded his struggles at the plate. There was also the sudden descent of the club from first place to a losing record in six weeks.

Fate again dealt Daulton another untimely blow when he suffered a torn anterior cruciate ligament in late August that would result in his seventh knee operation.

Daulton's better days were behind him. Two more knee surgeries would limit him to 89 games over the next two seasons. New manager Terry Francona was faced with working Daulton into right field and first base in 1997, as the club had a budding catcher named Mike Lieberthal on the horizon. Giles was still committed to Daulton, who was in the last year of his contract.

Surprisingly, Daulton performed well in right field, hitting 11 homers and driving in 42 runs. But his Phillies career came to an end in mid-July when he was dealt to the Florida Marlins.

He finally gained his championship ring, as he delivered a key hit in Game 3 of the World Series, in which he hit .389 with a pair of doubles and a homer. He announced his retirement shortly after the season at the age of 37. He had played 1,109 of his 1,161 games in Phillies pinstripes.

Today Daulton does some work in private industries and sharpens his golf game on Florida's gulf coast.

Darren Daulton Phillies Statistics

Year	G	AB	R	H	2B	3B	HR	RBI	AVG	OBP	SLGP
1983	2	3	1	1	0	0	0	0	.333	.500	.333
1985	36	103	14	21	3	1	4	11	.204	.311	.369
1986	49	138	18	31	4	0	8	21	.225	.391	.428
1987	53	129	10	25	6	0	3	13	.194	.281	.310
1988	58	144	13	30	6	0	1	12	.208	.288	.271
1989	131	368	29	74	12	2	8	44	.201	.303	.310
1990	143	459	62	123	30	1	12	57	.268	.367	.416
1991	89	285	36	56	12	0	12	42	.196	.297	.365
1992	145	485	80	131	32	5	27	109	.270	.385	.524
1993	147	510	90	131	35	4	24	105	.257	.392	.482
1994	69	257	43	77	17	1	15	56	.300	.380	.549
1995	98	342	44	85	19	3	9	55	.249	.359	.401
1996	5	12	3	2	0	0	0	0	.167	.500	.167
1997	84	269	46	71	13	6	11	42	.264	.391	.480
Totals	1,109	3,504	489	858	189	23	134	567	.245	.357	.427

Seventeen

Lenny Dykstra

MVP of the 1993 Phillies

by Jeff Moeller

There are few players in Phillies history who thoroughly exemplify their nickname. Lenny "Nails" Dykstra was one of them.

In his eight seasons with the Phillies, Dykstra used a low-key, approach to baseball and life. Throughout his career, he endured his share of highlights, along with four knee surgeries, back surgery, an appendectomy; broken bones in his arm, cheekbone, and left hand; and a pair of broken collarbones.

Dykstra set the table as the club's leadoff hitter and catalyst during the 1993 season, a year in which he scored a major league-leading 143 runs, the most in the National League since former Phillie Chuck Klein scored 152 runs in 1932.

Dykstra also became the first player to lead the league in walks and at-bats in the same season, as he finished with 773 plate appearances, two more than Pete Rose's previous record of 771. His 129 walks set a new team record.

Overall, Dykstra led the National League in runs, walks, at-bats, and hits and was second in doubles and third in on-base percentage. A pair of statistics often overlooked about Dykstra in 1993 were his season highs in homers and RBIs, as he belted 19 round-trippers and drove in 66 runs.

Dykstra credits most of his success to his dedication to baseball as he was growing up. He wasn't the guy who you would find attending dances or proms, but one who would be working on his batting stance during times normally reserved for teenage social events.

When he retired in the spring of 1998 due to a bad back, and before a contract extension kicked in, Dykstra had played in 1,278 games, averaging .285 during his 12 seasons with the Mets and Phillies.

His World Series ring with the 1986 Mets remains high on his list of personal highlights, but Dykstra certainly relishes his run on the 1993 team.

"It got to a point where we all were so anxious to get to the ballpark to see who the next hero would be every day," he said. "There was just so much excitement around that year.

"It was a great year in a great sports town."

After a stellar regular season in '93, Dykstra kept his offensive spark throughout the postseason, as he hit .280 with a pair of homers in the NLCS against Atlanta and then went on to hit .348 in the World Series against Toronto.

Dykstra was easily the team's choice for MVP against the Blue Jays. In Game 2, his leadoff walk helped open the gates for a five-run third inning. He also made two spectacular catches, robbing Devon White to save a run in the third and later grabbing a shot off the bat of Roberto Alomar in the fourth.

He would save his best shot for the sixth. With Toronto cutting the deficit to 5-3 in the sixth, Dykstra smashed one of his four Series homers, giving the Phillies a 6-4 cushion and the eventual win.

In Game 4, Dykstra had a night that baseball fans everywhere will remember. He cracked a pair of two-run homers and barely missed a third, while scoring a record-tying four runs in a World Series game.

In his unique and frank style, Dykstra told the media after the game that he "couldn't care less about what I did." He cited, instead, the state of the team.

"We can't sit and pout about it," said Dykstra about the club's wild 15-14 loss. "You don't have to be a baseball genius to figure that out. Now we've just got to find a way to get back to Toronto."

Dykstra and his teammates did, mainly due to a spectacular Series-saving mound performance from Curt Schilling in a 2-0 victory, one in which Dykstra had his 13-game postseason hitting streak snapped. In response to his streak, Dykstra "couldn't have cared less."

"We came in here and just said, 'Screw it,'" he added. "It showed you what a great game baseball is. We couldn't have had a worse loss than we did the other night.

"But it's still the same game as when you're eight years old. You've still got to hit, run, catch, and throw. Last night I hit two home runs and scored four runs. But this night, I liked better. I had no hits, but we won.

"You just have to go and let it rip. I know one thing. We're going to fight until the end. We also didn't want them to celebrate on our turf."

Dykstra certainly did his share to fight until the end. With his club down, 5-1, Dykstra brought the Phils back with a dramatic three-run homer in the seventh and Mariano Duncan scored the tying run an inning later.

"I can't say enough about him in the Series," said teammate Darren Daulton. "He certainly gave us the spark, but he did that the whole '93 season.

"Without a doubt, he was our MVP of the Series. Nothing amazed me about the guy at the end of the season. I saw him do too much, things I never thought of."

"He sticks out in my mind as the guy who jump-started their offense that year," said Paul Molitor, who edged out Dykstra as MVP of the Series after batting .500. "He was very patient at the plate and could hit for power."

Dykstra's reputation as a spark plug carried over from his days with the Mets, from whom he was acquired in a controversial midseason 1989 deal for Juan Samuel. His brand of playing was often interpreted as "cocky," but he was a guy who any team would be glad to have on its side.

"He's got that competitiveness," said former manager Nick Leyva of Dykstra shortly after he joined the team in 1989. "He's like a mosquito when you're outdoors. You're always waiting for him to bite you."

Former general manager Lee Thomas had similar thoughts.

"I disliked him when he played against us," Thomas said. "He always seemed to get the big hits. I liked to acquire players people don't like. Ain't too many players you'd say that about."

"The greatest compliment I could pay Lenny Dykstra is that he was an easy guy to dislike," said the late Richie Ashburn about Dykstra early in his Phillies career. "But you've got to admire him. He's not big on fraternization, like so many guys are today. He goes out to beat you. He doesn't want to be your friend."

In addition to his steady offense, Dykstra finished his career with a .987 fielding percentage, a mark that reminds many of Ashburn at the height of his career.

"In the first 20 games he played with us, I saw him make one false break," recalled third-base coach John Vukovich. "Even when he did that, he ended up catching the ball. He was a good center fielder with good instincts. He worked on getting help on his game coming up, and it showed."

Today, Dykstra lives in Southern California and owns a string of car washes.

Among club career marks, Dykstra ranks eighth in stolen bases with 174 and third in on-base percentage with a .388 clip. He led the team in stolen bases five consecutive seasons from 1990 to 1994 with totals of 38, 28, 35, 49, and 19.

Lenny Dykstra Phillies Statistics

Year	G	AB	R	H	2B	3B	HR	RBI	AVG	OBP	SLGP
1989	90	352	39	78	20	3	4	19	.222	.297	.330
1990	149	590	106	192	35	3	9	60	.325	.418	.441
1991	63	246	48	73	13	5	3	12	.297	.391	.427
1992	85	345	53	104	18	0	6	39	.301	.375	.406
1993	161	637	143	194	44	6	19	66	.305	.420	.482
1994	84	315	68	86	26	5	5	24	.273	.404	.435
1995	62	254	37	67	15	1	2	18	.264	.353	.354
1996	40	134	21	35	6	3	3	13	.261	.387	.418
Totals	734	2,873	515	829	177	26	51	251	.289	.388	.422

Eighteen

Del Ennis

Phillies' All-Time Slugging Great

by Skip Clayton

Twice the Phillies have had two all-time teams selected by the fans. Each time, Del Ennis was picked as one of the outfielders.

And rightfully so. In his 11 years with the Phillies, Ennis established himself as one of the top hitters in club history.

Playing with the team from 1946 to 1957, the native of the Olney section of Philadelphia hit .286 for the Phillies with 259 home runs—at the time he left the team, a club record. Ennis drove in more than 100 runs six times and hit 20 or more home runs eight times during his career with the Phillies.

Ennis still ranks among the leaders in many of the club's career hitting categories. He is second in home runs (259), third in RBIs (1,124) and total bases (3,029), fourth in hits (1,812) and extra-base hits (634), and fifth in games played (1,630), at-bats (6,327), and doubles (310).

In a career that extended three years beyond his time with the Phillies, Ennis posted a lifetime batting average of .284 with 288 home runs, 2,063 hits, and 1,284 RBIs.

One of the premier hitters of his era in the National League, Ennis, a three-time member of the senior circuit's All-Star team, was *The Sporting News* Rookie of the Year in 1946. Del led the league in RBIs with 126 in 1950, when he helped spark the Whiz Kids to the team's first pennant in 35 years. He was also a top contender for the Most Valuable Player award that year, finishing fourth.

Despite his years of outstanding hitting, Ennis was probably booed more than any player in Phillies history. It was largely because he was a hometown player and the fans expected too much of him.

Del remained a resident of the Philadelphia area until he died on Feb. 8, 1996. He was a co-owner of a bowling establishment in Huntingdon Valley from 1958 to 1991. Ennis was signed by the Phillies right out of high school in 1942.

"I was in my senior year at Olney High when Jocko Collins came out to one of our games," Ennis recalled. "I think I drove in about 12 runs against Bok High School with three homers and a double.

"I signed with the Phillies and played the 1943 season at Trenton in the Inter-State League."

Ennis had an excellent year at Trenton, hitting .346. Del led the league in total bases with 320, cracking 37 doubles, 18 homers, and a league-leading 16 triples. Ennis drove in 93 runs while scoring 104.

Del missed the next two seasons while serving in the Navy. He was out in time to join the 1946 Phillies.

"In 1946, I didn't really expect to stay with the Phillies, but they had to keep me because I was on the national defense list and they had to give me a 30-day trial," Ennis said. "I never had any spring training."

Del hit .313 in his rookie year with 17 home runs, which at the time, was a club rookie record.

"Personally, Schoolboy Rowe helped me the most," he said. "He told me that I should know the pitchers. He used to sit on the bench when he wasn't pitching and help me with the pitchers."

Ennis had two big moments in his rookie year. He was voted to the All-Star team and saw action in Fenway Park. He also had a Del Ennis Night in June at Shibe Park.

"We beat St. Louis and I had a couple of hits," said Ennis. "They had over 35,000 that night."

After a fine rookie season, Del saw his average drop to .275 in 1947, and he hit only 12 home runs. But he drove in 81 runs, eight more than in 1946. And he had a 19-game hitting streak, the longest of his career.

Ennis came back strong in 1948, hitting .290, driving in 95 runs, and smashing 30 homers. He also established the club record (at the time) for most homers in a season on the road with 22.

The following year, the Phillies finally escaped the second division by moving up to third place. The Whiz Kids were starting to come together.

"In the last six weeks, we were all starting to mature as ballplayers," Ennis said. "We were all starting to concentrate and learn how to play."

Del helped the Phillies with a strong finish, as he hit .302, with 25 home runs and 110 RBIs. His 39 doubles were second most in the league, two behind the leader, Stan Musial.

Del was also a part of history that year when the Phillies tied the National League record for the most home runs in an inning with five, against Cincinnati at Shibe Park. Del hit the first. Andy Seminick hit two, while Rowe and Willie Jones each hit one.

The 1950 season was the best of Del's career. The Whiz Kids captured the pennant on the last day of the season, and Ennis hit .311, led the league in runs batted in with 126, and hit 31 homers.

The Whiz Kids had taken the lead for good on July 25, but ran into bad luck in September. On the last day of the season, the Phillies had a one-game lead over the Brooklyn Dodgers. The Phillies won the final game, 4-1, in 10 innings on Dick Sisler's three-run homer.

Brooklyn had almost won in the ninth. With Cal Abrams on second and Pee Wee Reese on first, Duke Snider hit a single to center off Robin Roberts. Richie Ashburn threw out Abrams trying to score. After Jackie Robinson was given an intentional walk, Carl Furillo popped out to Eddie Waitkus at first. Gil Hodges then flied out to Ennis in right.

"I have a recording of that out in the ninth," Ennis said. "Gene Kelly said, 'There's a fly ball to Del Ennis in right field. He is under it and he got it.' It wasn't that easy. What made it so tough was, it was a line drive instead of a fly ball. It was lost in the sun, and I didn't see it too good.

"After we won the pennant, the World Series was an aftermath," Ennis added. "It was a big thrill for us to win the pennant on the last day of the season, going down to the wire. If we had won earlier, we might have given the Yankees a much better battle. We had real good pitching.

"It was wonderful to play with a bunch of guys who worked together so well. We had 25 guys on that club and everyone stuck up for one another. To win, you have to work together. It was a team effort."

Del had one of the biggest days of his career in 1950, when he tied the National League record for most RBIs in two consecutive innings. He drove in seven against the Cubs at Shibe Park on July 27. Ennis doubled with the bases loaded in the seventh and hit a grand slam in the eighth.

After the Phillies were swept in four games by the Yankees, they dropped to fifth in 1951. Ennis made the All-Star team as the starting right fielder. But his average fell to .267, he drove in only 73 runs, and he finished with just 15 homers. By the end of the season, the booing of Ennis had begun.

"The booing didn't bother me much," he said. "At first, when it started, I thought about it. But I made up my mind I was going to play ball or go home. I kept it out of my mind."

Ennis had hurt his back that year. "I had hurt my two back muscles," he said. "That hit me late in May and I couldn't get rid of it the rest of the year. The only cure was to rest, and that didn't come until the off-season."

Del came back strong in 1952, and the Phillies moved up to fourth place, playing the best baseball in the majors over the last three months. Ennis was third in the league in runs batted in with 107, hit 20 homers, and had a .289 batting average. He also came through with one of the biggest clutch hits of his career on Sept. 6 when the Phillies beat the Boston Braves at Shibe Park, 7-6, in 17 innings. Roberts went the distance for his 23rd win of the year, and Del won it when he led off the bottom of the 17th with a homer into the left-field stands.

"I broke my wrist during that game and didn't know it," Ennis said. "I did it in about the third inning. They kept icing it during the game. I had no feeling in it when I hit the homer. But I missed only two games."

Del had another fine season in 1953, hitting .285 with 29 homers and 125 RBIs, fourth in the league. His average dipped to .261 in 1954, but he was fifth in the league with 119 runs batted in, and he also hit 25 homers.

The 1955 season began with Ennis hurt. He and Richie Ashburn collided chasing a line drive by Mickey Mantle in a game against the Yankees in Wilmington right before the home opener. Ennis missed the first three games. He went on to hit .296 with 29 homers. His 120 RBIs were third in the National League.

Not only was Ennis voted to the All-Star team as the starting left fielder that year, but he also had one of his biggest days as a hitter. On July 23, he hit three home runs and drove in seven runs against the Cardinals at Connie Mack Stadium.

On Aug. 9, he picked up his 1,000th RBI. Del was honored on Aug. 25 that year. The second Del Ennis Night drew 38,535 to Connie Mack Stadium.

"That was a night I will never forget," Ennis said. "I had four hits, we won both games, and I missed a grand-slam homer when I hit a foul ball over the roof in left. That would have been the payoff. Next pitch, the pitcher hit me."

Del's average slipped to .260 in 1956. He hit 26 home runs, but his RBI total dropped to 95. It was a good year for a lot of players, but Ennis had had better years for the Phillies. That November, he was traded to the Cardinals for Rip Repulski and Bobby Morgan. It wasn't a good trade for the Phillies.

"We almost won the pennant in St. Louis in 1957," Ennis said. "We lost in the last week to the Braves. I drove in 105 runs batting in front of Musial, who was also my roommate."

The 1957 season was Del's last big year. After spending 1958 with St. Louis, he played briefly with Cincinnati and the Chicago White Sox in 1959 before calling it a career on June 20.

Between 1946 and 1959, Ennis drove in 1,284 runs. Only Stan Musial, with 1,678, drove in more runs in that period. Del was certainly one of the greatest players in Phillies history.

Del Ennis Phillies Statistics

Year	G	AB	R	H	2B	3B	HR	RBI	AVG	OBP	SLGP
1946	141	540	70	169	30	6	17	73	.313	.364	.485
1947	139	541	71	149	25	6	12	81	.275	.325	.410
1948	152	589	86	171	40	4	30	95	.290	.345	.525
1949	154	610	92	184	39	11	25	110	.367	.367	.525
1950	153	595	92	185	34	8	31	126	.311	.372	.551
1951	144	532	76	142	20	5	15	73	.267	.352	.408
1952	151	592	90	171	30	10	20	107	.289	.341	.475
1953	152	578	79	165	22	3	29	125	.285	.355	.484
1954	145	556	73	145	23	2	25	119	.261	.318	.444
1955	146	564	82	167	24	7	29	120	.296	.346	.518
1956	153	630	80	164	23	3	26	94	.260	.299	.430
Totals	1,630	6,327	891	1,812	310	65	259	1,124	.286	.344	.479

Nineteen

Bill Giles

The Only Phillies President with Two Pennants

by Skip Clayton

N ame the baseball job and Bill Giles has done it, going all the way back to 1948 and starting with the Cincinnati Reds, where his father, Warren, was the president and general manager. Warren became president of the National League in 1951. In 1965, Bill headed to Houston to help the Astros open the Astrodome. He also had some fun with the new message scoreboard when umpire John Kibler missed a couple of calls, and flashed a message, "Kibler did it again."

Bill found out the umpires weren't amused. A phone call from the National League president the following morning was put in to Bill. He found out in a hurry that his father wasn't amused.

Meantime, Bill was doing an outstanding job of getting people to the ballpark in Houston. During the 1969 season, the Phillies were looking for somebody to do the same. He got Pete Rose to Philadelphia, and that resulted in two pennants and one World Series championship. He has been active in the community and has been the only Phillies president to have two pennant winners.

His big job has been trying to get a new stadium for the Phillies. Giles has served in other major league capacities, such as on the Official Rules Committee, the Television Committee, and the Schedule Format Committee.

The Phillies were facing a big problem during the 1969 season when they were getting ready to vacate Connie Mack Stadium in time for the 1970 season. They would move to a park that seated 56,000 people, leaving behind a park that held only 33,000.

Bob Carpenter, who was the president of the Phillies, turned to Warren Giles, who would be stepping down as league president that year.

"My father told me about this later, about the story of how I came to the Phillies," recalled Giles. "He was having a cocktail before a game at Connie Mack Stadium in 1969. Bob Carpenter and George Harrison told him that they were going into this new stadium and needed a new marketing guy. Who would you recommend in baseball to do that? My dad mentioned Dick Wagner and a couple of other people. Bob Carpenter said, 'What about your son?' My dad said he would not speak for me or recommend me. You have to make your own decisions. They called me up and asked to interview me to be Vice-President of Business Operations. I asked my boss if it would be OK, and he said fine.

"I came up and was interviewed at Bob Carpenter's house, and Ruly [Carpenter] and George [Harrison] were there. They asked me a lot of questions, and a week or so later, they offered me the job. A couple of days later, I accepted."

The Phillies never did get into the Vet in 1970, but instead spent the whole season at Connie Mack Stadium. Their attendance jumped from 519,414 to 708,247.

"I never forgot that last game at Connie Mack Stadium," said Giles. "I had the brilliant idea of giving out seat slats. We had 5,000 seat slats that were used to replace broken ones at Connie Mack Stadium. I said, 'We don't need these anymore, so why don't we give them out as a souvenir?' In about the fifth or sixth inning, people started taking those seat slats and were pounding them. It was the most eerie sound. People came through the gates carrying wrenches, screwdrivers, hammers, and saws. They just demolished the place. I remember the game went into extra innings and the crowd was really getting kind of scary. We won the game in the 10th, 2-1.

"My plan was to have a helicopter fly in and take home plate out of Connie Mack Stadium and fly it down to the Vet, where home plate was going to be. I was down in the dugout with all of the city officials, and there was no way the helicopter could get down because everybody was on the field."

The first year at the Vet, the Phillies drew 1,511,223 to set an attendance record.

The Phillies became contenders in 1974 and reeled off three East Division championships (1976-78), but lost the National League Championship Series three times. It was at this time that Pete Rose became a free agent. Rose came to Philadelphia for a brief conference. It looked like a sure deal that Rose wouldn't be coming to the Phillies until Giles moved, and moved quickly.

"I never forgot that because I was the one really pushing for Rose," Giles said. "We met with Pete and his lawyer [Reuven Katz] at Ruly's house and Ruly and I said all the great things about Philadelphia. We had in mind to offer him $500,000 a year. Katz said, 'The figure has to be a seven-figure number.' Ruly started counting on his fingers and said, 'That is a million dollars or more a year.' Katz said, 'That is right.' Ruly said, 'Let's have lunch. That is the end of the discussion.'

"We came back to the Vet and announced that Pete wasn't coming to Philadelphia.

"I drove them back to the airport. I walked him into the airport, and his lawyer told me that he really wants to come to Philadelphia. He told me to see if I could get $600,000 a year out of the Carpenters.

"I went back to Bob and Ruly and told them if we can get $600,000 a year, he might sign with us. Ruly said, 'We can't afford that.' I asked them to give me a couple of days. I called WPHL-TV 17 and told them you are paying us so much for the rights. If we get Pete Rose, your ratings will go up and you are going to make more money, so why don't you throw in a couple of hundred thousand extra a year? A day or two later, they said yes. That was one of my prouder moments. People were lined up in the middle of the winter waiting to buy season tickets. We paid for his contract right away."

It finally paid off in 1980, when the club won the World Series for the only time. The way they were rolling in 1981 prior to the strike, they probably would have won their second.

"The 1981 team was probably our best team," said Giles. "I thought the 1977 team was the best team at the time. We were playing better in June 1981 than any team I have ever seen. Then the strike hit, and we were awarded first place. When we came back, we had no momentum."

Ruly Carpenter had announced in spring training that the Phillies were up for sale.

"I was shocked," Giles said. "Within 24 hours, I talked to my lawyer friend, Bill Webb, and 24 hours later, I talked to the Carpenters. I told them I would like to buy the team. They said they wanted me to buy the team and they would be happy to see me own the team because I love baseball and won't screw it up. On June 15, I got a call from Dudley Taft, who said, 'We just had a board meeting, and we have decided that we will put up any amount of money that you want up to $30 million in exchange for the television rights, and we will pay you a fair market price on the rights.' I had already raised $13.5 million. So I asked for $15 million and told him we will make an offer. I had $28.5 million and borrowed $1.5 million and that was it."

The sale of the Phillies was announced on Oct. 29, 1981. In addition to Bill and Taft Broadcasting, the other limited partners were J.D.B. Associates, Tri-Play Associates, Fitz Dixon (who had sold the Philadelphia 76ers earlier in the year), and Rochelle Levy.

The Phillies won 89 games in 1982, but finished second, three games behind the St. Louis Cardinals. The 1983 season was better, as the club, also nicknamed the Wheeze Kids, won the pennant. So far, the Phillies were winning pennants every 30-35 years (1915, 1950, and 1980), but after 1980, Phillies fans only had to wait three years to win another one.

The Phillies weren't as fortunate in the 1983 World Series, losing to the Baltimore Orioles in five games. Things started to go downhill after that. Between 1984 and 1992, they only posted one winning season, 1986. The Phillies shocked many people in 1993 when they won the pennant, then lost the World Series in six games to the Toronto Blue Jays. This made Bill Giles the only club president in Phillies history to have two pennant winners.

"That 1993 season was by far the most exciting and most fun I ever had here," Giles said. "We did win it in my second season [1983] and I thought it would be easy.

There was always that hope after 1983 that the club would string together a bunch of pennants, but it didn't.

"My biggest mistake was not recognizing how bad our farm system was in the late eighties," Giles said. "I think believing the wrong people as far as the talent of our farm system was probably the biggest mistake I made."

Meantime, Bill went through five managers and three general managers. There were trades that didn't pan out, like trading Ryne Sandberg, although nobody seemed concerned at first when the deal was announced. There were also trades that brought in Joe Morgan, Al Holland, and John Denny, moves which brought a pennant to Philadelphia.

Giles turned the reins over to David Montgomery on June 20, 1997. Bill became chairman of the Phillies. New stadiums are popping up all over both leagues, and even though the Phillies drew more than three million in attendance in 1993, a new park was needed.

"When the strike hit in 1994, that took a lot out of me," Giles said. "I really wasn't as effective a leader as I had been in losing the postseason play in 1994. That really hurt me emotionally. Then we got into that J.D. Drew thing where Scott Boras pulled all of that stuff. That was the final straw. I said, 'I can't handle this anymore.' I said that the only way we were going to survive here for any long period of time is to get the revenue these new stadiums provide. I said, 'Dave [Phillies executive vice president at the time], you take over and run the club and I'll do whatever I can do to get the public money to get us a stadium.' That is what I have been doing."

Knowing how hard Bill Giles has worked to accomplish this, look for a new stadium by 2002 or 2003. The Phillies are as big a part of the city as anything and have been here longer than any other team has been in its current city.

Giles has been a big part of that history and had a lot to do with some of the success the team has had.

Twenty

Dallas Green

Led Phillies to the 1980 World Series

by Skip Clayton

He had been through it all, the 23-game losing streak, the loss of the 1964 pennant in the final two weeks and finally, some good news, the 1980 World Series.

From 1955 to 1981, Dallas Green had been a big part of the Phillies organization as a player, minor league pitching coach, minor league manager, and assistant director of minor leagues to Paul Owens. He then took over Owens' job as farm director in 1972 when Owens was promoted to general manager. Finally, he became the manager of the club for a little over two years.

Green, who was born in Newport, Del. was signed by the Phillies in 1955 and stayed in the minors until he was called up during the 1960 season.

Dallas was called up and made his debut on June 18, 1960, at San Francisco but lost to the Giants, 7-4. Ten days later, Green posted his first victory, a three-hitter, shutting out the Dodgers at Connie Mack Stadium.

"I remember that first win," Green said. "Everybody has a ray of sunshine somewhere along the line, and that was one of mine. I remember pitching pretty good a couple of times against the Dodgers."

Green was 3-6 in 1960 and followed up with a 2-4 record in 1961. Both of those years, the Phillies finished last in the eight-team National League.

"I also pitched good against the Giants," Green remembered. "Everybody else, I was pretty lousy against. I know one of my biggest thrills came against the Giants in their home opener in 1961. I struck out Willie Mays with the bases loaded. We won the game, which was great. I didn't have too many days in the sunshine, but that was one of them."

The 1961 season saw the Phillies go 47-107 and suffer through a 23-game losing streak. Nine pitchers lost one or more of those 23, but Dallas was not among them.

"We were young and trying to learn the game," Green recalled. "We were getting our lumps daily.

"I can remember we snapped the streak in Milwaukee, in the second game of a doubleheader, and I remember Frank Sullivan and Sammy White, who were on that club, were dreading going back to Philadelphia.

"We got back and there were 5,000 fans at the airport cheering us. It just showed the kind of fans we had. They were in our corner.

"To Gene Mauch's credit, he taught us how to play the game. If you remember, he was pretty rough on the fundamental stuff."

Dallas went 6-6 in 1962 as the Phillies finished seventh. The following year, Dallas was 7-5. The Phillies finished the season on the road with 11 games. They started by taking two from the Mets in the last games played in the Polo Grounds.

Moving on to Houston, they split the first two of a three-game series. The final game was a loss when an unknown at the time, Joe Morgan, singled in the winning run.

When the players came into the clubhouse for their after-game snack, they found there was no food on the table. Mauch had flipped it.

"We were surprised when Mauch flipped the table," Green said. "We knew Gene had a temper. We knew he was volatile. It was the first time he really cleaned our clock. Covington and Gonzalez got new suits. Most of the food went in their lockers and in their pockets.

"It showed one part of Gene that I respected and liked—that he couldn't stand to lose. He taught us that losing shouldn't be a part of our agenda and shouldn't be a part of our thinking. Guys took that to heart."

The Phillies finished by winning five out of six to finish one game ahead of Cincinnati and one game behind third-place San Francisco.

The 1964 season saw Dallas' pitching career go in a different direction. He was 2-1 in 25 games and was sent down in July for about six weeks. He was recalled in time to see the club suffer through its 10-game losing streak and the loss of the pennant.

"I had really pitched so-so in 1964 when I was sent down," Green said. "That was one of my most disappointing times of my baseball career."

Green left the Phillies and pitched with the Washington Senators (1965) and the New York Mets (1966). He spent part of the 1967 season as the pitching coach with Reading and also pitched for the Phillies.

Green retired with a 20-22 record. He pitched in 185 games and threw 562.1 innings, striking out 268 and posting a 4.26 earned run average.

"I had told Pope [Paul Owens], who was my mentor and one of my best friends, that I was done, and I was ready to come into the front office. Pope said, 'No, you are going to be a minor league manager for two years.' He had me go to Huron, S. Dak., to manage a rookie club. Then I went to Pulaski, Va., in another rookie league, and won a championship there. After that, they brought me into the front office."

Dallas became an assistant to Owens, and when Paul was made the general manager, taking over for John Quinn on June 4, 1972, Green took over Paul's job.

"Pope and I had grown together and did what we could for the Phillies," Green added. "We had a lot of great kids come through the farm system, but the scouts get credit for that."

Danny Ozark came in to manage in 1973, and the club got to the top, beginning in 1976, winning the National League East three straight years. In all three years, they lost the National League Championship Series.

The 1979 Phillies were hit by injuries, and after losing eight of nine on a homestand at the end of August, the front office was concerned and deciding what to do next. They decided that Ozark would be replaced by Green.

Under Ozark, the Phillies had gone 65-67 and were in fifth place, 12 1/2 games out of first. Under Green, the Phillies went 19-11 and finished in fourth place.

Dallas was listed as the interim manager, but during the off-season, it was announced that Green would be the manager for 1980.

"I had really enjoyed being the manager," Green said. "I told Paul I knew the club, I knew what we had in the minor leagues, and I know you and I know Ruly. We got a better club. It is not a big deal. They know how to play."

"My sense of the club being down there was no competition," Green said. "Danny favored the group that was there. My feeling was to create some competition on the club, that there had to be a better mix of veterans and young kids. The kids could push a little bit. The only way I could push was to sit them down. I didn't have any other weapons."

The Phillies spent only 16 days in first place, 12 of them after Sept. 1.

"We went through a lot of adversity," Green said. "First, I was the manager and a lot of guys weren't happy about that. Then Larry Bowa was popping off because Garry Templeton from St. Louis got a bigger contract. They had a big stink about that. Same time, Maddox hadn't signed his contract and we didn't know if he was going to sign or quit. We lost 10 days of spring training because we almost had a strike during that year.

"I was determined that they were not going to call the shots anymore because that is what they had done with Danny, in my opinion. We battled and battled.

"Pope made his big speech in San Francisco on Sept. 1 after I made mine a few weeks earlier in Pittsburgh. After that, I didn't have to manage a lot. Those guys played like heck. They finally put all the petty bull aside and decided to play baseball. They could play when they wanted to. Pope let everybody have it, backed me, and the fact was, we woke up and played baseball."

The Phillies and the Expos were tied for first as the two teams got ready to square off for the final three games of the year. The Phillies won the first, 2-1, and the second, 6-4, in 10 innings on Mike Schmidt's two-run homer, and the East Division championship belonged to the Phillies for the fourth time in five years. The Phillies met the Astros in the playoffs and won the series in five games.

"I still don't watch the tapes," Green said. "I know what happened but I don't watch. Beyond a doubt, that had to be the greatest five-game series in the history of baseball. Four games went extra innings and we had our backs against the wall. We had things going against us.

"I could sense that our guys didn't want to quit, and to their credit, they got off the floor a lot of times and came after those guys with some heart. That is what made that club."

The pennant was only the third in the team's history and its first in 30 years. The Phillies hadn't won a World Series, but that streak came to an end when they beat Kansas City in six games, wrapping it up at the Vet.

"Pete Rose had told me, if we win the playoffs, you will find the World Series will be a piece of cake," Green said. "We just took it to them.

"I had worked for a long time [25 years] with the Phillies and knew the Carpenter family. We had a great feeling and a great organization. Everybody was close, and it was a great feeling to be a part of a championship."

Green became the 17th manager to win a pennant in his rookie year, but only the fourth to win the World Series.

"There is no question we would have won it in 1981 if there wasn't a strike," Green said. "We started like a house on fire and won the first half. They called it a first half. We would have gone through the whole year like that. We played super the first half.

"We came back, and they had that formula that we were already in the playoffs. We couldn't get any of our guys to get it going back and didn't have to. We were already in the playoffs. In the playoffs, Montreal beat Steve Carlton twice, and that is truly doing something. We didn't carry it to the end of the year."

After the 1981 season, Dallas took over as the general manager of the Cubs. He remained there through 1988 and managed the New York Yankees for most of the 1989 season. Later on, he was a scout and manager for the New York Mets. In 1998, Dallas returned to the Phillies as a senior advisor to general manager Ed Wade.

Having Dallas Green back with the Phillies is one of the best moves the club has ever made.

Dallas Green Phillies Statistics

Year	W	L	SV	PCT	G	GS	CG	SH	IP	H	BB	SO	ERA
1960	3	6	0	.333	23	10	5	1	108.2	100	44	51	4.06
1961	2	4	1	.333	42	10	1	1	128.0	160	47	51	4.85
1962	6	6	1	.500	37	10	2	0	129.1	145	43	58	3.83
1963	7	5	2	.583	40	14	4	0	120.0	134	38	68	3.23
1964	2	1	0	.667	25	0	0	0	42.0	63	14	21	5.79
1967	0	0	0	.000	8	0	0	0	15.0	25	6	12	9.00
Totals	20	22	4	.476	175	46	12	2	543.0	627	192	261	4.28

Granny Hamner

Spark Plug and Captain of the Whiz Kids

by Skip Clayton

Anytime a discussion rolls around to the best shortstops in the history of the Phillies, one of the first players mentioned is Granny Hamner. Change the subject to the best second baseman in the club's history, and once again, the name Hamner pops up.

It's all with good reason. Granny was the first player to become an All-Star Game starter at both positions. Since then, other players have started in the mid-summer classic at two positions, but nobody else ever started at both second and shortstop.

Suffice it to say, Hamner was one of the finest middle infielders ever to pull on a Phillies uniform. One of the best clutch hitters of his day, Granny was the spark plug and captain of the 1950 Whiz Kids.

He first appeared with the Phillies as a 17-year-old in 1944, and played with the team until 1959. When he ended his career in 1962, Hamner had a lifetime batting average of .257 with 1,529 hits, 104 home runs, 708 RBIs, and 711 runs scored.

Granny ranks seventh on the Phillies' all-time list in at-bats and doubles, ninth in hits and games played. He ranks third in games played at shortstop. And he hit more career home runs than any Phillies shortstop (61).

Granny was signed out of high school in Richmond, Va., for an $8,000 bonus and joined the wartime Phils in September 1944. He played in 21 games that season, hitting .247.

"Coming to the Phillies in 1944 at the age of 17 wasn't as bad as it sounds," said Hamner. "We had a very poor club. It was during the war and there weren't many ballplayers around. I went back to high school after playing that season with the Phillies."

Hamner began the 1945 campaign with the Phils, but was sent to Utica after 14 games. Before he got a chance to play there, though, he was drafted. Granny spent the rest of 1945 and most of 1946 in the service, finally reporting back to the Phillies at the end of '46.

It was back to Utica in 1947 before once again rejoining the Phillies for the final two games of the year. This time, though, Hamner was with the Phillies to stay.

"I was a utility infielder in the beginning of 1948, but Emil Verban sprained his ankle on opening day, and I played there that season. Eddie Miller was our regular shortstop. The following year, I was moved to short and Eddie moved to second base," he said.

The 1948 Phillies finished in sixth place. The next year, they moved up to third place. That season—Granny's first full year at shortstop—he led the National League in chances, double plays, and assists (506) while hitting .263.

"I don't think anybody took us seriously in 1950," said Hamner. "We were so young and we seemed to have so little power. We had good pitching, and we were a fighting, late-scoring club. And we had Jim Konstanty. When we came from behind and tied a game, we had a 95 percent chance of winning it, once we got Jim on the mound. He was outstanding.

"We had great starters in Robin Roberts and Curt Simmons, and we had the nucleus of a good club. We averaged over four runs a game. That wins a lot of games."

After bouncing in and out of the lead, the Whiz Kids took over first place for good on July 25 when they blanked the Cubs twice at Shibe Park, 7-0 and 1-0, behind Bubba Church and Roberts. By Sept. 17, the Phillies had a seven and a half-game lead as they came into a Sunday game with the Pittsburgh Pirates. That day was "Granny Hamner Day."

"That was one of the highlights of my career," recalled Hamner. "The fans were wonderful to me. They gave me a house full of wonderful gifts and some cash, which I could use at the time. As luck would have it, I had a real good day at the plate. It was a happy day all around. It was the only big-league game that my father ever saw me play before he died. I was tickled that it was such a good day."

Granny hit a three-run homer that afternoon as the Phillies beat the Pirates, 5-3.

Eventually, the Whiz Kids won the pennant on the last day of the season, beating the Dodgers in Brooklyn, 4-1, in 10 innings. Hamner hit .270 for the season with 82 RBIs.

Although the Phillies lost the World Series in four straight to the Yankees—the first three games by one run—Granny led the team in hitting with a .429 average.

Hamner would like to forget the third game. With two outs in the bottom of the eighth, the Yankees had the bases loaded and Bobby Brown hit a grounder to short. Granny bobbled it, the tying run scored, and the Yankees went on to win in the ninth inning.

In 1950, Hamner had 513 assists, although he did not lead the league.

"I had good range, which I was proud of," added Hamner, "and I had a good arm. The only balls I ever had trouble with were the ones hit right at me."

The Phillies, who had lost Simmons to the service with three weeks to go in the 1950 season, were still without Curt in 1951. The club dropped to fifth. Granny's average dropped to .255, although he drove in 72 runs.

The Phillies came back in 1952 to finish fourth. Hamner set club records for shortstops with 17 homers and 87 runs batted in. He was also voted the starting shortstop for the National League All-Star team.

"It meant a lot to me to be voted the starter," said Hamner. "I had to beat out some great shortstops in those days like Pee Wee Reese, Marty Marion, Al Dark, and Roy McMillan."

Hopes were high for 1953. Hamner started out having another good season, but in June, the club called up shortstop Ted Kazanski from the minors. He took over at short and Granny moved to second.

"It didn't help any for me to move to second because I wasn't a good second baseman," said Hamner. "I wasn't a good pivot man. I had a good arm, but I wasn't quick enough getting rid of the ball. Kazanski couldn't play second, and we didn't have any other infielders."

After hitting .275 in 1952, Hamner upped his average one point in 1953. He also set club records for second basemen with most homers in a season (21) and most runs batted in (92). Those marks held up until Juan Samuel broke them in 1987.

Again, Hamner made the All-Star team as a reserve infielder.

In 1954, Granny stayed at second. He raised his average to a career-high .299 with 13 homers and 89 RBIs, as the Phillies finished in fourth place.

When Hamner was voted the starting second baseman on the All-Star team, he became the first player in the history of the game to be selected as a starter at two different positions.

Granny moved back to shortstop in 1955, but was hurt early in the year. "I dove for a ball and hurt my left shoulder," he recalled. "Eventually, I had to have an operation."

When Granny got back, he returned to second, but hit only .257 in 104 games.

The following year, Hamner was back at short playing in 110 games, and he also tried pitching. "After the operation, I couldn't swing a bat, so I started throwing a knuckleball and a fastball. I never had a curveball. The first time I pitched in a game was in Milwaukee. They were laughing at me. They didn't take me seriously, but I was serious."

Granny pitched one inning, faced three batters and struck out two of them. Later, he pitched in two more games, finishing the season with a 4.50 ERA and an 0-1 record in eight innings.

Granny reported to spring training as a pitcher in 1957. That season the Phillies got off to a poor start. Three weeks into the season, Hamner—after pitching in one game—returned to second and the Phillies began playing better. Hamner wound up with .227 average.

Granny got off to a great start in 1958 and was hitting .301, but sustained a knee injury while playing second that put him out for the year.

"That was a bad injury," said Hamner. "One doctor said I wouldn't play again. They couldn't operate on it, so they just put a cast on it. It was never supposed to be right again, but then I ran into a doctor who said he could fix it. And he did. I played a couple of more years. I thought that was great, but I never could play the infield again."

A month into the 1959 season, Granny, who had come back to short, was hitting .297 when he was traded to Cleveland. "I didn't like it, cried like a baby, but I couldn't play every day," said Hamner.

After retiring at the end of the 1959 season, Hamner returned for three games to the majors in 1962 with the Kansas City A's as a relief pitcher. Then he retired again and was out of baseball until 1973, when he rejoined the Phillies' minor league system as an instructor. Later, he became a minor league supervisor. He stayed with the Phillies' organization through the 1988 season.

In 1982, Granny was crossing the Skyway Bridge to Sarasota when a freighter rammed the bridge, knocking a section of it into Tampa Bay, killing 34 people.

"I was driving across and I saw a guy's taillights flashing," said Hamner. "I stopped and somebody said the bridge was out. I got out and looked, and this boat had just demolished the bridge. All I did was help some other traffic turn around.

"I went back, and after I got off the bridge, I kept hearing about the deaths. Then I started to get more nervous and more nervous. I didn't know that all of those people had gone over until I had gotten off the bridge."

There were only a couple of cars in front of Granny that didn't go off the bridge.

Counting 16 years as a player and 16 years in the minor league organization, Granny spent 32 years with the Phillies. He did everything in uniform except manage in the majors.

Granny died on Sept. 12, 1993, in Philadelphia while attending the reunion of the Whiz Kids at a baseball card show.

As a player or as an employee in the Phillies organization, Granny did an excellent job and was voted into the Philadelphia Baseball Hall of Fame in 1987, an honor he richly deserved.

Granny Hamner Phillies Statistics

Year	G	AB	R	H	2B	3B	HR	RBI	AVG	OBP	SLGP
1944	21	77	6	19	1	0	0	5	.247	.275	.260
1945	14	41	3	7	2	0	0	6	.171	.190	.220
1946	2	7	0	1	0	0	0	0	.143	.143	.143
1947	2	7	1	2	0	0	0	0	.286	.375	.286
1948	129	446	42	116	21	5	3	48	.260	.298	.350
1949	154	662	83	174	32	5	6	53	.263	.290	.353
1950	157	637	78	172	27	5	11	82	.270	.314	.380
1951	150	589	61	150	23	7	9	72	.255	.290	.363
1952	151	596	74	164	30	5	17	87	.275	.307	.428
1953	154	609	90	168	30	8	21	92	.276	.313	.455
1954	152	596	83	178	39	11	13	89	.299	.351	.466
1955	104	405	57	104	12	4	5	43	.257	.323	.343
1956	122	401	42	90	24	3	4	42	.224	.276	.329
1957	133	502	59	114	19	5	10	62	.227	.274	.345
1958	35	133	18	40	7	3	2	18	.301	.340	.444
1959	21	64	10	19	4	0	2	6	.297	.348	.453
Totals	1,501	5,772	707	1,518	271	61	103	705	.263	.305	.385

Twenty-two

Willie Jones

1950s Third Baseman

by Skip Clayton

Third base has been one position on the Phillies that hasn't been a problem over the years. From Pinky Whitney to Scott Rolen, the hot corner has been held down by a lot of great talent. In between, you had the likes of Pinky May, Dick Allen, and Mike Schmidt.

Outside of Schmidt, nobody held down third base longer than Willie Jones, who used to tell everybody that the only time his sore feet hurt was when they touched the ground.

Had they been giving out a Gold Glove Award then, Willie (who was also referred to as "Puddin' Head") would have had a few on display in his trophy case. He holds the National League record among third basemen for the most consecutive years leading the league in fielding with four (1953-1956) and led the league in putouts and assists in 1949 and 1950.

Jones started his career in the Phillies' farm system, playing at Terre Haute as a shortstop in 1947. He came up to the Phillies at the end of the year and played 18 games and hit .226. Jones was put at third base. The shortstop of the future with the Phillies would be Granny Hamner, and the pair would be on the same side of the infield for good, starting late in the 1948 season.

Jones returned to the minors at the start of 1948, playing 18 games at Utica in the Eastern League, then was moved up to Toronto. In 118 games, he hit .275 and led International League third basemen in putouts and assists. Willie was called up at the end of the season.

"Eddie Sawyer gave me a lot confidence," Jones said. "He gave me my break in major league baseball."

After that call-up to the Phillies, he would stay until he was traded to Cleveland on June 3, 1959. In 1948, he got into 17 games, hit .333, and banged out two homers.

Although he hit only .244 in 1949, Willie walloped 19 home runs, including two at the end of the year that almost prevented the Dodgers from clinching the pennant on the final weekend of the season.

Willie got his name in the record book in the beginning of the year when he tied the major league record for the most consecutive doubles in a game with four.

"One of those doubles should have been a triple, but I tripped going around second," Jones said. "When I came up for the fourth time, somebody yelled out, 'Double or nothing.'"

Meantime, Brooklyn came into Shibe Park for the final two games of the 1949 season with a one-game lead over St. Louis. In the first game, Jones homered in the eighth with one on to give the Phillies a 6-4 win. The Dodgers caught a break when St. Louis lost to Chicago, and that kept their one-game lead. Brooklyn came back to beat the Phillies in 10 innings the next day and wrapped up the pennant, although Willie connected for another homer.

Jones started 1950 by hitting safely in the first 16 games. That, along with his six-game hitting streak at the end of 1949, gave him a string of 22 straight. Jones hit his first grand slam against Brooklyn in Ebbets Field on April 27, as Robin Roberts beat the Dodgers for the second time in nine days. By the time the All-Star Game arrived, Jones was hitting .322 and had been voted in as the starter. He set an All-Star Game record for the most innings played at third base (14) when the National League beat the American League, 4-3, in 14 innings. In seven trips to the plate, Willie picked up one hit.

The 1950 Phillies, now being referred to as the Whiz Kids, took over first place on July 25, when they swept the Cubs at Shibe Park, 7-0 and 1-0. Bubba Church and Robin Roberts spun a pair of shutouts. This put the Phillies in front to stay.

During the last two months, Willie saw his batting average drop, but he still chipped in with some game-winning hits.

Twice he singled in the winning run in the ninth inning against Boston and St. Louis in key September games.

By the time the last day of the season arrived, the Phillies had a one-game lead over Brooklyn, with their final game scheduled against the Dodgers in Ebbets Field. Win it and the pennant would be the Phillies' first in 35 years. Lose the game and the Phillies would face the Dodgers in a two-out-of-three playoff.

Two-out singles in the sixth by Dick Sisler and Del Ennis brought Willie to the plate. He promptly singled in Sisler with the first run of the game. The Dodgers tied it in the bottom of the inning when Pee Wee Reese hit a ball to right that hit the screen, then fell on a ledge and stayed there. Reese had a fluke homer, and the Phillies found themselves in a tie game.

In the bottom of the ninth, Richie Ashburn saved the pennant when he threw Cal Abrams out at home. In the top of the 10th, Sisler hit a three-run homer, giving the Phillies a 4-1 lead. Roberts set the Dodgers down in order in the bottom of the 10th.

Willie hit .267 in 1950 with 25 homers, and he drove in 88 runs. He tied the National League record for the most games played at third in a 154-game season (157), since the Phillies were involved in three ties. For the second year in a row, Willie led all National League third basemen in putouts and assists.

The Phillies met the Yankees in the World Series but lost four straight, the first three each by one run. Willie hit .286, the second-highest average on the team.

"That was a terrific ball club that year," Jones said. "Everybody played and pulled together. I enjoyed it very much. About all I can say about the World Series, we were there for four games, but the first three games were by one run. We left too many runners on third base with none and one out, but with a little luck, we could have won a couple of those games."

In 1951, Willie upped his average to .285, hit 22 homers, and drove in 81 runs. He also made the All-Star team as a reserve and batted twice without a hit. Jones also was the fifth of six players in Phillies history to hit an inside-the-park grand slam, connecting in Forbes Field against the Pirates.

This was the year that the Dodgers would like to forget. They coughed up a 13 1/2-game lead. In the final nine days against the Phillies, they split six games. Willie had a lot to do with their losing two of those games. On the next-to-last weekend of the season at Ebbets Field, Willie hit his fourth lifetime grand slam, and his third against the Dodgers. The Phillies went on to beat Brooklyn, 9-6.

On the final weekend, the Dodgers were in Philadelphia for their final three. In the first game, Jones singled in Ashburn with the winning run, and the Dodgers and Giants were tied for first. Both Brooklyn and New York won their final two to set up their famous playoff.

Willie's average dropped to .250 in 1952, but he hit 18 homers. The following year, Jones hit 19 homers and drove in 70 runs, but his average dropped to .225. Batting in the leadoff spot in the first half of the 1954 season, Willie got his average up to .271, although his home run production dropped to 12.

The Phillies finished in the first division for the fourth straight year in 1955, and Jones drove home 81 runs and hit 16 homers. He also added his fifth lifetime grand slam in Connie Mack Stadium, and it was his fourth against the Dodgers. He followed in 1956 with a .277 average, 17 homers, and 78 runs batted in. Willie also tied the club record at the time for the most career grand slams when he got his sixth, against the Cubs, in Connie Mack Stadium. From 1953 to 1956, he set the National League record for the most consecutive years (four) as the leading third basemen in fielding. He also led the league in 1958. Between 1952 and 1956, Willie led all National League third basemen in putouts and tied the league record for most years leading third basemen in putouts with seven.

Willie's average dropped to .218 in 1957, but he rebounded to hit .271 in 1958. Jones also tied the club record for most RBIs, in a game with eight against the Cardinals at Busch Stadium.

Jones was off to a good start in 1959 when he was traded to Cleveland on June 6 for outfielder Jim Bolger and cash. On July 1, the Indians sold Willie to Cincinnati.

Willie stayed with the Reds into the early part of the 1961 season, when he was released. He continued to live in Cincinnati and took a job as a car salesman.

His career average was .258, and he hit 190 homers and drove home 812 runs.

On Oct. 18, 1983, he died in Cincinnati. He certainly will be remembered as one of the best third basemen in Phillies history. In 1969, when baseball celebrated its 100th anniversary, he was voted the best third baseman in Phillies history, an honor he later relinquished to Mike Schmidt. In 1995, Jones was voted into the Philadelphia Baseball Hall of Fame.

Willie Jones Phillies Statistics

Year	G	AB	R	H	2B	3B	HR	RBI	AVG	OBP	SLGP
1947	18	62	5	14	0	1	0	10	.226	.304	.258
1948	17	60	9	20	2	0	2	9	.333	.365	.467
1949	149	532	71	130	35	1	19	77	.244	.328	.421
1950	157	610	100	163	28	6	25	88	.267	.337	.456
1951	148	564	79	161	28	5	22	81	.285	.358	.470
1952	147	541	60	135	12	3	18	72	.250	.323	.383
1953	149	481	61	108	16	2	19	70	.225	.342	.385
1954	142	535	64	145	28	3	12	56	.271	.342	.402
1955	146	516	65	133	20	3	16	81	.258	.352	.401
1956	149	520	88	144	20	4	17	78	.277	.383	.429
1957	133	440	58	96	19	2	9	47	.218	.310	.332
1958	118	398	52	108	15	1	14	60	.271	.399	.420
1959	47	160	23	43	9	1	7	24	.269	.343	.469
Totals	**1,520**	**5,419**	**735**	**1,400**	**232**	**32**	**180**	**753**	**.258**	**.343**	**.413**

Twenty-three

Harry Kalas

Phillies' Top Broadcaster

by Skip Clayton

The Phillies were set to open Veterans Stadium in 1971 after closing down Connie Mack Stadium on Oct. 1, 1970. After the season, it was announced that Harry Kalas was joining the Phillies broadcasting team. "I was ready to leave Houston because they had three play-by-play guys," Kalas said. "There weren't any color analysts. We kind of divided the game up. I had gone to Kansas City. I talked to them. I had also gone to Cincinnati and was actually offered a job by Bob Howsam and Dick Wagner for radio only. The contract was there. Prior to meeting with Howsam and Wagner, my then-wife called me and said that Bill Giles had said not to sign anything until I talked to him. I finished my meeting and went back to the hotel room and called Bill and he said, 'I want you here in Philadelphia.' So I was very happy it worked out and I didn't sign with Cincinnati. Glad I came to Philadelphia.

"I had the opportunity to do radio and television. I knew Bill Giles from the days in Houston. I traveled to Philadelphia, liked the city, and knew that it was a great sports town. I took the job.

"I was told that I would be an addition. I would be the new guy and that everybody would remain. As it turned out, they let Bill Campbell go. So, there was some negative publicity. I'm not saying I wouldn't have taken the job had I known, but I didn't know at the time. I hated to see Bill lose his job, because he is one of the great broadcasters in Philadelphia."

Kalas had started broadcasting baseball with Hawaii in the Pacific Coast League and also did high school and college football and basketball on KGU in Honolulu.

The Phillies started the 1971 season on the road, then finally, on April 10, opened the Vet. Harry had the honor of introducing everybody from down on the field. When it was over, he realized that he had neglected to introduce one person—the National League president.

"I forgot to introduce Chub Feeney," Kalas recalled. "I felt badly and I apologized and he was real good about it."

The Phillies fans took to Harry right away, and it wasn't long before they were saying he was the best who ever called baseball in Philadelphia. He and Richie Ashburn blended together as though they had known each other all their lives.

"We worked 27 years together in the booth, and it was just a joy to work with him and be around him, both in the booth and off the field away from the ballpark," Kalas said. "He was such a pleasure to be around.

"We just had a rapport that evolved over the years. It just happened. You just can't work on things like what-are-we-going-to-talk-about things. It just evolved. It was spontaneous.

"I worked with so many color analysts in football and baseball over the years, but Richie and I had a special relationship. It is hard to say why it came about, but it just did. It is just one of those special things that happen in broadcasting. He is probably my best friend ever. So I miss him.

"I love working with Larry Andersen. I am glad that it is he that came in the booth. That first broadcast that I did after Richie died was the hardest broadcast I ever did. That was difficult, but you felt his presence. We kept a chair in the booth right there. That was Richie's chair. No one sat in it. We felt like he was there. We felt like he was carrying us through the game and he would have wanted us to have done it. We felt his presence and we still do feel his presence. We feel his presence all the time."

Richie Ashburn died in New York on Tuesday, Sept. 9, 1997. The Phillies' next home game was Thursday, and prior to the game, Kalas read a poem that he had written to honor Ashburn on his induction into the Hall of Fame and which he updated. At his funeral that Saturday, Harry delivered the eulogy.

Fans not only have heard Harry on Phillies games since 1971, but he is also heard on NFL Films each week during the season and also narrates other features for NFL Films.

He did Notre Dame football for six years before NBC-TV picked up the full package. Prior to joining the Phillies, Kalas also had broadcast University of Houston football games.

When Harry came to the Phillies, the team was more used to being in the bottom of the division rather than the top. That changed in 1976 when they reeled off three straight East Division championships. Finally, in 1980, the Phillies won it all, but all Harry and the rest of the broadcast team could do was look on. The networks had their own announcers since 1976.

"That was disappointing not to do the 1980 World Series," Kalas said. "Broadcasters around baseball now have the Philadelphia public to thank for them being able to do the games on their flagship station only on radio. We did in 1983 and 1993.

"There really was a public outcry that we didn't get the opportunity to do the games on radio. Fans not only called the Phillies' front office, but they called the commissioner's office, the National League office, and the TV stations. They wrote letters and raised cain and they changed the policy."

Nothing against Joe Garagiola, but it would have been better and more exciting to have Harry talking into the mike, "The Phillies win the World Series."

There is one call, though, that Phillies fans can identify Harry with, and that is his home run call, "Outta here, home run."

Kalas didn't start with that call when he first came to the Phillies. "It started, I think, in the late '70s," Kalas recalled. "I was standing around the batting cage when the Phillies were taking batting practice, and Greg Luzinski was hitting some bolts and Larry Bowa was standing around the batting cage waiting his turn and he was saying something like, 'Oh, that one is way outta here.' I thought, that has a neat ring to it. So I just started using it at that point.

'Of course, everyone heard the one when I called Mike Schmidt's 500th home run. That one is still played. One that was almost lost in the shuffle was Eddie Mathews' 500th home run. He had his Hall of Fame career, for the most part, with the Braves, but he finished his career with the Astros.

"I was at Houston at the time, and I was on the air when he hit his 500th in 1967. It came in Candlestick Park."

One of the most exciting days for Kalas came as a spectator when he was on hand for the induction of Ashburn and Schmidt into the Hall of Fame in 1995.

There have been other exciting days, watching the Phillies win the 1980 World Series and also broadcasting all the first-place teams the team has had.

Kalas has been the Pennsylvania Sportscaster of the Year 17 times. In addition to doing the Phillies games and NFL Films now, he also does pro football games for the Westwood One radio network after the Phillies' season ends.

There is still one honor for Kalas to receive, and that is his induction into the Baseball Hall of Fame. Inducting broadcasters and giving them the Ford C. Frick Award began back in 1978. Kalas should receive it someday, preferably sooner instead of later. Others have gotten the award while still broadcasting games; Harry should be no different.

People mention the game's great broadcasters—Mel Allen, Red Barber, Vin Scully, and Ernie Harwell. Put Harry Kalas in that group.

Twenty-four

Chuck Klein

Hall of Fame Outfielder

by Jeff Moeller

Chuck Klein was a hitter who was ahead of his time. After his retirement in 1944, it took 36 more seasons until he was inducted into the Hall of Fame.

Klein finished his career with 300 homers, 1,201 RBIs, a .320 batting average, a .543 slugging percentage and holds more than a dozen Phillies, National League, and major league baseball records.

The outfielder has held a number of National League records, including most total bases by a left-handed hitter (445), most RBIs by a left-handed batter in one season (170), most consecutive years with 400 or more total bases (two), most games with one or more hits in a season (135), and most runs scored in two consecutive games (eight).

Amazingly, Klein set these marks in just 12 major league seasons as a regular and 17 overall.

Among Phillies records, Klein is fourth overall in runs scored (963), sixth in hits (1,705), fourth in RBIs (983), 10th in singles (1,062), fourth in doubles (336), third in homers (243), fourth in total bases (2,898), third in extra-base hits (643), fifth in batting average (.326), and fourth in on-base percentage (.383).

He hit 10 or more homers in a month during July 1929 (14); June 1932 (12); May 1929 (11); July 1930 (10); and May 1932 (10). Klein's 243 homers are the most by a Phillies left-handed batter in a career. He hit three grand slams in 1929 and 1932, and hit two or more homers in a season 23 times. His 43 homers in 1929 rank third overall behind Mike Schmidt for most homers in a season by a Phillie.

Part of his identity crisis among baseball critics was playing in Baker Bowl, a park with very inviting distances for left-handed hitters.

Still, Klein was the symbol of the prototypical ballplayer of the 1920, '30s, and '40s. The Indiana native was a solid 190 pounds on a six-foot frame and utilized his strength in a sweet, compact swing.

Klein grew up on a farm and enjoyed the simple pleasures in life, such as baseball, basketball, farm work, fishing, and taking a dive into an old swimming hole. He developed his muscles while working in a steel mill, where he carried ingots weighing hundreds of pounds.

Most of his nights and weekends were spent playing semipro ball around Indianapolis, and he signed his first pro contract with Evansville. He hit .327 before a broken ankle sidelined him, and Klein was later sold over the winter to Fort Wayne.

In 1928, he hit .331 there and slugged 26 homers. The Phillies were one of several clubs interested in him, and they purchased Klein for $5,000.

He moved into right field and shared time there with reigning home run king Cy Williams, who was 39 at the time. But the following year, Klein moved into the spot permanently and began a monstrous five-year run.

During that time, Klein averaged 36 homers, 139 RBIs, 224 hits, 132 runs, a .359 batting average, and a .635 slugging percentage. He captured four home run titles and won the triple crown in 1933 (28 homers, 120 RBIs, .368). The previous year, Klein was named MVP and became the only player at the time to lead the league in home runs (38) and stolen bases (20).

In 1929, Klein hit .356, but his season was overshadowed by Lefty O'Doul's league-leading .398 average. Klein hit what was then a National League record 43 homers, drove in 145 runs, and scored 126. He also hit a homer in every park; in July alone, he hit 14 homers and drove in 40 runs.

He was the team's main ticket draw, as the club wallowed near the bottom of the standings. In the years in which he batted at least 300 times, Klein never drew more than 60 walks or fanned more than 61 times. Twice he went through seasons striking out just 21 times.

One of Klein's biggest obstacles was the Phillies' front office. Team owner William F. Baker had an additional 20 feet of fence placed atop the right-field wall, mainly to prevent power hitters from getting homers of the "cheap" variety. Later, financially strapped, Baker sent Klein to the Cubs for three players and $65,000.

Before Baker sent him away, he would often pay for broken windshields resulting from Klein's homers flying over the right-field wall, onto Broad Street. On more than one occasion, Klein's homers would cross Broad Street and land on the Reading Railroad tracks.

The move to Chicago took its toll on Klein, as his average dropped below .300 for the first time in his career in 1935. He hit 21 homers and batted .293 to help the Cubs to the World Series, and he hit a two-run homer in Game 5 to highlight his .333 overall average.

Just over a month into the 1936 season, Klein was dealt back to the Phillies, along with a pitcher, for $50,000. His homecoming provided him with some fire as he hit 25 homers and drove in 104 runs.

During 1936, Klein hit four homers in one game. He hit homers in four consecutive at-bats, including the game-winner in the 10th. His shots had reportedly measured more than 350 feet into the right-field stands. At the time, he was one of four players to hit four homers in a game, joining Bobby Lowe, Ed Delahanty, and Lou Gehrig. Klein drove in six of the Phillies' nine runs in a 9-6 victory.

Klein hit .325 in 1937, but it would be his last year of double-digit homers, as he finished with 15. He hit just eight homers and his average dipped to .247 at age 34 the following season.

In 1939, Klein played in just 25 games before the club released him in June. He was signed by the Pirates and hit .300 in 85 games for a combined average of

.284. Ironically, the Pirates released him during the winter and the Phillies re-signed him.

Klein spent his last season as regular in 1940, but he apparently lost his game, as his average was an embarrassing .218 with seven homers. He remained with the Phillies over the next four years as a pinch hitter and coach. He hit the last of his 300 homers in 1941 and rapped his final hit, a single, three years later.

But Klein's deterioration on the field was due in part to his battle with the demons of alcohol, and he eventually developed some severe medical problems. After he retired, Klein operated a bar in Philadelphia for a period before returning to Indianapolis in 1947.

In 1956, his 20-year marriage broke up, his health deteriorated, and he became partially disabled. Klein died of a cerebral hemorrhage at the age of 53 in 1959. In 1980, he was elected to the Hall of Fame.

Chuck Klein Phillies Statistics

Year	G	AB	R	H	2B	3B	HR	RBI	AVG	OBP	SLGP
1928	64	253	41	91	14	4	11	34	.360	.396	.577
1929	149	616	126	219	45	6	43	145	.356	.407	.657
1930	156	648	158	250	59	8	40	170	.386	.436	.687
1931	148	594	121	200	34	10	31	121	.337	.398	.584
1932	154	650	152	226	50	15	38	137	.348	.404	.646
1933	152	606	101	223	44	7	28	120	.368	.422	.602
1936	117	492	83	152	30	7	20	86	.309	.352	.520
1937	115	406	74	132	20	2	15	57	.325	.386	.495
1938	129	458	53	113	22	2	8	61	.247	.304	.356
1939	25	47	8	9	2	1	1	9	.191	.333	.340
1940	116	354	39	77	16	2	7	37	.218	.304	.333
1941	50	73	6	9	0	0	1	3	.123	.229	.164
1942	14	14	0	1	0	0	0	0	.071	.071	.071
1943	12	20	0	2	0	0	0	3	.100	.100	.100
1944	4	7	1	1	0	0	0	0	.143	.143	.143
Totals	1,405	5,238	963	1,705	336	64	243	983	.326	.382	.553

Twenty-five

Jim Konstanty

© 2000 Phillies

MVP of the 1950 Pennant-Winning Whiz Kids

by Skip Clayton

The Phillies were playing the Chicago Cubs at Shibe Park on Sept. 17, 1948. Trailing 2-0 going into the bottom of the fifth, the Phillies picked up four and took the lead, 4-2. Manager Eddie Sawyer went to the bullpen and brought in Jim Konstanty. This was only his second appearance for the Phillies since they brought him up from Toronto but this was the first time he was being called upon to save a game.

Konstanty gave up only one run in four innings and the Phillies won the game, 6-3. Konstanty pitched in six games in 1948, saving two games and winning one. Sawyer knew that having a closer for the following year would help the club move up the ladder.

Konstanty, who was born on March 2, 1917, in Strykersville, New York, pitched for the Cincinnati Reds and the Boston Braves before joining the Phillies.

He started in the minors with Springfield in 1941, pitched for Syracuse beginning in 1942, and joined the Reds in 1944. Konstanty pitched in 20 games, posted a 6-4 record, then spent the 1945 season in the service.

In 1946, he was traded to the Boston Braves, with cash, for outfielder Max West. Konstanty was sent to Toronto during the 1946 season and stayed there until he came up to the Phillies in 1948. By then, he was throwing a slider and a palm ball.

Konstanty appeared in 53 games in 1949 and was 9-5 with seven saves.

Konstanty also showed he could still pitch a complete game. In early June at Shibe Park, the Phillies found themselves in an 18-inning game against Pittsburgh.

Konstanty came on in the 10th and held the Pirates scoreless for nine innings before the Phillies won it in the 18th.

Not too many picked the Phillies—now the Whiz Kids—to win the pennant in 1950, even though they had played the best ball in the National League in the final six weeks of 1949.

At the All-Star break, the Phillies were in first place by a game over St. Louis. Konstanty was 7-3 with 11 saves and was selected to the All-Star team. He pitched the sixth inning in Comiskey Park, struck out Hoot Evers and Jim Hegan, and got Bobby Doerr to ground to short.

On July 25, the Phillies shut out the Chicago Cubs, 7-0 and 1-0, and took over first place for good.

Meanwhile, on July 20, Konstanty had retired the final two batters against the Pirates. Jim didn't give up a run in his next 13 games, a span covering 22 1/3 innings. His streak ended in Pittsburgh when he came in with the score tied, 6-6, in the bottom of the seventh. In the top of the 10th, after Andy Seminick homered to put the Phillies ahead, 7-6, Ralph Kiner homered off Konstanty to end his streak and tie the game. The Phillies got two in the 15th to win it, 9-7, as Konstanty went nine innings for the win.

The Phillies got back to Shibe Park in September with a seven-game lead over Brooklyn. The pennant was anything but clinched with 27 games to go.

In the second game of a doubleheader against Cincinnati at Shibe Park, Jim was called upon to pitch 10 innings, before coming out of the game in the 18th for a pinch hitter. The Phillies won the game, 8-7, in 19 innings, the longest Phillies game ever played at Shibe Park.

The Phillies didn't clinch the pennant until the final day of the season, when they beat the Dodgers in Brooklyn, 4-1, in 10 innings.

Konstanty finished with a 16-7 record and 22 saves. His earned run average was 2.66. He set two pitching records that year—most games pitched (74) and most games finished (57).

Anytime Konstanty ever got into a slump, which wasn't often, he would always call on his friend Andy Skinner, who was an undertaker. Skinner would visit Jim and catch up with him and tell him what he had been doing wrong.

Up next were the New York Yankees in the World Series. Sawyer surprised everyone when he picked Konstanty, who hadn't started all year, to start Game 1 at Shibe Park.

The Phillies lost, 1-0, as Vic Raschi pitched perhaps his greatest game. The Yankees' lone run came in the fourth when Bobby Brown led off with a double and scored on two long fly balls.

After Roberts lost Game 2 in 10 innings, 2-1, when Joe DiMaggio homered to snap the tie, the series moved to Yankee Stadium. Ken Heintzelman started the third game and held the Bronx Bombers in check into the eighth and the Phillies ahead, 2-1. With two out and the bases loaded, Konstanty came into the game and got Brown to hit a grounder to Granny Hamner, who fumbled the ball as the tying run scored. The Yankees won it in the ninth after Konstanty had come out for a pinch hitter.

The following day, Konstanty came into the fourth game after Miller gave up two runs and retired only one batter. He held the Bronx Bombers scoreless until the sixth, when they scored three runs. The Phillies lost the game, 5-2, and the World Series in four straight.

After the end of the season, announcements were made for the Most Valuable Player award. Konstanty won it with 286 points, including 18 of 24 first-place votes. Stan Musial was second with 158 points.

The Phillies dropped to fifth in 1951, and Konstanty's record fell to 4-11 with nine saves. He rebounded to 5-3 in 1952 with six saves and started two games late in the season and went the distance. The Phillies rebounded, moving up to fourth with 87 wins, only four fewer than the 1950 pennant winner.

In 1953, Konstanty divided his time as a starter and a relief pitcher, going 14-10 with five saves as the Phillies climbed into a tie for third with the Cardinals. On Aug. 22, 1954, after going 2-3 with three saves, Konstanty was sold to the Yankees.

He led the Yankees in saves with 11 in 1955 and posted a 7-2 record. The Yankees won the pennant but lost the World Series in seven games to the Brooklyn Dodgers, who won their first title. Ironically, Jim didn't get to pitch in the World Series.

He started the 1956 season with the Yankees, but was sold to the St. Louis Cardinals during the season. In 1957, Konstanty pitched for San Francisco in the Pacific Coast League. At the end of the year, he retired at the age of 40 with a 66-48 record, an earned run average of 3.46, and 74 saves—54 of those with the Phillies.

Later, Konstanty was a minor league pitching coach for the St. Louis Cardinals and Yankees. He became the athletic director at Hartwick College in Oneonta in 1968 and stayed there until 1972.

Konstanty was one of the first closers in baseball and proved how important it was to save a game. Jim wasn't called on just to pitch one inning, but sometimes two, three, or four innings. Pitchers turned in more complete games in that era.

In 1950, the Phillies had 57 complete games, and they had 80 in 1952, so the chances weren't as great then for a save.

On June 11, 1976, Konstanty died at Oneonta, N.Y., of cancer. He was 59.

There have been Phillies pitchers who saved more games than Konstanty, but in 1983, he was voted the Phillies' all-time best right-handed relief pitcher. To this day, he still is one of the best closers in Phillies history.

Jim Konstanty Phillies Statistics

Year	W	L	SV	PCT	G	GS	CG	SH	IP	H	BB	SO	ERA
1948	1	0	2	1.00	6	0	0	0	9.2	7	2	7	0.93
1949	9	5	7	.643	53	0	0	0	97.0	98	29	43	3.25
1950	16	7	22	.696	74	0	0	0	152.0	108	50	56	2.66
1951	4	11	9	.267	58	1	0	0	115.2	127	31	27	4.05
1952	5	3	6	.625	42	2	2	1	80.0	87	21	16	3.94
1953	14	10	5	.583	48	19	7	0	170.0	198	42	45	4.43
1954	2	3	3	.400	33	1	0	0	50.1	62	12	11	3.75
Totals	51	39	54	.567	314	23	9	1	675.1	687	187	205	3.64

Twenty-six

John Kruk

The One and Only Krukker

by Jeff Moeller

John Kruk will never forget his days as a pitcher. Yes, a pitcher. But no one ever said those days were official.

It was the night after a Saturday-evening game, and Kruk decided to stay overnight on the couch in the video room. Rather than driving home, the "Krukker" had spent many a Saturday night in the confines of Veterans Stadium.

This was an especially pleasing night because Kruk had been informed by manager Jim Fregosi that he was out of the lineup for Sunday's game.

Early Sunday morning, Kruk engaged in a Wiffle ball game with members of the Phillies' ground crew. He took to the mound and hurled 30 to 40 innings.

Time apparently stood still with the baseball gods, and the hours leading to seven in the morning felt more like meager minutes. Kruk caught an hour-long catnap, assuming he would have a rather quiet day in the field.

Kruk never should have assumed anything. He recalled how projected starter Wes Chamberlain was a late scratch from the lineup due to a pulled muscle.

"I finally got to sleep about 7:30 and woke up about 8:30," recalled Kruk. "Fregosi told me that I was in left field and I almost fell over."

"I couldn't even lift my leg. I had pitched all night. My hip was so sore. I had some pain in my shoulder, and I thought it was going to be the most miserable day in my life."

"I ended up getting three hits that day. Hopefully, they were three singles."

It was just one in a series of anecdotes that captured the essence of the West Virginia native who captured the fancy of Philadelphia fans for five and a half seasons. Kruk was a relatively unknown hitter when he was acquired, along with utility man Randy Ready, from San Diego for promising young outfielder Chris James in a June 1989 deal, a trade that ranks among the best in Phillies history, as James never quite fulfilled his promise. Kruk was a no-nonsense, true-grit, throwback type of player who spoke his mind, yet carried a soft interior in spite of his usual moody, scruffy exterior.

Perhaps the most moving moment of his Phillies career was his appearance on the opening day of the 1994 season.

A few months earlier, though, Kruk was experiencing pain in his groin area. Visits to a doctor and later tests revealed testicular cancer. A preliminary diagnosis called for surgery followed by radiation treatments and a hopeful return by late May.

On opening day, during a ceremony in which the Phillies received their National League championship rings, the loudest ovation came for one of their beloved heroes, John Kruk.

Kruk was in the opening-day lineup and had three hits in five at-bats. The man also often referred to as "Jake" didn't miss a beat. In fact, he led the team in hitting with a .378 average through the first 21 games.

"It was amazing how he didn't need spring training and had three hits," recalled teammate Darren Daulton. "He was a one-of-a-kind ballplayer. He was a main reason why it was so fun to be around the 1993 team."

Kruk's finest season as a Phillie came in 1993, when he appeared in 150 games and hit .316 with 14 homers and 85 RBIs. He made an All-Star appearance for the second consecutive season and hit over .300. Kruk posted a career-high .323 mark with 10 homers and 70 RBIs.

But numbers aside, "Macho Row" will always be his baseball home.

"The thing about being on the 1993 team was that it was the most fun anyone could ever have in baseball," Kruk said. "There was always something going on. Someone was going to fight someone. Someone was getting ragged on.

"It was just a blast. You would come in there every day, and you never knew if someone was going to play a joke on you or kick your butt.

"It kept you on your toes. I enjoyed it."

The magic of the '93 season didn't last long, and "Macho Row" and the rest of the clubhouse venues began to take a different route. Kruk played in just 75 games during the 1994 season, but he still hit .302.

Like many from the '93 team, Kruk was traded before the start of the 1995 season. His new home was in Chicago with the White Sox, where he would primarily be a designated hitter at age 34, but it wouldn't be for long.

Keeping pace with his unorthodox style, Kruk retired in his 45th game with the White Sox.

"I told everybody that I was going to retire on Friday before the weekend series was over," said Kruk, who was hitting .308 at the time. "Robin Ventura and Ozzie Guillen told me to get a hit and walk off the field.

"That's what happened. I'm glad I got a hit. The way I was swinging the bat, it could have been two to three weeks until I got another one.

"I had enough. I felt that I lost it. I lost my love for the game when I left Philadelphia. Players weren't the same. Too many players now are businessmen. It's supposed to be fun. When I was on the White Sox, I didn't see too many people having fun."

John Kruk Phillies Statistics

Year	G	AB	R	H	2B	3B	HR	RBI	AVG	OBP	SLGP
1989	81	281	46	93	13	6	5	38	.331	.386	.473
1990	142	443	52	129	25	8	7	67	.291	.386	.431
1991	152	538	84	158	27	6	21	92	.294	.367	.483
1992	144	507	86	164	30	4	10	70	.323	.423	.458
1993	150	535	100	169	33	5	14	85	.316	.430	.475
1994	75	255	35	77	17	0	5	38	.302	.395	.427
Totals	**744**	**2,559**	**403**	**790**	**145**	**29**	**62**	**390**	**.309**	**.400**	**.461**

Twenty-seven

Stan Lopata

Heavy-Hitting Catcher of the '50s

by Skip Clayton

I n the long history of Phillies baseball, the club has had some outstanding catchers.

Jack Clements, Bill Killefer, Jimmie Wilson, Spud Davis, Andy Seminick, Bob Boone, Darren Daulton, and Mike Lieberthal have all been excellent backstops for the Phillies. None, however, hit more home runs in a season than Stan Lopata.

Lopata was the club's regular catcher in the mid-1950s. A strapping 6-2, 210-pounder, Stan broke in with the Phillies in 1948 and played with them until 1958.

In 1956, Lopata set the club record at the time for the most homers (32) by a right-handed hitter in a season. Big Stash, as he was often called, was in the midst of a four-year spree in which he hit 86 home runs, including quite a few over the roof at Connie Mack Stadium.

Lopata, who ended his career in 1960 with the Milwaukee Braves, had a career batting average of .254 with 116 home runs and 397 RBIs in 853 games.

In 1950, it was Lopata who took Richie Ashburn's throw from center field and tagged out the Brooklyn Dodgers' Cal Abrams at the plate in what would have been the winning run in the ninth inning of the last game of the season. The Phillies went on to ride Dick Sisler's three-run homer in the top of 10th to their first pennant in 35 years.

At the time, Lopata was the backup backstop to Andy Seminick, who, while playing on a broken ankle, had been taken out of the game for a pinch runner. Stan remembers the play well.

"Richie's throw had Abrams out by about 20 to 25 feet," he said. "In a way, I was surprised they sent him in because they had nobody out and Jackie Robinson, Carl Furillo, and Gil Hodges coming up. It was the perfect throw from Richie. There was still only one out, but Robbie [Robin Roberts]—and it seemed like anytime he got into a problem, I don't know where he got it—reached back and got that little extra. Very few pitchers can do this. He reached back and got them out. When Tommy Brown popped to Eddie Waitkus for the final out in the 10th, we just charged the mound. We were so happy, especially after what we went through the final week of the season."

The Phillies never had another season quite like that during Lopata's stay in Philadelphia. But Stan is glad to have been a Phillie, nonetheless.

Today, Lopata is retired and living in Arizona. A native of Delray, Mich., a suburb of Detroit, Lopata was signed by Phillies' scout Eddie Krajnik in time for him to join Terre Haute of the Three-I League. He received a $20,000 bonus for signing.

After hitting .292 at Terre Haute in 1946, Stan moved up to Utica of the Eastern League, where he was named the Most Valuable Player after hitting .325 in 1947. The following year, Lopata was up to Toronto of the International League. He hit .279 with 15 homers. In one game at Jersey City, he doubled with two on, homered with two on, and then hit a grand slam.

The Phillies brought up Lopata at the end of the 1948 season. He stayed with the club in 1949 and 1950 as a backup catcher to Seminick, hitting .271 and .209, respectively.

Lopata began the 1951 season in Philadelphia, but by then the Phillies had acquired catcher Del Wilber. Stan was farmed out to the Triple-A team in Baltimore.

After the season, the Phillies sent Seminick to the Cincinnati Reds in a major trade which brought Smoky Burgess to Philadelphia. Lopata was recalled for the 1952 season, and for the next three years, he and Burgess platooned behind the plate, Stan playing mostly against left-handed pitchers. Lopata hit .274 in 1952 and .239 in 1953. In 1954, the big story was the sudden improvement in his hitting, as he went up to .290.

Lopata completely revamped his batting stance, changing to a crouch. It has often been reported that the switch was the result of a suggestion by Hall of Famer Rogers Hornsby, but Stan denies it.

"It really and truly was my own idea," said Lopata. "Rogers stayed at the Edgewater Beach Hotel in Chicago where we stayed. I roomed with Johnny Wyrostek, and he knew Rogers pretty well. Johnny and I went to see Rogers, and Johnny asked him, 'What about Stan?' He had seen me on television. He said that I missed too many balls. He meant that anytime you swing a bat, you are supposed to get a piece of the ball.

"So that day, I went out to the ballpark, I did crouch a little and felt real good, and I saw the ball better. The second time up, I got down a little lower, and the third time, I got down even lower. I saw the ball better, and it seemed I could pull the ball better."

With his .290 average, Lopata hit 14 homers and had 42 RBIs in only 259 times at bat.

Early in the 1955 season, Burgess was traded back to Cincinnati and Seminick returned to the Phillies. Dividing his time between catcher and first base, Lopata had a .271 average in 303 times at the plate.

In 1956, Stan established four club records for catchers—most doubles in one season (33), most triples (seven), most homers (32) and most RBI (95). All of those records are still held by Stan except the RBI record, which Darren Daulton broke in 1992 with 110.

"I had a real good year in 1956, but I didn't know how good a year it was until I saw all of the records in the Phillies media guide," Lopata said. "It is nice to hold them as long as possible."

In 1956, Lopata was named to the National League All-Star team for the second straight year. On defense, Stan was the only catcher playing 100 or more games to have only one passed ball.

Some of his homers that year were estimated to have carried from 450 to 500 feet. At Connie Mack Stadium, few home runs went over the roof, but Lopata hit a number that traveled that far.

Injuries slowed Stan in 1957. He hit only .237 with 18 homers. In one stretch of 14 games, Stan hit eight homers, including one in four straight games.

"I hurt my knee at Connie Mack Stadium in a rundown between third and home," Lopata said. "I had no business catching, but we were in a pennant race. I couldn't crouch well, but the doctor said I wouldn't damage my knee. I was taking batting practice, and after the workout, [clubhouse manager] Unk Russell told me that Roy Hamey, our general manager, wanted to see me. He said, 'There is nothing wrong with your knee. The doctor says you can play. Nothing is going to happen with it.'

"I knew what my condition was, and I was peeved. I said I would go down and try it, even though it was all messed up. Mayo Smith, our manager, wasn't in yet. I left a note on his desk and told him the same thing I told Hamey. He said to go out and see how it feels. I told him—and this was a Saturday game—that we had a doubleheader coming up on Sunday and that if I caught today, I am not going to catch anything tomorrow. He let me sit and I hit a three-run pinch-homer in the ninth to beat Cincinnati. I caught the second game the next day and hit two more homers. I kept catching, but my knee bothered me the rest of the year. I couldn't crouch too well behind the plate. Toward the end of the year, I was told that the first-base coaches were picking off my signs. I had the right leg stuck out, and that was why they picked off the sign."

In 1958, Stan got off to a good start, but was beaned by Larry Jackson in St. Louis. Stan had hit six homers, but he had only three more after that, while splitting the catching duties with Carl Sawatski. He wound up with a .248 average.

During spring training of 1959, he was traded to the Milwaukee Braves, along with Johnny O'Brien and Ted Kazanski, for Gene Conley, Joe Koppe, and Harry Hanebrink.

"In a way, I was surprised at the trade and a little disappointed," Lopata recalled. "But I was still in the big leagues and that was the main thing. I made friends, especially with the people in the Phillies organization."

Stan spent two years with Milwaukee, playing in only 56 games. Del Crandall was the No. 1 catcher, and coming up from the minors was Joe Torre. In 1960, Stan went back to the minors and helped Louisville of the American Association capture the Junior World Series.

Had Stan not suffered injuries in the 1957 and 1958 seasons, there is no telling how many more homers he might have hit. His total of 116 Phillies home runs is 13th best in the club's history. Lopata also did a good job at first base when he played there, although in the late innings, when the Phillies had the lead, Marv Blaylock took over.

Stan Lopata Phillies Statistics

Year	G	AB	R	H	2B	3B	HR	RBI	AVG	OBP	SLGP
1948	6	15	2	2	1	0	0	2	.133	.133	.200
1949	83	240	31	65	9	2	8	27	.271	.330	.425
1950	58	129	10	27	2	2	1	11	.209	.325	.279
1951	3	5	0	0	0	0	0	0	.000	.000	.000
1952	57	179	25	49	9	1	4	27	.274	.395	.402
1953	81	234	34	56	12	3	8	31	.239	.321	.419
1954	86	259	42	75	14	5	14	42	.290	.369	.544
1955	99	303	49	82	9	3	22	58	.271	.388	.538
1956	146	535	96	143	33	7	32	95	.267	.353	.535
1957	116	388	50	92	18	2	18	67	.237	.331	.433
1958	86	258	36	64	9	0	9	33	.248	.391	.388
Totals	821	2545	375	655	116	25	116	393	.257	.355	.459

Twenty-eight

Greg Luzinski

The Bull

by Jeff Moeller

His home run blasts were synonymous with his nickname.
As baseball headed into the 2000 season, Greg "The Bull" Luzinski ranked in the top 10 in nine of the team's offensive categories: RBIs (seventh, 811); doubles (10th, 253); home runs (fourth, 223); total bases (ninth, 2,263); extra-base hits (eighth, 497); walks (eighth, 572); intentional walks (fourth, 74); strikeouts (second, 1,098); and sacrifice flies (second, 53). The Bull started in four consecutive All-Star games from 1975 to 1978.

He and Mike Schmidt were the "Bash Brothers" version of the mid- to late-1970s, as Luzinski hit 30-plus homers three times, including 39 in 1977, while Schmidt hit 38. The following season, he hit 35 and Schmidt hit just 21, but their power was instrumental in helping the team return to the postseason again.

But it was the 1977 National League Championship Series that left a black mark on his Phillies career and a sour taste that lingers with Philadelphia fans.

Luzinski dropped a fly ball off the bat of Manny Mota against the left-field fence in the ninth inning. The game went from a 5-3 win to a 6-5 defeat, and it would eventually play a part in the firing of manager Danny Ozark less than two years later, as the skipper routinely failed to replace Luzinski for late-inning defensive purposes.

Still, Luzinski had a stellar Phillies career for the better part of nine seasons.

Paul Owens, then the Phillies farm director, discovered Luzinski at Notre Dame High School in Chicago in 1968. Owens initially believed Luzinski would be a catcher or first baseman, mainly due to his compact 6-foot-1, 220-pound frame, which garnered him his share of football offers from colleges as a linebacker.

Three years later, Luzinski made a cameo appearance with the big club, stopping in for 28 games during the 1971 season. The following year, he played in 150 games and hit 18 homers with a solid .281 average.

But it was in 1973 that Luzinski and Schmidt splashed onto the scene together. The Bull rocked 29 homers, and he continued to shine with his overall hitting ability, as he raised his average to .285 with 26 doubles.

Luzinski shattered his knee in June of the following year in left field. His season was cut to 85 games, and he hit only seven homers. But he recovered and began with Schmidt a power barrage as impressive as any duo's in recent years.

After 1978, though, Luzinski's power numbers and his overall average began to dip. His homers dropped from 35 to 18 and his batting average fell to a mediocre .252.

It was ironic, too, that Luzinski had developed a personality problem with manager Dallas Green, who was his first manager at Rookie League Huron in

1968. It was then that Luzinski and Green had a good relationship, but it wasn't the case in 1979.

Luzinski's name also came up in numerous trade talks before the winter meetings, and owner Ruly Carpenter drove to Luzinski's home to curb any problems before they got worse.

Carpenter reportedly told Luzinski to get down to a playing weight of 215 instead of his ballooned 240—a favorite catcall of the fans when he struggled.

Luzinski started the 1980 season strong, but he soon swooned due to nagging injuries and personal problems. His relationship with Green didn't change much, and a promising rookie outfielder named Lonnie Smith was on the horizon.

He slid into second base during an early July game in St. Louis and felt a pain in his right knee, the same one he had surgery on in 1974. The pain subsided a little, and he was placed on the disabled list shortly after the All-Star break. Luzinski underwent surgery to remove loose cartilage in late July and didn't return to the lineup until mid-August.

But he did come through with two hits in four at-bats in a September game against Montreal that locked up the division title. Luzinski also responded in the wild playoff series against Houston with a clutch homer in the first game, four RBIs overall, and a .294 average.

During the World Series, however, Luzinski was bothered by the flu and Green played him in just three of the six games, opting for Smith and veterans Del Unser and Greg Gross in left field.

Despite all his problems, Luzinski still cherishes the 1980 season.

"Obviously, it was a great year, especially after getting so close three other times. To finally win the Series was something we'll never forget," Luzinski said.

"The whole year, at different times, everybody helped to win the division, and the division series was big. We finally got over the hump, through the division series, and the pressure was off. We made it to the World Series, so it was a little easier playing."

During the postgame celebration after Game 6, Luzinski was spotted huddling with Owens, a good friend who had approached Luzinski in mid-September to talk about his swing.

It was apparent that Luzinski's career as a Phillie was over, and he was sold to the Chicago White Sox before the start of the 1981 season.

Greg Luzinski Phillies Statistics

Year	G	AB	R	H	2B	3B	HR	RBI	AVG	OBP	SLGP
1970	8	12	0	2	0	0	0	0	.167	.333	.167
1971	28	100	13	30	8	0	3	15	.300	.386	.470
1972	150	563	66	158	33	5	18	68	.281	.332	.453
1973	161	610	76	174	26	4	29	97	.285	.346	.484
1974	85	302	29	82	14	1	7	48	.272	.330	.394
1975	161	596	85	179	35	3	34	120	.300	.394	.540
1976	149	533	74	162	28	1	21	95	.304	.369	.478
1977	149	554	99	171	35	3	39	130	.309	.394	.594
1978	155	540	85	143	32	2	35	101	.265	.388	.526
1979	137	452	47	114	23	1	18	81	.252	.343	.427
1980	106	368	44	84	19	1	19	56	.228	.342	.440
Totals	1,289	4,630	618	1,299	253	21	223	811	.281	.363	.489

Twenty-nine

Garry Maddox

Secretary of Defense

by Jeff Moeller

Through the years, few Phillies can be immediately recognized in the same breath by their nicknames as well as their regular names. Garry Lee Maddox, better known as the "Secretary of Defense," was one of them.

In his 11 years with the Phillies, Maddox won eight straight Gold Gloves and had a career fielding average of .983. He made just 78 errors in 4,621 chances while recording 4,449 putouts and 94 assists.

The slender outfielder with long, loping strides was basically an unknown when the Phillies acquired him from San Francisco on May 4, 1975, for the popular Willie Montanez.

But it didn't take long for Philadelphia fans to appreciate his defensive prowess and his uncanny ability to run down fly balls that appeared to be headed into extra-base gaps.

In part, Maddox was often overlooked when it came to his offensive production. In his first full season with the Phillies in 1976, Maddox finished second in the National League in hitting with a .330 average and swiped 29 bases.

The following season, Maddox began a string of four consecutive seasons where he hit double figures in homers—a career-high 14 in 1977—and hit better than .280 in three of those seasons.

Maddox went on to hit .429 in the National League Championship Series against the Dodgers with a pair of RBIs.

"I can remember one game against Chicago," recalled then-general manager Paul Owens during the 1980 season. "We were down in the 15th inning by two runs and came back to beat them, and he got the big hit then with two outs. He was a clutch hitter."

However, Maddox will always be remembered in certain circles for uncharacteristically dropping a routine fly ball in Game 4 of the 1978 National League Championship Series against the Dodgers that allowed the game-winning, and series-winning, run to score.

But there was also another moment that will always be remembered, one in which Maddox vindicated himself and his team two years later.

Maddox made a running catch in right-center of a line drive off the bat of Houston's Enos Cabell in the 10th inning of the 1980 National League Championship Series that gave the Phillies their first pennant in 30 years. He also drove in the winning run during the game.

It would be enough at the time to defuse and deflate the negativity that surrounded Maddox's regular season.

His problems started in spring training when his agent began contract demands with Maddox as Garry entered his option year. Rumors circulated of Maddox being dealt elsewhere, and manager Dallas Green began to search for an alternative plan for center field.

By late March, the Phillies had signed Maddox to a six-year deal, the first four years containing a no-trade clause. But Maddox realized his game would suffer.

His average would hover around the .250 mark throughout the season, and he finished the regular campaign with a .259 mark. He had developed a personality conflict with Green, who blasted him in the press for fielding miscues.

In an Aug. 31 game against San Diego, Maddox lost two balls in the Southern California sun and Green blamed him for not wearing sunglasses. The following day, general manager Paul Owens held a meeting in which he singled out Maddox and Larry Bowa for not playing well.

As a result, Maddox was benched for all three upcoming games against San Francisco and two of the four upcoming games against Los Angeles.

However, in the second game of the Giants series, Green planned to use Maddox as a middle-inning replacement. When Green called on Maddox, the outfielder had been in the clubhouse to use the bathroom and get a cup of coffee. As it turned out, Maddox had asked coach Lee Elia for permission and Elia later informed Green.

But things got worse before they got better for the duo. Maddox missed a fly ball in a nationally televised game against Montreal. This time, he had his sunglasses on but not down. Green was again critical and benched him, along with Bob Boone and Greg Luzinski, for an upcoming series against Chicago.

The following season, the conflict between Green and Maddox continued, and Maddox tailed off slightly with a .263 average in 94 games. He still remained a key part of the club and hit .333 in three at-bats in the 1981 division series playoff against Montreal.

In 1982, Green moved on to Chicago and Maddox moved back into the driver's seat. He upped his average back to .284 and played in 119 games under new manager Pat Corrales.

In 1983, the 33-year-old Maddox began to fit in with the "Wheeze Kids." Involved in an outfield platoon under manager Paul Owens, Maddox played in 97 games but still hit .275.

During a game in late July, however, Maddox had balked at entering a game against Atlanta in which the Phillies had been trailing by a couple of runs. Maddox felt he was simply being used as a "mop-up" guy. Owens blew up and used Maddox as an example of the "I-ism" attitude that he believed was affecting his club.

Maddox's playing time was hampered by back problems, and the club had been looking at a young, speedy outfielder named Bob Dernier. Maddox's supporters often said the veteran was simply shy and sensitive, and they feared he had been a victim of Agent Orange from his Vietnam tour of duty from 1968 to 1970.

"Winning is contagious, and you know when the atmosphere on the team is winning, it is hard not to get caught up in it," Maddox said during the 1983 season. "Everyone just looks for a chance to get out there and play."

Yet he hit .273 in three games of the NLCS against the Dodgers. And his home run in Game 1 of the World Series against Baltimore gave the club its lone victory. Maddox hit .250 in the Series.

At the time, Owens preferred to leave Maddox in center field until his contract was scheduled to run out in 1985. Still, Dernier played heavy in their plans.

"Right now, Garry Maddox is, very candidly, a late-inning replacement and an insurance policy for Dernier, and an expensive one at that," said president Bill Giles.

The Phillies had tried to trade him, but a reported deal with the Yankees fell through when the Phils refused to take pitcher Rudy May. Maddox had also been involved in trade talks with San Diego for pitcher John Montefusco, but the Padres were concerned about his salary and his age.

Maddox remained a Phillie and took the season in stride. He also realized he wasn't alone on that club.

"I think a few guys who started the season as regulars, no one likes to have anyone give up on them, and that's what happenend in this case," Maddox said during the season. "Guys got off to a slow start, and it forced the team to do a lot of different things. So we never got back to our original format, the way we planned to play the season.

"Guys felt, 'Hey, I was given up on. That's kind of hard to take.' But a lot of times you have to swallow the pride and go out there and do it. Believe me, I swallowed it.

"It was definitely my most difficult season. Almost being traded, asking me to waive my no-trade clause and all that."

The next two seasons, Maddox's playing time began to diminish as the club began to rebuild and retool with young upstarts such as Glenn Wilson, Von Hayes, and Sixto Lezcano.

Maddox also began to be bothered more and more by back problems, and at age 36, he announced his retirement six games into the 1986 season. Among the club's all-time records, he ranks third in sacrifice flies (51), sixth in stolen bases (189), and 10th in intentional walks (51).

Through the years, Maddox was involved with the Child Guidance Clinic and had sponsored events such as the Garry Maddox Celebrity Bowling Benefit. He has also been involved with the Fellowship of Christian Athletes and spent time as a Phillies broadcaster.

Garry Maddox Phillies Statistics

Year	G	AB	R	H	2B	3B	HR	RBI	AVG	OBP	SLGP
1975	99	374	50	109	25	8	4	46	.291	.359	.433
1976	146	531	75	175	37	6	6	68	.330	.377	.456
1977	139	571	85	167	27	10	14	74	.292	.323	.448
1978	155	598	62	172	34	3	11	68	.288	.332	.410
1979	148	548	70	154	28	6	13	61	.281	.304	.425
1980	143	549	59	142	31	3	11	73	.259	.278	.386
1981	94	323	37	85	7	1	5	40	.263	.295	.337
1982	119	412	39	117	27	2	8	61	.284	.303	.417
1983	97	324	27	89	14	2	4	32	.275	.312	.367
1984	77	241	29	68	11	0	5	19	.282	.316	.390
1985	105	218	22	52	8	1	4	23	.239	.281	.339
1986	6	7	1	3	0	0	0	1	.429	.556	.429
Totals	1,328	4,696	556	1,333	249	42	85	566	.284	.320	.409

Thirty

Gene Mauch

In a Class by Himself

by Skip Clayton

I n the 117-year history of the Phillies, the club has been managed by 48 different men.

Some of them have been good, some of them have been bad, and most of them have been somewhere in between. None, however, was in the same category as Gene Mauch.

Mauch was in a class by himself, a fiery general who knew as much about managing as anybody who ever skippered a team. He was controversial, he was smart, and he was tough. He whipped, cajoled, and maneuvered his teams in an effort to get the best out of them.

And in his nine years with the Phillies, that's exactly what he usually got.

Mauch piloted the Phillies from the third game of the season in 1960 to the middle of the season in 1968. In 1,331 games during that time, his teams won 645, lost 684, and tied two for a .485 percentage. No Phils' skipper managed the team in more games, only one (Harry Wright) won more games, and none lost as many.

Mauch is the only manager in the team's history to have led his club to six straight winning seasons. Four times he finished in the first division, his highest finish being in 1964, when the club wound up in a tie for second place after leading the league most of the season.

When the club hired Gene to replace Eddie Sawyer, who quit after the first game of the 1960 season, few people knew much about him. By the time he left, he was a household name.

Mauch had spent parts of nine years in the major leagues, most of them as a utility infielder for the Brooklyn Dodgers, Pittsburgh Pirates, Chicago Cubs, Boston Braves, St. Louis Cardinals, and Boston Red Sox.

Mauch took his first shot at running a club in 1953 as player-manager of the Atlanta Crackers of the Southern Association. After finishing third that year, he resumed a full-time playing career until 1958, when he became pilot of the Minneapolis Millers of the American Association. In two years in Minneapolis, Mauch's teams won the Junior World Series one year, sweeping Buffalo in 1958, and lost in seven games to Havana in the Series in 1959.

Meantime, the Phillies had finished last both years.

"After the 1959 season, I had an opportunity to manage in the big leagues and I had turned it down," recalled Mauch. "I actually had two offers. Then in 1960, we were in Florida and it was the last week of spring training with Minneapolis. John Quinn called me about the Phillies job.

"I knew they had a bad baseball team in Philadelphia. But I agreed to come up there. Eddie Sawyer had said that his reason for resigning was that he was 49 and wanted to live to be 50. I was 34, so I said, 'What the hell, I'll make it to 50. I don't care how bad it is.'

"I always agreed with what Mr. Mack said about pitching being a high percentage of the game of baseball," Gene continued. "I knew the quality of arms on that Phillies staff—Dick Farrell, Jim Owens, Don Cardwell, and Jack Meyer. But inasmuch as they did have those great arms, that was a starting point.

"One thing I didn't really realize, though, was how little protection those arms had in the field. It was a pretty bad situation, and John Quinn told me that right from the beginning," he said. "We tried to rebuild the club. We made all kinds of deals. We traded away veterans for younger players.

The 1960 Phillies were 59-95 and finished last for the third year in a row.

"It was obvious we needed everyday players," said Mauch. "We kind of struggled through 1960 while I learned the National League. I don't think a manager can make much of a contribution to any club unless he knows the people he is playing against. I spent the first couple of years learning what I was up against. There were some truly great teams."

Mauch also began building his reputation as an innovator. In one of his early moves, he switched bullpens, moving the Phillies to the right-field pen and putting the visitors in left. Since 1909, when Connie Mack Stadium opened, the home team had always had its bullpen in left field, down the line from its dugout. Mauch had his reasons for making the change.

"I saw countless times when balls were hit off that high wall in right," he explained. "The player on first didn't know whether the ball was off the wall or not. He would hesitate, and we would end up with guys on second and third. I said, 'Not us.' I put our bullpen in right and had a guy there with a towel. If the ball was hit off the wall, that towel was waved. Guys were flying around the bases, scoring from second or first."

Mauch's creative ideas, however, didn't do much to help the 1961 team, which won only 47 games.

"In 1961 it was pretty much of a nightmare," Mauch conceded. "We lost 23 in a row. But we knew what we were doing. Expansion was coming, and once it was established in our minds and in the minds of the fans that this was a pretty bad club, we almost went on a campaign to make it even worse—if that makes sense.

"After the middle of the season, we tried, almost on a daily basis, to see how bad we could make the club. The idea was that there was a certain number of players the Mets and the Colt 45s had to take from our club. If there is any successful aspect of that 1961 season, it was jamming our lineup and our 25-man roster full of older players so that our key young players in the minors were prevented from being taken—like Ray Culp and Richie Allen."

In 1962, the Phillies moved up to seventh, posting a winning record for the first time since 1953. They were 81-80, winning 19 of their last 26 games.

"In 1963, we had the opportunity to finish in the first division for the first time in eight years. That was the year the spare ribs went haywire after we lost in Houston. [Mauch in, a fit of anger in the clubhouse, knocked over a table containing the postgame meal.] After that, we went to San Francisco and beat the Giants two out of three. Then we beat the Dodgers in Los Angeles three in a row. We won 87 games, then made a real good deal that winter with Detroit in which we got Jim Bunning and Gus Triandos for Don Demeter and Jack Hamilton."

Despite getting Bunning, and with Dick Allen coming up from the minors, only 10 writers out of 232 in a wire-service poll picked the Phillies to win the pennant in 1964.

"We only won five more games than we did the year before, but we won them pretty quickly," said Mauch. In the first 150, we won 90. Then I took a couple of dumb pills or something. We couldn't turn the corner.

"But in those first 150 games of the 1964 season, we played as perfectly as I have seen a team play. I have never seen a team that had as many guys who knew exactly how the game was supposed to be played and enjoyed playing it the right way. My only regret is that they were never rewarded for playing such astute baseball as they did for the first 150 games."

The Phillies, who led by one and a half games on Aug. 7, helped themselves by picking up Frank Thomas from the Mets. Thomas helped the Phillies build their lead to six and a half, but got hurt on Sept. 8. By Sept. 21, the lead was still six and a half with 12 games to go. Then the Phillies lost 10 in a row before winning their final two and finishing in a tie for second.

Much has been written and said that Mauch pitched Bunning and Short too often during the 10-game losing streak. In the final week, Mauch had no choice but to pitch those two pitchers.

"I wouldn't do a thing differently," Mauch said. "Not with that club. I don't think people really realize what our options were. Dennis Bennett was down. Ray Culp was down. Jack Baldschun was down.

"I knew I was going to manage that team again, and I was perfectly willing to take the full responsibility. And it is a manager's responsibility when you lose. But I wasn't going to point fingers at people. There was no place to point, anyway. They played as good as they could play and as hard as they could play."

Players such as Jim Bunning, Chris Short, Tony Taylor, Cookie Rojas, Bobby Wine, and Ruben Amaro have never blamed Mauch for the slide. Moreover, during the month of September, the Phillies never had a day off. The injury to Thomas hurt the club, too. Despite the loss of the pennant, Mauch was chosen as the National League Manager of the Year for the second time in three years (He first took the honor in 1962).

The Phillies dropped to sixth in 1965, despite a record of 85-76, and moved up to fourth place, winning 87 games, in 1966. In 1967, the Phillies finished fifth with an 82-80 record.

Two months into the 1968 season, Mauch was fired with the team in a tie for fifth place with a 27-27 record. Since then, no manager has been with the Phillies as long as Mauch was. Mauch wasn't out of work long. The following year, he joined the expansion Montreal Expos, managing them until 1975. He piloted the Minnesota Twins from 1976 to 1980, then took over the California Angels in 1981, leading them to the West Division championship in the American League in 1982 and 1986.

Mauch stepped down as manager nine days before the 1988 season opened. He finished his 26 years as a manager with a 1,902-2,037 record, much of it compiled with noncontenders.

Mauch came back in 1995 as a bench coach with the Kansas City Royals to help out his former catcher with the Angels, Bob Boone. Gene is now retired and living in Rancho Mirage, Calif.

Although it has been 32 years since he last pulled on a Phillies uniform, Mauch still has a warm spot for the club and the city in which it played.

"The greatest thing that could happen to any young manager like me was, when a guy wins 59 games the first year and 47 his second, he is gone," Mauch said. "But I associated myself with John Quinn and Bob Carpenter, who were great people and great baseball people. I mean great.

"They stuck with me. I learned. I got a little better each year. The situation got a little better. It was a good break for me to break in under those conditions.

"Overall, being with the Phillies was a wonderful experience. I loved the team, and it was a great, great town."

Thirty-one

Bake McBride

Key Player on Phillies' Title Teams

by Skip Clayton

P aul Owens, the Phillies' general manager, faced two challenges on the night of June 15, 1977.

He didn't need to look at the clock to know that the midnight trading deadline was approaching.

And he didn't need the National League East standings or a copy of his team's roster to know that the Phillies were one player away from repeating as division champions.

They trailed the first-place Chicago Cubs by eight games and didn't look at all like the team that had won 101 games the previous year.

The main reason was the lack of a true leadoff hitter. Dave Cash, the catalyst who had helped convince the team that it was a winner, had gone to the Montreal Expos as a free agent during the winter, and his absence left a gaping hole at the top of the lineup.

It was after midnight, Philadelphia time, when Owens filled the gap, getting Bake McBride from the St. Louis Cardinals.

The price: left-handed pitcher Tommy Underwood, plus prospects Dane Iorg and Rick Bosetti.

McBride helped the Phillies to three division titles, one National League championship and the 1980 World Series crown. His home run in Game 1 against the Kansas City Royals helped the Phillies to a comeback victory.

McBride became the leadoff hitter and the base-stealing threat the Phillies needed. He was also more than capable in the outfield before his bad knees cut his career short. After Pete Rose joined the club, Bake batted in different spots. When he led off, he got on. When he batted third or fourth, he hit and he drove in runs.

"I was shocked by the trade," McBride recalled. "I couldn't believe they would trade me to one of the clubs in the same division. But in the end, it worked out best for myself and the Phillies."

McBride, who had hit .300 or better in his first four seasons with the Cardinals, was batting just .262 at the time of the trade. But he recovered his batting eye and hit .339 for the Phillies.

A lifelong center fielder, he was switched to right by the Phillies because Garry Maddox was the best center fielder in baseball.

McBride started his career in the Cardinals organization in 1970 and spent close to four years with farm teams. He came to St. Louis late in 1973, and in 1974 he was named Rookie of the Year.

"I went to a tryout camp for the Cardinals, and they signed me out of the camp," McBride said. "Baseball wasn't important to me when I was in high school or college. At the time, I didn't like it. I liked basketball, football, and track.

"When I started playing baseball, it was something new to me. It was a totally different world. I felt that the only reason the Cardinals signed me was because of my speed. I didn't know anything about hitting and didn't know anything about the outfield, because at Westminster College, I pitched.

"I had never dreamed of playing professional baseball. I wanted to play professional basketball."

McBride's play helped the Phils finally reach first place on Aug. 5. Once they got there, they never looked back, finishing five games in front of the Pittsburgh Pirates. The Los Angeles Dodgers captured the West Division with 98 wins, three fewer than the Phillies.

With the series tied at one win apiece, the third game was a nightmare for the Phillies, as the Dodgers scored three in the ninth after two were out to win, 6-5. The Dodgers wrapped up the finale the next night in the rain, 4-1.

"It hurt everybody when we lost it, and it hurt again in 1978 when we lost again to the Dodgers," McBride said. "It seemed like we were always one game away from winning the playoffs, but we never could. It was something we finally accomplished in 1980."

The 1978 Phillies had to go to the final weekend to wrap up the East Division against the Pirates, after blowing most of an 11 1/2-game lead. Injuries slowed Bake down in 1978. He hit .269 but led the outfielders in fielding with a .996 average.

McBride's average jumped to .280 in 1979, and he reached double figures in doubles, triples, home runs, and stolen bases, but the Phillies slipped to fourth place despite the addition of Pete Rose to their lineup.

But everything came together in 1980. The Phillies won the only world championship in their history, and McBride had a splendid season, batting .309 and driving in a career-high 87 runs.

The Phillies and the Expos were in the battle for the title all year, and on the next-to-last weekend of the season, Montreal came to the Vet for three games. The Phillies won the first, 2-1, when McBride homered in the ninth off David Palmer, giving the team a one-and-a-half-game lead.

Montreal won the next two games and regained first by a half-game. The Expos went home to play the Cards three games. The Phillies played host to the Cubs for four. Then the two would meet in Montreal in another three-game series. The Phillies swept the Cubs, and the Expos took three from St. Louis. The two teams were tied for first.

The Phillies won the first game, 2-1, and the second game the following afternoon, 6-4, in 11 innings and reached the National League Championship Series for the fourth time in five seasons.

They beat the Houston Astros in five memorable games and made it to their first World Series in 30 years, against the Kansas City Royals.

The Phillies were down, 4-0, in the third inning of Game 1 at the Vet, when they came back with five runs, three of them on Bake's homer, putting them in the lead for good.

"The thing about that homer, I had heard that Dennis Leonard was the hardest thrower they had over in the American League. The first time up, I made an out. I came back and told Larry Bowa, 'Next time up, I am going to hit a home run off this guy. This guy can't throw that hard. He doesn't throw as hard as the guys in the National League.'

"I admit I didn't think I was going to do it. Really, it was one of those things, just something that was meant to be at that time."

The Phillies went on to win the Series in six games as McBride hit .304, driving in five runs.

McBride played in 58 games in the strike-torn 1981 season, hitting .271. On Feb. 16, 1982, he was traded to Cleveland for pitcher Sid Monge. McBride played in just 97 games in two seasons with the Indians before he retired.

"I had a problem with my eyes," he said. "After all the problems I had with my knees and eyes, I felt if I could get my 10 years in, that would be good enough. I was fortunate to get my 10 years, and I didn't have a disappointment."

McBride finished with a .299 career average in 1,071 games. He was only 34 when he retired.

McBride remained in baseball as a roving instructor for some time in the New York Mets farm system and later worked in the St. Louis Cardinals organization.

Today, Bake lives in Owensboro, Ky., and is an area manager for the World Wide cleaning company in Kentucky, Illinois, and Indiana.

If you were to list the best trades in Phillies history, the Bake McBride deal was one of them.

Bake McBride Phillies Statistics

Year	G	AB	R	H	2B	3B	HR	RBI	AVG	OBP	SLGP
1977	85	280	55	95	20	5	11	41	.339	.392	.564
1978	122	472	68	127	20	4	10	49	.269	.315	.392
1979	151	582	82	163	16	12	12	60	.280	.328	.411
1980	137	554	68	171	33	10	9	87	.309	.342	.453
1981	58	221	26	60	17	1	2	21	.271	.303	.385
Totals	553	2,109	299	616	106	32	44	258	.292	.335	.435

Thirty-two

Tug McGraw

1980 World Series Hero

by Skip Clayton

N
ot one Philadelphia sports fan forgot where he was at 11:29 p.m. on Oct. 21, 1980. The Phillies were seconds away from finally winning the World Series.

When Tug McGraw struck out Willie Wilson to end the final game, excitement hit the city like no other time in 30 years, dating back to when the Whiz Kids won the pennant on the last day of the 1950 season.

The Phillies had gone from 1968 to 1974 without a winning season, but things were starting to improve. One of the Phillies' needs was a left-handed reliever. General manager Paul Owens didn't wait long and got McGraw from the New York Mets, along with Don Hahn and Dave Schneck, for Del Unser, Mac Scarce, and John Stearns.

"My response to getting traded to the Phillies was split right down the middle," McGraw said. "I had an older brother, Hank, who was playing in the Phillies' organization. I knew a whole bunch of the Phillies that my brother played with in the minor leagues. I had some real good feelings about the kind of ballplayers that they were going to become. The reports my brother gave me on the Phillies' organization were all real good.

"When I was traded, it was like being a castoff because I had seen a lot of guys come and go. I thought I was different and that my relationship with the Mets was going to be one that would keep me there my entire career. I also had a shoulder injury and the Mets were unable to determine what was the cause of it.

"They came to the conclusion, the old Branch Rickey theory, to trade a guy a little too soon than a little too late. On one hand, I was extremely disappointed and angry with the Mets, in particular with Joe MacDonald, the new Mets' general manager, but on the other hand, I was excited to join Paul Owens and the Phillies. Once I got to spring training, Dr. Phillip Marone was able to address my shoulder problem. We got that taken care of, and from then on, I felt wonderful about everything."

McGraw was signed by the Mets in 1964 and was back and forth in the minors and New York from 1965 to 1968. In 1969, he helped the Miracle Mets win it all with a 9-3 record and 12 saves. When the Mets won the 1973 pennant, McGraw, who had been a starter until 1969, saved 25 games.

In McGraw's final five years with the Mets, he was 43-36 and posted 85 saves. He pitched in the 1972 All-Star Game in Atlanta. He hurled two innings and struck out four. It was in the 1973 World Series in Game 2 against the A's in Oakland that Tug had his biggest thrill ever.

"I was the short reliever," McGraw said, "and I went six innings, batted three times, including a bunt single in the 12th. Willie Mays got a base hit up the middle in the 12th to send in the go-ahead run with two out. We won it, 10-7."

McGraw also saved the fifth game for the Mets, but Oakland came back to win the final two games and the World Series.

"I never understood as a Met, when we played the Phillies, that they were never a better team," McGraw said. "I always enjoyed coming to Philadelphia, and I enjoyed the old park, Connie Mack Stadium. I remember players like Jim Bunning, Dick Allen, Johnny Callison, Tony Taylor, and Bobby Wine. I never understood the reasons why the Phillies weren't winning. I was a little bit naive. I didn't understand baseball as well as a lot of players did when they were younger. I was kind of a slow learner when I got traded to the Phillies. I never viewed it in the context that I was joining an organization that had never won.

"I was looking forward to joining a team that had hitters like Tommy Hutton—who wore out Tom Seaver—Tony Taylor, Dave Cash, Larry Bowa, and Mike Schmidt. I had pitched against Schmidt, and it was going to be more fun having him on my team than pitching against him. They also had Greg Luzinski, Bob Boone, and Willie Montanez. I thought, 'Hey, this is going to be fun.' At the time, they were developing a pitching staff: Larry Christenson, Dick Ruthven, Jim Kaat, Jim Lonborg, Ron Scheuler, Wayne Twitchell, and Steve Carlton, of course. When I joined the Phillies staff, I really understood the definition of short reliever. I was 5-10 and all the pitchers were over six foot, as were all the other starters except Bowa and Cash."

McGraw pitched with the Phillies from 1975 to 1984. The club had nine straight winning seasons, fell to .500 in 1984, and started having more losing seasons than winning ones after McGraw retired.

The Phillies finished second in 1975, and McGraw went 9-6 with 14 saves. At the time, the Phillies had Gene Garber and Tug. This gave the club two closers. The Phillies picked up Ron Reed in 1976. When Garber was traded on June 15, 1978, to Atlanta, they got Ruthven back. The Phillies had three pitchers who could save a game. Among the three of them, they had 36 saves in 1976 and 43 in 1977.

"What I remember was, I had help," McGraw added. "I was a short reliever."

Through 1979, McGraw had saved 59 games for the Phillies, but in 1979, he tied a record that he would just as soon foget—giving up four grand slams in one year, all by left-handed batters.

McGraw had as good a season as any Phillies relief pitcher in 1980. He came off the disabled list July 17, after a flare-up of tendinitis in his left shoulder. For the rest of the year, he gave up only three earned runs in 51.1 innings. McGraw finished with 20 saves and a 5-4 record.

The Phillies and the Expos had been tied with three games to play in the 1980 season. They would meet in a three-game series in Montreal. The Phillies won the first, 2-1, as McGraw saved it, pitching two innings and striking out five. The following day, the Phillies won, 6-4, in 11 innings as Mike Schmidt's two-run homer won it. McGraw was the winning pitcher, allowing one hit and striking out four in three innings.

"After Schmitty hit the two-run homer, we still had to get the Expos out and Don McCormack was catching. In fact, he caught the last three innings," said McGraw. "I was looking in for signs and he was back there smiling, and he was so excited to be back there and get involved in this type of situation after just being called up from the minor leagues. It was a pleasure to pitch to him and I had every pitch at my command. I was in such a groove and I could use all my pitches in any fashion. Every time I see [McCormack], the first thing he does is give me that big smile. We share a lifetime memory together."

McGraw mowed down the Expos 1-2-3 to end it and give the Phillies their fourth East Division crown in five years.

After that tense playoff series with the Houston Astros, where the Phillies were always coming from behind, they got ready to play Kansas City in the World Series with only one day off. The Royals had been off three days.

In the Series, McGraw saved the first game, lost the third, won the fifth, and saved the sixth game back at the Vet. Ron Reed saved the second game, and in the four games that the Phillies won, the last batter for the Royals struck out.

In the sixth game, McGraw had come in for Carlton in the bottom of the eighth with two on and nobody out. The Royals got one in the inning, but once the ninth started, you could feel that McGraw was going to save it. The Royals had refused to go down without a fight. They loaded the bases with one out, when Frank White hit a foul in front of the Phillies dugout. Boone was ready to make the catch, but the ball popped out of his glove. Rose was there to grab it for the second out. Willie Wilson was next, and Tug struck him out swinging and the Phillies were the world champions.

"Initially, none of the players except Pete [Rose] had experienced a World Series before, and it's not like everybody knew what to do when we won it," McGraw said. "I kind of jumped up. Boone was exhausted. He had a bad ankle, bad knees, and a bad back. I wasn't going to jump on him. That wasn't the thing to do.

"I had a humorous conversation with Schmitty before the game, because I was always striking out the last guy in the last month and getting my picture in the paper and being the hero. He was the real hero, driving in the runs and making the plays and getting all the hits. He was joking that when the game was over, he was going to run over and dive on top of me and get his picture in the paper and screen me out. I turned toward third, and here came Schmitty with that look in his eye. He was going to dive on me and I got myself set for that. He got there about the time everybody else did, and sure enough, all the photos used the next day were Schmitty diving on top of me. He got his due plus the MVP."

Injuries slowed McGraw in his final four years, and when he retired after the 1984 season, he was tops in Phillies history with 94 saves. His overall record with the Mets and Phillies was 96-92 with 180 saves. He was on another pennant winner in 1983, but at his request, he was left off the 25-man roster for the playoffs, allowing another player to fill his spot.

Today, McGraw lives in Media, Pa., and owns McGraw & Company, which is involved in sports and entertainment marketing. He is also the chairman of marketing for Major League Baseball Players Alumni.

In 1983, the Phillies selected their greatest team by position, and McGraw was picked as the best left-handed relief pitcher in the team's history. Today he is still the best to come out of the bullpen for the Phillies.

Tug McGraw Phillies Statistics

Year	W	L	SV	PCT	G	GS	CG	SH	IP	H	BB	SO	ERA
1975	9	6	14	.600	56	0	0	0	102.2	84	36	55	2.98
1976	7	6	11	.538	58	0	0	0	97.1	81	42	76	2.50
1977	7	3	9	.700	45	0	0	0	79.0	62	24	58	2.62
1978	8	7	9	.533	55	1	0	0	89.2	82	23	63	3.21
1979	4	3	16	.571	65	1	0	0	83.2	83	29	57	5.16
1980	5	4	20	.556	57	0	0	0	92.1	62	23	75	1.46
1981	2	4	10	.333	34	0	0	0	44.0	35	14	26	2.66
1982	3	3	5	.500	34	0	0	0	39.2	50	12	25	4.31
1983	2	1	0	.667	34	1	0	0	55.2	58	19	30	3.56
1984	2	0	0	1.000	25	0	0	0	38.0	36	10	26	3.79
Totals	**49**	**37**	**94**	**.570**	**463**	**3**	**0**	**0**	**722.0**	**633**	**232**	**491**	**3.10**

Thirty-three

Hugh Mulcahy

Hard-Luck Hurler in Lean Years

by Skip Clayton

Although he was a pitcher of considerable ability, it was Hugh Mulcahy's misfortune to hurl for the Phillies during the bleakest era in club history.

From 1933 to 1945, the Phillies never finished higher than seventh or eighth. That was not Mulcahy's fault, despite the fact that he won only 45 games during all or parts of eight seasons with the club.

Hugh was a big right-hander with a crackling fastball and plenty of talent. A tireless worker, he was one of the Phillies' top hurlers from 1937 to 1940. Unfortunately, during that period, the Phillies had some hopelessly terrible clubs, and Mulcahy always labored with little or no support.

Hugh never seemed to get a break while he was on the mound. In 1941 he was the first major league player drafted into World War II.

A native of Brighton, Mass., who now makes his home in Beaver, Pa., Mulcahy posted a 45-89 career record with a 4.49 ERA in 220 games. In 1,161.1 innings pitched, he gave up 1,271 hits while striking out 314 and walking 487. Hugh completed 63 of the 143 games he started.

In his four main years with the Phillies, Mulcahy pitched well over 200 innings each season. Twice he led the National league in losses (1938, 1940) and once in walks (1937) and hits (1940). In 1940 he was also among the league leaders in complete games with 21. That year, he was selected to the National League All-Star team.

Mulcahy joined the Phillies in 1935. "I came to the club in July, when they were playing in Pittsburgh," he recalled. "I had been sold by the Albany club to Philadelphia, and the first time I got into a game, I was mopping up against Pittsburgh. I had to pitch against Paul Waner, Lloyd Waner, and Arky Vaughan.

"I pitched one inning and Jimmie Wilson, our manager, asked me, 'How do you feel?' I said, 'Pretty good.' But he said, 'Don't tell me that stuff. Your knees were shaking out there.'

"He was right. I had been reading about these guys all the time; then here I was facing them. Fortunately, I got them out.

"I was very fortunate to be with the Phillies under Jimmie Wilson," added Mulcahy. "He helped my pitching a lot."

Hugh got into 18 games with the Phillies in 1935, but was only 1-5. The Phillies finished seventh.

In 1936, Mulcahy was sent to Hazelton of the New York-Penn League. He posted a 25-14 record before being called back to the Phillies late in the season. He was 1-1 with the Phils after his recall.

The following year, Mulcahy became a regular on the Phils' staff. He was 8-18 as the Phillies finished seventh. Hugh led the league in games pitched with 56 (26 starts), which, at the time, set a National League record.

The 1938 Phillies sank into the basement, winning only 45 games. It was one of the worst seasons in Phillies history. Hugh was able to win 10 games, but lost 20, as the club hit just .254 as a team and poled only 40 home runs.

That year, the Phillies moved from Baker Bowl to Shibe Park.

"I never thought too much about changing ballparks that year," said Mulcahy. "The hitter was still 60 feet, six inches away. We thought that Shibe Park was a better ballpark all the way around. We were kind of glad to leave Baker Bowl. Shibe Park held more people, but I don't know if we drew any more people when we got there.

"I almost had a no-hit game in Baker Bowl, which is kind of unusual, I guess," added Mulcahy. "It was against the Boston Braves. I had a no-hitter for seven innings. Vince DiMaggio got a single in the eighth, and I allowed a double in the ninth. I finished up with a two-hitter.

"I had a no-hitter going at Shibe Park, too, against Cincinnati. But Ernie Lombardi got a single in the eighth, and I allowed another single in the ninth."

The Phillies in 1939 won only 45 games once again. Hugh posted a 9-16 record and saved four games, but the Phillies finished in last for the second straight year with no help on the way.

In 1940, the Phillies went 50-103 and finished last once again. Hugh won 13 and lost 22, at one point losing 12 in a row, equaling a club record.

"If you were with the Phillies, they said, you ought to moan and groan," said Mulcahy. "They said the only way you can be kicked is to be kicked upstairs or sold. But I was just never that way. I figured if they signed me, I was going to try and do the best I could to help the team. I never thought, I wish I was pitching with somebody else."

By 1940, World War II had broken out. Although the United States hadn't yet entered the war, it had started the draft. Mulcahy was the first major league player to be taken.

"They caught me quickly," Mulcahy said. "They said I probably wouldn't be called until the end of the 1941 season. I was getting ready to go to spring training when greetings came through from the Army. It was about nine or 10 months before Pearl Harbor. They were getting ready to discharge some of the fellows who had been in quite awhile when Pearl Harbor hit. They just kept everybody then.

"I lost 1941, 1942, 1943, 1944, and the biggest part of 1945. I went in when I was 27 and came out when I was 32. When I went overseas, I weighed 200 pounds. When I was discharged, I weighed 170. I was in New Guinea and the Philippines. A lot of guys got sick, so we couldn't put the weight back on."

Hugh was finally discharged in time to pitch in five games at the end of the 1945 season. He won only one game while losing three.

"I spent the winter in St. Petersburg trying to put some weight back on, building myself back up again," said Mulcahy.

Unfortunately for Hugh, he wasn't part of the future with the Phillies. After posting a 2-4 record in 16 games in 1946, he finished his major league career with the Pittsburgh Pirates.

"When I came back, I think I made a mistake not coming up with a knuckleball, a screwball, or some kind of a freak pitch," Mulcahy said. "My speed was going, and I couldn't get back to throwing as hard as I had. Pittsburgh picked me up in 1947. Then I went out to Oakland of the Pacific Coast League and played under Casey Stengel later that year. Casey was a pretty smart baseball man."

When Hugh retired from pitching after the season, he got another job right away. "I was the pitching coach for the Chicago White Sox minor league clubs and was also supervisor for the minor league training camp for 25 years," he said. "I retired in 1976."

Mulcahy will always be remembered as the first major league player to be drafted during World War II. But he should also be remembered as a good pitcher who didn't have the best of luck.

Hugh Mulcahy Phillies Statistics

Year	W	L	SV	PCT	G	GS	CG	SH	IP	H	BB	SO	ERA
1935	1	5	1	.167	18	5	0	0	52.2	62	25	11	4.78
1936	1	1	0	.500	3	2	2	0	22.2	20	12	2	3.18
1937	8	18	3	.308	56	26	9	1	215.2	256	97	54	5.13
1938	10	20	1	.333	46	34	15	0	267.1	294	120	90	4.61
1939	9	16	4	.360	38	32	14	1	225.2	246	93	59	4.99
1940	13	22	0	.371	36	36	21	3	280.0	283	91	82	3.60
1945	1	3	0	.250	5	4	1	0	28.1	33	9	2	3.81
1946	2	4	0	.333	16	5	1	0	62.2	69	33	12	4.45
Totals	**45**	**89**	**9**	**.336**	**218**	**144**	**63**	**5**	**1,155.0**	**1,263**	**480**	**312**	**4.49**

Thirty-four

Joe Oeschger

1915 Phillies Pitcher

by Skip Clayton

I n 1915, the Phillies won their first National League pennant and proceeded to the World Series, where they were defeated by the Boston Red Sox.

When the Phillies returned to the World Series in 1983, only one member from that 1915 team was still alive. That was Joe Oeschger, a right-handed pitcher who played for the local club from 1914 to 1919 and again during part of 1924.

Joe was 95 when he died on July 29, 1986, and was a resident of Ferndale, Calif. Oeschger had a 29-48 record for the Phillies. He was 1-0 in six games in 1915.

Overall, Joe posted an 83-116 record during a 12-year big-league career that also included stints with the New York Giants, Boston Braves, and Brooklyn Dodgers.

Of course, he is best known for the famous 26-inning game he pitched in 1920 while playing for the Braves. Joe and his opponent, Leon Cadore of the Dodgers (also called the Robins) each went the distance, eventually settling for a 1-1 tie in what remains the longest game in major league history.

Oeschger, a native of Chicago, Ill., earned a bachelor's degree in civil engineering at St. Mary's College and a master's degree in physical education at Stanford University. After retiring from baseball in 1925, he spent most of the rest of his working career with the San Francisco Board of Education as a physical education teacher.

Following his undergraduate studies, Oeschger got his first exposure to the major leagues in 1914, when he played briefly for the Phillies before spending most of the summer in the minors.

"The first time I pitched against a major league team was in the City Series in 1914 against the A's," recalled Oeschger. "The City Series was quite intense. It was quite a rivalry. I won two ball games. Connie Mack still had a great club."

In 1915, the Phillies brought in new manager Pat Moran. "He was a good manager and very considerate of everybody," said Oeschger. "He was very intense."

Connie Mack sold all his star players before the start of the 1915 season, and that wiped out any chance of an all-Philadelphia World Series. The A's dropped to last place, while the Phillies captured the pennant.

The Phillies wrapped up the pennant on Sept. 29 at Braves Field when they beat Boston, 5-0. Grover Cleveland Alexander pitched his fourth one-hitter of the year and Gavvy Cravath hit a three-run homer in the first inning.

"The key feature of the 1915 club was hitting," said Oeschger. "We had power hitters in Cravath and Fred Luderus. We won a lot of close games. Of course, Alexander was our top pitcher. If you got him one or two runs, you would win the game."

Oeschger rated Alexander the finest hurler of his day. "If I were to classify all of the pitchers that I had contact with or witnessed, I would say that Alexander was the greatest. He was fantastic.

"Alexander worked every fourth day," said Oeschger. "He never had to be relieved. In those days, if you couldn't pitch nine innings, you better start looking for another job."

In the 1915 World Series, the Phillies beat the Boston Red Sox, 3-1, in the first game. After that, Boston captured four straight, each by one run.

"We faced some good pitchers in that series in Ernie Shore, George Foster, and Dutch Leonard," said Oeschger. "They had a good club with Duffy Lewis, Harry Hooper, and Tris Speaker in the outfield."

During Oeschger's career with the Phillies, the club played its home games at Baker Bowl. "Although it was quite high, the right-field fence was only 272 feet away," said Oeschger, remembering how mere pop flies used to fly over and against the wall.

Oeschger had his best year with the Phillies in 1917, when he posted a 15-14 record and, with it, picked up a nice bonus from the owner, William F. Baker. Many blamed Baker for the Phillies' problems in those days, but Oeschger refused to criticize the former president of the Phillies.

"He did a very honorable thing for me," said Oeschger. "I had a bonus clause in my contract. If I won 15 games, I would get an extra $500. Late in the season, I had 14 wins and was going to face the New York Giants. They had a terrific club. John McGraw, their manager, started first baseman George Kelly on the mound. They were going to make a pitcher out of him. He had terrific speed.

"But I thought this was good, because it gave us a chance to win. Well, Kelly started throwing the ball by our guys. After eight innings, we hadn't scored and they had gotten one run off me. I came into the bench at the end of the eighth and there was the president of the Phillies with a check in his hand. He said, 'Joe, you pitched good enough to win. Here is your bonus.' We still had an inning to go. I'll never forget that. Don't ever criticize W. F. Baker in my eyes. I think he did a very commendable thing."

In 1919, Oeschger pitched a 20-inning game for the Phillies, which tied him with Tully Sparks (who did it in 1905) for the longest-pitched game. It ended in a 9-9 tie, although both teams scored three runs in the 19th inning.

It was a good tune-up for the 26-inning tie game that Joe pitched May 1, 1920, against Brooklyn in Braves Field. By then, Joe had been traded by the Phillies to the Giants, who swapped him to Boston.

"I was tired at the end of that game, but I pitched some other games that I was more exhausted from," said Oeschger. "In fact, when I pitched 20 innings for the Phillies, I wasn't in the good shape that I was for the 26-inning game."

Joe gave up 15 hits during the 26 innings. They were all singles. He walked four and struck out seven.

Oeschger won 15 games in 1920 and another 20 the following year. During the 1919 season, his roommate was Jim Thorpe, whom the Braves had picked up from the New York Giants.

"Jim was a real good hitter," said Oeschger. "He was a great athlete. I remember one time when we were in New York. We were in the hotel, sitting around with some of the other players. The talk came up about some of the track records that Thorpe had set. One player asked him how far he jumped in the standing broad jump.

"The room had two single beds and a little stand in between. Jim couldn't remember the distance he jumped, but said from here to here. The other fellow says, 'You mean, you could stand there and jump over the two beds?' Jim said, 'That is what I said.' So the beds were made. Jim jumped across the beds and won the bets."

When Joe was at the 1983 World Series, he mentioned that he was still getting mail asking him for his autograph 63 years after pitching the 26-inning game.

When the Phillies captured the pennant in 1983, the club selected players from the three previous pennant winners to throw out the first ball in the World Series games at the Vet. Joe stood up for the 1915 Phillies.

"Coming back here to Philadelphia after 68 years and being invited to participate in the World Series overwhelmed me," Oeschger said. "It was probably the greatest event in my life. Here I am, the only remaining member of the 1915 Phillies—and this invitation—I don't know how to express my thanks for the wonderful reception and the way I have been received here by the Phillies. I have been entertained more or less by the Dodgers, but this supersedes everything. I can't even compare it."

It was great that Joe was able to come back for the 1983 World Series and hear the crowd once again.

Joe Oeschger Phillies Statistics

Year	W	L	SV	PCT	G	GS	CG	SH	IP	H	BB	SO	ERA
1914	4	8	1	.333	32	12	5	0	124.0	129	54	47	3.77
1915	1	0	0	1.000	6	1	1	0	23.2	21	9	8	3.42
1916	1	0	0	1.000	14	0	0	0	30.1	18	14	17	2.37
1917	15	14	1	.537	42	30	18	5	262.0	241	72	123	2.75
1918	6	18	3	.250	30	23	13	2	184.0	159	83	60	3.03
1919	0	1	0	.000	5	4	0	0	38.0	52	16	5	5.92
1924	2	7	0	.222	19	8	0	0	65.1	88	16	8	4.41
Totals	29	48	5	.377	148	78	37	7	727.1	708	264	268	3.32

Thirty-five

Paul Owens

Farm Director, Manager, and General Manager
Who Rebuilt the Phillies

by Skip Clayton

The Phillies made an announcement on May 22, 1965, that Paul Owens had been named the farm director. It wasn't a move that created headlines, but had Phillies fans known what this man was going to do for the big-league team, they might have thought of having a parade. He would rebuild the farm system, which was a wreck at the time. Later, he would become the general manager on June 3, 1972, replacing John Quinn. Owens would build the team into a solid contender that would finish first five times and win the 1980 World Series. In 1983, he would leave his office on the fourth floor of Veterans Stadium, and go down and manage the club to another pennant.

Owens, who was nicknamed "Pope," spent six full years in the minors (1951-1953 and 1955-1957), winning three batting championships and compiling a .374 average. Owens turned to managing in 1955.

"The Phillies had a farm team in Bradford, and they were going to move it to Olean in 1956, where I was managing," Owens said. "They asked me to stay on." In 1956, Owens' career was under way with the Phillies. He stayed with Olean through 1957, then moved to Bakersfield, Calif., for two years, beginning in 1958. After that, Owens turned to scouting for the Phillies, until he was named the farm director.

"They fired three of the four West Coast scouts after the 1959 season," Owens said. "I scouted until I became the farm director. Every spring, I would run the camp for the young kids from Class C and Class D in Leesburg, Fla. Ruly Carpenter came in 1964 as the business manager."

Paul was back out scouting in 1965 when he got a call that would change the whole history of the Phillies.

"John Quinn called and said that he and Bob Carpenter would like me to take over the farm system," Owens recalled. "The first draft was coming up in 10 days. That was all the time we had to get ready."

One of his first moves with Ruly Carpenter, who was assigned the job of working under Owens, was to evaluate all the scouts. Once that was done, Owens met with Carpenter and Quinn.

"I said that I wanted a one-hour meeting with Carpenter and Quinn, uninterrupted, with no phone calls or anything else," Owens said. "When I got done, I told Bob and John that was the way I wanted to do it. I cannot do this job, and I am not going to sit here for four years till you find out I can't, if you don't allow me to do the things I want to do to turn it around. Bob said, 'You go ahead and do what you want.'

"That fall, I let 10 scouts go and hired 10 new ones. I called each one personally and let him go, looking at him across the table."

During Owens' seven years, the farm system showed a rapid growth. He talked Bob Carpenter into building the Carpenter Complex in Clearwater, Fla. That was completed in 1967.

"I wanted all the players to be at the same place," Owens said. "I wanted them all to be taught the Phillies way, rather than have the teams scattered all over."

"I remember on June 3, 1972, I was in my office and Bob called me in," said Owens. "He said, 'Paul, we are going to make a change. I am going to have a press conference and announce that you are going to be the new general manager.' I liked John and we were good friends. You always feel bad."

When Owens took over as general manager, the Phillies hadn't had a winning season since 1967. He turned the farm system over to Dallas Green, who had been his assistant for three years.

In 1972, they won only 59 games, even though Steve Carlton was able to win 27 of those, but the club had some bright spots.

When Owens took over as general manager, the club was 16-27. Six weeks later, Owens fired manager Frank Lucchesi and took on the job himself. He needed somebody to go on a fact-finding mission for the team. There was only one way to find out, and that was to do it himself down on the field.

"I knew Frank Lucchesi well," Owens said. "I told him I didn't expect miracles, because you don't have half a team. Do the best you can with them. One thing I would like to see improved is the outfield play. I told him to start having workouts.

"Lucchesi told me OK. Instead, he was going to a luncheon every day. After telling him two more times, still no workouts. I talked to him. He told me he had commitments. I said, 'Frank, I told you once, I told you twice, and I am telling you again, I want workouts.' He told me he didn't believe in morning workouts. I told him he wanted to get in the good graces with people at luncheons at my expense. I told him that he was hired to be with these kids. He told me he had to be at these luncheons and dinners. I told him, 'You are not going to manage my ball club.' Lucchesi said, 'You don't mean that.' I said, 'I told you three times. You know me well enough that I am strong in what I believe in.'

"I told Bob and Ruly about the meeting and told them that the more I thought about it, I would manage those guys. If I live, sleep, and eat with those guys, I want to make sure I am going to make the right moves."

After the season, several moves were made. Danny Ozark was hired as the manager. Bob Carpenter retired as president and turned the reins over to his son, Ruly, and became chairman of the board.

"Bob had asked me over the last year or two whether Ruly was ready to take over," Owens recalled. "I told him he was ready. Bob said he was going to become chairman of the board. He was interested in the club, but never looked over our shoulder."

Next, Owens started to wheel and deal.

"I started off in stages," Owens said. "I fixed the pitching first. Then I started on the outfield. The kids were getting their feet wet."

It came together in 1976 when the club won 101 games, the most ever for a Phillies team. It brought the Phillies their first-ever East Division championship, but they lost in three straight to the Cincinnati Reds in the National League Championship Series.

The Phillies started off slowly in 1977, but as the trading deadline approached on June 15, they acquired Bake McBride from the St. Louis Cardinals. The club moved through the rest of the season like a Patton tank and won 101 games again. It looked like Philly would finally win the pennant.

In the playoffs, the Phils split with Los Angeles in Dodger Stadium, only to come home and lose the next two. The first home loss was the heartbreaker in which the Dodgers scored three in the ninth after two were out. Los Angeles wrapped up the pennant the next night in the rain.

The Phillies won their third straight East Division title in 1978, but lost in four games for the second straight year to the Dodgers in the National League Championship Series.

The Phillies picked up Pete Rose after the 1978 season, and everyone pretty much penciled in another trip to the playoffs.

"I felt bad about not getting Rose the first time we met with him after the 1978 season," said Owens. "I knew what he could do. Bill Giles gets the credit for what he did in getting extra money so we could sign him."

Injuries clobbered the 1979 team, as it limped home in fourth place. Ozark was let go as the manager at the end of August and was replaced by Green.

Rather then wheel and deal for 1980, the Phillies stood pat, except for bringing up some minor league help, which got them over the hump. They won the team's first World Series.

When Sept. 1 rolled around, the club had been a little lax, losing two games in San Diego. Owens decided to read the riot act. Even the September recalls who had arrived that day weren't spared. They were wearing Phillies uniforms, and Owens decided they might as well get used to what he had to say.

Down the stretch, the Phillies won 23 of their final 34 games, including six of their last seven. The Phillies went on to win the East by one game over the Montreal Expos.

They knocked off Houston in the playoffs in five games—four of which went extra innings—in the best and most exciting National League Championship Series.

The series with the Kansas City Royals wasn't nearly as tough as the Houston series. The Phillies won it in six games, taking the final game at Veterans Stadium on Oct. 21. When Tug McGraw struck out Willie Wilson at 11:29 p.m., the biggest celebration in Philadelphia sports history began.

"When [baseball commissioner] Bowie Kuhn handed Ruly and me the trophy for winning the World Series, I couldn't speak," said Owens. "I had tears running and I have the picture at home. It was all worthwhile, and it is what it was all about."

Things looked good for winning it all again in 1981, but the players' strike ruined the year. After the season, a group headed by Bill Giles purchased the Phillies from the Carpenter family.

Owens watched as the team finished second in 1982 and, during the 1983 season, took over for Pat Corrales as the manager. The Phillies won the East Division crown for the fifth time in eight years. After the Phils lost 11 of 12 to the Los Angeles Dodgers during the season, the two teams met in the National League Championship Series. This time the Phillies prevailed, winning three of four and moving into the World Series for the second time in four years, but losing to Baltimore in five games.

Owens got to manage the National League in the All-Star Game in 1984 and led the club to a 3-1 win over the American League, making it four wins in four tries for Phillies managers in the midsummer classic. Under Owens that year, the Phillies dropped to fourth, and Owens stepped down and became the assistant to the president. That title changed when he became senior advisor to the general manager in 1998.

"The thing I am the most proud of is that I gave them the best decade of Phillies baseball in their history from 1975 to 1984," Owens said. "I was tickled to be able to do that."

The biggest mystery during his term as general manager is why he was never voted the Major League Executive of the Year by the *Sporting News*. He should have won that award four or five times.

There is no doubt that Paul Owens is the best general manager the Phillies have ever had.

Thirty-six

Robin Roberts

Phillies Hall of Fame Hurler

by Skip Clayton

When it comes to listing the greatest players in Phillies history, the name of Robin Roberts is usually one of the first that comes to mind.

Probably the greatest right-handed pitcher in Phillies history (He gets some competition from Grover Cleveland Alexander), Roberts was one of the all-time best pitchers to play in the major leagues. Roberts was not only a star performer, but he was also one of the most popular players to wear a Phillies uniform.

From a statistical standpoint, Roberts' record was awesome. Between 1948 and 1961, he posted a 234-199 record for the Phillies, despite the fact that eight times over that period, they were mired in the second division including four seasons in last place. Yet Roberts won 20 or more games six times in a row; 12 times he won in double figures.

He pitched in 529 games for the Phillies, 472 of them as a starter, compiling a 3.46 earned run average. He also had 24 saves.

Roberts is the Phillies' career leader in games, innings (3,740), complete games (272), runs (1,501), earned runs (1,437), hits (3,661), and losses. He is second in wins and strikeouts (1,871) and third in shutouts (35) and walks (718).

During his entire big-league career, which stretched to 1966 and included stints with the Baltimore Orioles, Houston Astros, and Chicago Cubs, Roberts registered a 286-245 record and a 3.41 ERA in 676 games. In 4,688.2 innings, he gave up 4,582 hits, struck out 2,357, and walked 902, while hurling 45 shutouts and 305 complete games.

Of Roberts' many accomplishments, probably none is more significant than his All-Star Game record. He started five games for the National League while being named to the team seven times.

One of only four players (along with Richie Ashburn, Steve Carlton, and Mike Schmidt) to have his number retired by the Phillies, Roberts led the National League in wins and fewest walks allowed per nine innings four times, in complete games and innings pitched five times each, and in shutouts and strikeouts twice each. He held the National League record for pitching the most season openers (13) until it was broken by Tom Seaver.

Although he pitched three one-hitters, Roberts' greatest moment was unquestionably in 1950, when he won the final game of the season to give the Phillies the pennant with a 4-1 victory over the Brooklyn Dodgers.

With Philly ahead, 1-0, in the sixth inning at Ebbets Field, the Dodgers came back in the bottom half to tie the score on Pee Wee Reese's home run on a ball that had hit the right-field screen and lodged on a ledge instead of falling back onto the field, as balls usually did.

With the score still tied in the bottom of the ninth, Brooklyn threatened to win the game and set up a playoff for the pennant. With two on, Duke Snider laced a hit to center. Richie Ashburn fielded the ball and threw to the plate to nail Cal Abrams by 15 feet. Reese went to third on the throw, and Snider moved to second, with three dangerous Dodgers coming to bat next.

"Eddie Sawyer told us to put Jackie Robinson on," Roberts said. "Then, with the bases loaded, I got Carl Furillo to pop up a fastball to Eddie Waitkus at first and Gil Hodges to fly to Del Ennis in right.

"I led off the top of the 10th with a single, and Waitkus singled me to second," Roberts continued. "Richie tried to bunt us over, but I got thrown out at third. Then Dick Sisler came up and hit a 1-2 pitch hard into the left-field stands for a home run. Dick had four hits that day.

"I had no problems in the 10th," Roberts recalled. "I had good stuff all day [He allowed five hits], but in that last inning, I was throwing the ball as hard as I ever had in my life. I retired them in order."

It was precisely for that reason that Sawyer had selected Roberts to pitch the final, crucial game, although the hurler would be going to the mound for the fourth time in nine days.

Roberts had by then been rising to the occasion for a good many years. A native of Springfield, Ill., he had gone to Michigan State University on a basketball scholarship, and after starring in baseball and basketball, had been signed for a $25,000 bonus to a Phillies contract by scout Chuck Ward.

His minor league career was brief. Robbie played in just 11 games at Wilmington in the Class B Inter-State League. He had a 9-1 record with 121 strikeouts in 96 innings when he was called up to the Phillies in June 1948.

Roberts finished the season with a 7-9 record. He moved up to a 15-15 mark in 1949 as the Phillies began their climb up the National League ladder. By then, the big right-hander had attracted considerable attention with his crackling fastball, an awesome curve, and pinpoint control—all of which came out of an incredibly fluid motion.

"Cy Perkins was a big help to me," Roberts said of those early days. "He was a coach with the Phillies, and he did more for me mentally than anyone could ever expect another person to do. He made me realize the talent I had, and he expressed it in such a way that I believed I was as good as anybody who ever walked out there on the mound. He explained how well I threw the ball, how my easy delivery was a gift. That was something that many guys didn't have."

In 1950, Roberts got his first call as an opening-day starter and bested Don Newcombe and the Dodgers, 9-1. The two would face each other 23 times in what would be some of the most classic pitching duels of the 1950s.

From opening day in 1950, the Phillies launched what had the appearances of a fine season. But it wasn't until July that they went into first place permanently. Returning from a western trip, the Phillies swept the Chicago Cubs, 7-0 and 1-0, behind Bubba Church and Roberts. Robbie was pitching on just two days' rest.

Roberts followed that game by shutting out the Pirates. In his next start, against the Cardinals, he ran his scoreless streak to 32 innings before Enos Slaughter hit a homer into the light standard in a 4-2 Phillies win.

Although the Phillies built a seven-game lead by Sept. 1, the margin began to dwindle as the end of the season approached. With Curt Simmons called into the National Guard and Church and Bob Miller nursing injuries, most of the starting burden fell on Roberts. He was dead tired by the final game of the season, but being the great competitor he was, summoned the strength to win the second-most famous game in Phillies history.

In the World Series against the New York Yankees, Roberts started the second game, losing, 2-1, in 10 innings on Joe DiMaggio's home run.

Roberts, however was just getting started. He posted a 21-15 record in 1951, as the Phillies tumbled into fifth place. Then in 1952, he had his finest season, posting a 28-7 record with a 2.59 ERA as the Phillies moved up to fourth. Roberts was named Major League Player of the Year by the *Sporting News*, but, curiously, lost out in the MVP balloting to the Cubs' Hank Sauer, who hit .270 with 37 home runs and 121 RBIs.

During the season, Roberts had a 6-0 record against the pennant-bound Dodgers. His finest game, though, came in win No. 23, when he hurled 17 innings to beat the Boston Braves, 7-6, at Shibe Park. Del Ennis won it with a homer.

"I was tired. I knew I had pitched a long time, but it was no big deal. It was just a job well done. The 17 innings weren't that impressive then, but as I look back, that has become some ball game."

Roberts registered a 23-16 record in 1953 as the Phillies tied for third, and a 23-15 mark in 1954 as the club moved back to fourth. That year, he had two one-hitters, including one in which he retired 27 batters in a row.

"I am one of the few pitchers ever to pitch a whole game without using a stretch," Roberts said. "It was in the game against the Reds. Bobby Adams led off the first inning and hit a 2-1 fastball upstairs at Connie Mack Stadium. There was no pressure after that. The no-hitter was gone and the shutout was gone after the first batter. I just settled down, and we beat them, 8-1."

In his other one-hitter, against Milwaukee at County Stadium, Roberts gave up a third-inning double to Del Crandall en route to a 4-0 victory.

Roberts had another long game that year when he pitched 15 innings and beat the St. Louis Cardinals, 4-3, at Connie Mack Stadium and didn't allow a walk.

Roberts came close to a no-hitter again the following season. It came on opening day at Connie Mack Stadium against the New York Giants.

"I had a no-hitter after eight innings," he said. "I was a little nervous going into the ninth. Generally, I gave up hits early. I knew I had a no-hitter going. With one out, Alvin Dark hit a line drive to right for a hit." The Phillies won the game, 4-2.

Roberts had his sixth straight 20-win season in 1955 when he logged a 23-14 mark. Toward the end of the season, he beat Newcombe twice in one week for his 19th and 20th wins.

In 1955, Roberts won the *Sporting News'* Pitcher of the Year award for the second time in four years. The Phillies finished in fourth place, and it would be their last first-division finish until 1963.

Roberts' record dropped to 19-18 in 1956, although he lost seven one-run games, four by a 2-1 score. Then he fell to 10-22 in 1957, but rebounded to 17-14 in 1958. He lost three 1-0 games that year and won one when he doubled off Sad Sam Jones to drive in Chuck Essegian in the eighth at Connie Mack Stadium to beat the St. Louis Cardinals.

After records of 15-17 in 1959, 12-16 in 1960, and 1-10 in 1961, Roberts was sold to the Yankees on Oct. 16.

He never pitched for the Yankees, and after being on the roster for one month, was released. He then signed with the Baltimore Orioles. Roberts won 42 games for the Orioles over the next three and a half years. His record was 5-2 against the Yankees, and he beat Whitey Ford twice.

Roberts finished his career with the Astros and Cubs, bowing out of the big leagues after the 1966 season. He spent part of the 1967 season pitching with the Reading Phillies, but the call back to the big leagues that he had hoped for never came, and he retired to private business.

Roberts spent three years in the mid-1970s as a part-time broadcaster with the Phillies. In 1976, he became head baseball coach at the University of South Florida, a position he held until resigning after the 1985 season. He was a Phillies minor league instructor for a few years after that, but is retired today.

In 1976, Roberts was elected to the Hall of Fame, an honor that he richly deserved.

For Roberts, the part he remembers best about his career was the 1950 season when the Whiz Kids won the pennant.

"That was my biggest moment in Philadelphia," he said. "I was disappointed that we were never able to win a pennant again. We were a solid organization."

"There were people who thought the Dodgers were better than us in 1950, but they were wrong. For that one year, we were better than anybody."

And for many years, so was Robin Roberts.

Robin Roberts Phillies Statistics

Year	W	L	SV	PCT	G	GS	CG	SH	IP	H	BB	SO	ERA
1948	7	9	0	.438	20	20	9	0	146.2	148	61	84	3.19
1949	15	15	4	.500	43	31	11	3	226.2	229	75	95	3.69
1950	20	11	1	.645	40	39	21	5	304.1	282	77	146	3.02
1951	21	15	2	.583	44	39	22	6	315.0	284	64	127	3.03
1952	28	7	2	.800	39	37	30	3	330.0	292	45	148	2.59
1953	23	16	2	.590	44	41	33	5	346.2	324	61	198	2.75
1954	23	15	4	.605	45	38	29	4	336.2	289	56	185	2.97
1955	23	14	3	.622	41	38	26	1	305.0	292	53	160	3.28
1956	19	18	3	.514	43	37	22	1	297.1	328	40	157	4.45
1957	10	22	2	.313	39	32	14	2	249.2	246	43	128	4.07
1958	17	14	0	.548	35	34	21	1	269.2	270	51	130	3.24
1959	15	17	0	.469	35	35	19	2	257.1	267	35	137	4.27
1960	12	16	1	.429	35	33	13	2	237.1	256	34	122	4.02
1961	1	10	0	.091	26	18	2	0	117.0	154	23	54	5.85
Totals	**234**	**199**	**24**	**.540**	**529**	**500**	**272**	**35**	**3,740.0**	**3,661**	**718**	**1,871**	**3.46**

Thirty-seven

Cookie Rojas

The Phillies' All-Around Player

by Skip Clayton

Infielder, outfielder, catcher, pitcher—you name it, and Cookie Rojas played it.

Rojas was the ultimate utilityman who performed his jobs so well that, eventually, he couldn't be kept out of the regular lineup.

He played for the Phillies from 1963 to 1969, and in the big leagues from 1962 to 1977. During his 16 years in the majors, the Havana, Cuba, native had a batting average of .263, which included 1,660 hits. Rojas had 54 home runs, 593 RBIs, and 714 runs scored.

The stocky 5-10, 170-pounder played mainly at second base during his career, seeing action in 1,449 games there. But he also performed in 200 games in the outfield, 46 at third base, 39 at shortstop, seven at catcher, two at first base, and one at pitcher.

Regardless of where he played, Cookie always hustled as though his job was on the line. He was not endowed with great talent, but he stretched what he had as far as anybody possibly could.

Born Octavio Victor Rojas (Rivas) in 1939, Rojas was just a struggling minor leaguer with brief big-league experience before coming to the Phillies from the Cincinnati Reds on Nov. 27, 1962, for pitcher Jim Owens. Nobody realized it at the time, but the swap would turn out to be one of the best that Phils' general manager John Quinn ever made.

Rojas had spent six and a half unspectacular years in the minors, breaking into organized ball in 1956. Cookie finally reached Cincinnati in 1962, where he played in 39 games and hit just .221. Shortly after the season ended, he landed with the Phillies, where he was immediately cast in the role of utilityman.

"My natural position was second base when I came into the major leagues," said Rojas. "When I came to the Phillies, however, Tony Taylor was playing second and Bobby Wine was playing shortstop. Tony Gonzalez got thrown out of a game and Gene Mauch says, 'You are playing left field.' I had never played any other position except second base in my minor league career. But I wasn't going to turn it down because I was hoping for a chance to play. I went out and played left field, and after that, I started moving from one position to another."

Cookie played in only 64 games in 1963 and batted just .221. In 1964, he played in 109 games and hit .291.

"In spring training in 1964, nobody gave the Phillies a chance to be a contending ball club," said Rojas. "All of a sudden, with a lot of young players and with Mauch running the club perfectly, we became a contending team. Everybody criticized us because we blew the pennant. The fact was, we were at a higher place than anybody thought we would be."

The Phillies got there, in part, because of a deal they made on Aug. 7 when they obtained Frank Thomas from the Mets. At the time, the Phillies were one and a half games in front. One month later, with Thomas carrying a hot bat, the Phillies had built a six-game lead. But Frank broke his thumb on Sept. 8. Two weeks later, the Phillies started the 10-game losing streak that knocked them out of the pennant race.

"Losing Thomas, the way he had been playing, definitely hurt us," recalled Rojas. "That could have been the difference. Who knows? There were so many things that happened during those 10 games."

Rojas improved his stats in 1965, batting .303 in one of the two .300 seasons of his career. Rojas made the All-Star team as a second baseman. He got into the game as a pinch-hitter but flied out.

"It meant a lot to make the All-Star team that year, because I played so many different positions," Rojas said. "It was a great honor. I went to the American League in 1970 and made the All-Star team four straight times, because I was playing one position every day—second base."

The Phillies in 1965 had dropped back to sixth place, but they came back in 1966 to finish fourth. Cookie's average fell to .268, but he became the club's regular second baseman for the next four years.

By 1967, Cookie had played every position on the field for the Phillies except pitcher. That would take place that season.

"I got to pitch in the second game of a doubleheader against the Giants at Connie Mack Stadium," said Rojas. "We had won the first game, but were losing the second game, 12-3. Mauch had used a lot of pitchers, so he said, 'Why don't you pitch?' It felt strange to go out and pitch, especially because I had to face Willie Mays. The only thing on my mind when he came to bat was, I didn't care how far he hit the ball, as long as he didn't hit it through the middle. As it was, he popped up. I think he was more afraid of me hitting him than anything else."

Cookie pitched one inning and held the Giants scoreless.

That season, Rojas hit .259 as the Phillies dropped to fifth place, although they were two games over .500.

The Phillies dropped to a tie for seventh in 1968. In 1969, when the National League split into two divisions, the Phillies finished in fifth. Over the three-year period from 1967 to 1969, their wins decreased from 82 to 76 to 63.

Cookie was traded after the 1969 season to the St. Louis Cardinals with Dick Allen and Jerry Johnson. The Phillies received By Browne, Curt Flood, Joe Hoerner and Tim McCarver.(Flood refused to report, and the Phils eventually got Willie Montanez in his place).

"I wanted to stay here," Rojas said. "I don't think any player wants to be traded, unless he isn't playing and has the chance to play someplace else. I was playing for the Phillies. But you have to accept trades. They're part of baseball."

Before the 1970 season was over, Rojas was traded to the Kansas City Royals. He was the Royals' regular second baseman until 1976, when Frank White took over.

Rojas retired after the 1977 season. For the next four years, he was a coach with the Chicago Cubs. When Rojas went to the California Angels as a scout in 1982, Gene Mauch was the manager. "It was great to work with Gene again," said Cookie. "I have great respect for him. I learned a lot about the game from him when we were in Philadelphia. I think he has so much knowledge.

"Go through his record and look at the clubs that he took over. He made them contenders. Then somebody else came along and maybe got the credit. But the man who put together those teams and taught a lot of good fundamental baseball to the players was Gene Mauch."

Rojas took over as manager of the Angels when Mauch left in 1988. He was let go with eight games left after posting a 75-79 record. He became a scout with the Angels once again before heading to the expansion Florida Marlins as a coach beginning in 1993. Rojas switched to the Mets as a coach in 1997, and he still coaches them today.

Cookie also received an honor with the Phillies when he was selected as the team's best second baseman in 1969.

Having a Cookie Rojas on your team as a player, a scout, or a coach was always an asset to that team.

Cookie Rojas Phillies Statistics

Year	G	AB	R	H	2B	3B	HR	RBI	AVG	OBP	SLGP
1963	64	77	18	17	0	1	1	2	.221	.259	.286
1964	109	340	58	99	19	5	2	31	.291	.334	.394
1965	142	521	78	158	25	3	3	42	.303	.356	.380
1966	156	626	77	168	18	1	6	55	.268	.310	.329
1967	147	528	60	137	21	2	4	45	.259	.297	.330
1968	152	621	53	144	19	0	9	48	.232	.248	.306
1969	110	391	35	89	11	1	4	30	.228	.269	.292
Totals	880	3,104	379	812	113	13	29	253	.262	.300	.334

Thirty-eight

Pete Rose

All-Time Batting King

by Jeff Moeller

“ The team really learned how to win. It learned how to win what I called racehorse baseball."

Those words were spoken nearly a month after the 1980 season by Pete Rose, the man the Phillies recognize for playing an integral part in bringing a world championship to Philadelphia.

He was a major piece of the puzzle, and one that nearly wasn't affordable. Rose signed a three-year, $3.2 million deal before the 1979 season, and it took some extra effort to get it done.

During the summer of 1978, Rose let his desire to play in Philadelphia be known. He also knew it would be difficult to turn down some hefty offers from Atlanta, Kansas City, Pittsburgh, and St. Louis, all known for flaunting open checkbooks at that time.

It finally took a $600,000 commitment from the club's cable outlet, WPHL-TV, and Rose's desire to play in the National League to break Stan Musial's hit record (3,630).

In his first year with the Phillies, Rose hit .331 and passed Honus Wagner as the National League's all-time singles hitter with 2,427. During the championship run, Rose's daily leadership and intensity on and off the field overshadowed his first season under the .300 mark since 1974 as he hit .282 with a league-high 42 doubles.

Rose hit .261 in the Series, and he played a rather subdued role in the celebration, a moment he had seen before in his days with Cincinnati.

"I had been there before and I was more happy for everyone else," said Rose during the postgame celebration. "I gained a lot of satisfaction knowing that I played an important part."

What will be a lasting memory of Rose will be his dramatic catch of a foul pop in Game 6.

With one out, the bases loaded, and the Phils leading 4-1, Kansas City's Frank White popped up a ball down the first-base line that sent both Rose and catcher Bob Boone chasing after it. The ball hit Boone's mitt, popped up, and landed in Rose's glove.

"Everyone always asks me about that play," Rose said. "I didn't want to call Boonie off. When it popped up, I just snapped it up. I think the reason I reacted so fast was that I didn't know if Tug McGraw was covering home plate or not."

During the last game before the in-season strike in 1981, Rose tied the National League record for most hits with a single off Houston's Nolan Ryan. Sixty days later, the first day after the strike, Rose become the all-time hits leader with a single off St. Louis' Mark Littell. He finished the season with a .325 average.

Rose played in all 162 games the following season, but his average dropped to .271. With an influx of younger players, along with aging veterans, Rose's time was reduced and he showed some signs of slowing down. Even though he played in 151 games, his average slipped even further to an un-Rose-like .245.

He was well aware of the swing of emotions during a roller-coaster season that nearly collapsed during an infamous Aug. 10, 1980 doubleheader loss to Pittsburgh, where Dallas Green's famous 20-minute tirade between games took place. In the second game, Green went toe-to-toe with relief pitcher Ron Reed, and the two nearly came to blows. In all, the club lost four straight.

The Phils moved into Chicago and won two of three and then swept the Mets in five games.

Rose recounted after the four-game loss in Pittsburgh how the players appeared determined enough on their flight to Chicago. He believed the team's sweep of the Mets—seven and a half games out at the time—was crucial, as it knocked the Mets out of the race.

Rose never lost his ability to perform in the clutch. He had a .375 mark in the National League Championship Series against the Dodgers and posted a .313 clip in the World Series against Baltimore.

In the NLCS, Rose set records for playing in all games (seven) and most times on a winning club (six). He and teammate Joe Morgan shared the record for most series played (seven). At age 42, Rose also became the oldest nonpitcher ever to play in a league championship series.

Yet Rose realized his days as a Phillie were about to end. The club didn't renew his contract, but he took the move in stride and truly had no ill feelings or regrets. Rose still wanted to be a full-time player, but the Phillies envisioned him as a part-time player.

Rose would leave the Phillies 10 hits shy of 4,000 and 202 away from breaking Ty Cobb's record of 4,191. He ended up breaking Cobb's record when he was the player-manager of the Reds and finished his career with 4,256 hits.

He stated shortly after the 1983 season that his greatest thrill in the game was "riding down Broad Street after the World Series parade."

"Just to see the smiles on people's faces. That's something I'll never forget. There were a million people on the streets and another million in the stadium. All those people—it was the most awesome sight I ever saw.

"I left Philadelphia with a lot of good memories. It was all fun. I wasn't mad at anyone. The Phillies have a great organization."

Even though Rose had many memories in a Phillies uniform that he cherished, he had a special relationship with Mike Schmidt, who still campaigns for Rose's induction into the Hall of Fame.

Schmidt has taken advantage of his many opportunities to support Rose, including one in which he thanked Rose when Schmidt received his MVP award from the 1980 season.

"I probably would not be standing here if it were not for Pete Rose," Schmidt said. "He instilled in me the vitality that was the turning point in my career.

"Pete gave me a new outlook on the game as well as life. He taught me how to have fun playing the game. We still have a close relationship."

"Mike Schmidt was the best player in the game during the '80s and especially in 1980," said Rose. "He probably never realized how much ability he had. He finally started to realize it after the Series."

Rose, who won three batting titles, spent his first 16 years (1963-1978) in Cincinnati. He spent five years with the Phillies, helping them win the 1980 World Series and the 1983 pennant.

After spending the first half of the 1984 season with Montreal, he came back to Cincinnati. Rose retired as a player at the end of the 1986 season and continued to manage the Reds until he was suspended from baseball for life by baseball commissioner Bart Giamatti on Aug. 24, 1989.

Pete Rose was certainly one of the greatest players of all time.

Pete Rose Phillies Statistics

Year	G	AB	R	H	2B	3B	HR	RBI	AVG	OBP	SLGP
1979	163	628	90	208	40	5	4	59	.331	.418	.430
1980	162	655	95	185	42	1	1	64	.282	.352	.354
1981	107	431	73	140	18	5	0	33	.325	.391	.390
1982	162	634	80	172	25	4	3	54	.271	.345	.338
1983	151	493	52	121	14	3	0	45	.245	.316	.286
Totals	**745**	**2,841**	**390**	**826**	**139**	**18**	**8**	**255**	**.291**	**.365**	**.361**

Thirty-nine

Eddie Sawyer

© 2000 Phillies

Led the 1950 Whiz Kids to the Pennant

by Skip Clayton

When Bob Carpenter took over as president of the Phillies on Nov. 23, 1943, the team was coming off of its 11th straight second-division finish. The farm system had hardly any good players, and the job of rebuilding the Phillies into a contender was going to take time and money.

Carpenter's first move was to hire Herb Pennock as his general manager. Together, the pair decided that building up the club would be done through the farm system.

Before long, the Phillies established a farm team at Utica, and Pennock quickly hired a manager for the Eastern League club. His name was Eddie Sawyer, a hard-hitting minor league outfielder who turned to managing in the New York Yankees farm system in 1939. Sawyer had just finished the 1943 season as manager of the Yankees' team in Binghamton, also in the Eastern League.

A college professor during the off-season, Sawyer would go on to become one of the top managers in Phillies history. Before his career ended, he would become one of only five men to lead the Phillies to a National League pennant, guiding the club to the title in 1950.

That year, Sawyer and his Whiz Kids captured the nation's fancy with their youth and exciting style of play. It was by far Eddie's best year as a manager.

In two stints as the skipper of the Phillies, Sawyer compiled a 390-425 record. His wins and games managed both rank sixth on the club's all-time list.

Sawyer, a native of Westerly, R.I., was retired and living in the Philadelphia area when he died on Sept. 22, 1997, at the age of 87. Before he died, Sawyer looked back fondly at his days as the Phillies' pilot, especially when he was directing the Whiz Kids.

"The Whiz Kids actually started in Utica, but were not known as the Whiz Kids then," said Sawyer. "We had players such as Richie Ashburn, Putsy Caballero, and Granny Hamner. In 1945, I had nine first-year men in a real tough league, and we won the pennant. We had an excellent team in 1945. We made very few mistakes because we tried to take care of that in morning and afternoon workouts. The games were played at night."

Eddie's first year in Utica had been 1944, when the club finished third. In 1945, when the young players started to arrive, the club finished first, six games ahead of Wilkes-Barre. The following year, Sawyer lost Ashburn and Hamner to the Army and the club finished in a tie for sixth. Richie and Granny returned in 1947 to help Utica finish 10 games ahead of Albany. In the playoffs, Utica won the championship.

In 1948, the Phillies signed their first working agreement with a Triple A farm team—Toronto of the International League. Sawyer was appointed Toronto's manager.

Toronto was in third place in late July when Carpenter decided that the time had come to bring Sawyer up as his manager. With the Phillies in sixth place, Ben Chapman was fired and Dusty Cooke was named to fill in until Sawyer arrived on July 26.

The Phillies finished the year in sixth place and moved up to third in 1949. In mid-August, the team was in fifth place, three games under .500. All of a sudden, it caught fire, and went on to capture 27 of its final 43 games.

"We were a surprise club," recalled Sawyer. "Nobody thought we were going to be that good. They didn't know whether we were here to stay or not.

"Our pitching had gotten better. We had enough talent by then, although we didn't have the reserves that we needed. The youth movement was on, and we wanted to make sure they would be there a long time, and we proved we were right in most cases."

The fans were excited about the club that was starting to be called the Whiz Kids.

"I told them to come back ready to play in 1950 and that we were going to win the pennant. I said that to the players because it left something in their minds to keep them in shape and to keep them thinking baseball over the winter. I wanted them to come to spring training thinking they were going to win. I also knew at the time that we had four clubs to contend with—Brooklyn, New York, Boston, and St. Louis. We could finish anywhere from first to fifth.

The club moved in and out of first several times, until it went into the lead for good on July 25 after taking two from the Cubs at home, 7-0 and 1-0, behind Bubba Church and Robin Roberts.

With three weeks left in the season, the Phillies had a six-and-a-half-game lead. But suddenly, the team started to fall apart. First, it lost Curt Simmons—a 17-game winner—to the Army. Church, Bob Miller, Andy Seminick, and Dick Sisler were hurt, and Bill Nicholson was diagnosed with diabetes.

The pennant boiled down to the last day of the season for the Phillies. If they beat the Dodgers in Ebbets Field, the flag would be the first for the club since 1915. If they lost to Brooklyn, the two teams would meet in a two-out-of-three playoff.

It was Roberts against Don Newcombe. Robbie beat Don, 4-1, in 10 innings as Sisler hit a three-run homer to give the Whiz Kids the flag.

"Robbie had pitched a lot when that last game came around, but he always pitched well when things were the toughest," said Sawyer. "He always pitched well in Ebbets Field, too. I don't ever recall him pitching a bad ball game there. He always pitched well against Brooklyn, and he always pitched well against Don Newcombe.

"Robbie had a reasonable amount of rest," Sawyer added. "Two days off were reasonable for him at that time. I knew he would be ready because he always rose to the occasion."

The World Series was another story, as the Yankees swept the Phillies in four games. Three of the losses were by one run.

In 1951, the club dropped to fifth. Simmons was still in the service and many of the regulars had bad seasons.

"We really missed Curt," said Sawyer. "We were 23 games out when the regular season ended. Take those 17 games he won, which probably would have been 20 if he hadn't been taken, and there is no telling what would have happened. It's hard to believe that one person could make that much difference."

In 1952, the Phillies had Simmons coming back, and hopes for a pennant were high. But the Phillies got off to a bad start. With the club in seventh place with a 28-35 record, Carpenter fired Sawyer.

Sawyer remained out of baseball from the middle of the 1952 season until he returned to the Phillies as manager in July 1958. In the six years he was away, Eddie was working in sales for a golf ball manufacturer.

From 1952 to 1957, the Phillies had four finishes in the first division and two in fifth place. But the club was sliding downhill fast in 1958, and it wouldn't get back into the first division until 1963.

The 1958 Phillies got off to a great start under Sawyer. The night he returned, they swept a pair from the Giants at Connie Mack Stadium. But they finished with a 69-85 record, which put them in the basement. Ashburn won the batting title with a .350 average while Roberts won 17 games, but it wasn't the same club that Sawyer had seen the first time around.

The following season was even worse. The Phillies, under Eddie, finished last once again with a 64-90 record.

"Most of the Whiz Kids that were still there were on the way out," said Sawyer. "The Phillies had decided they were going to get rid of a lot of them. I think the club wanted me back as a hatchet man who would tell those players that they had had it with the Phillies. Also, there were some changes in the front office [e.g., John Quinn had replaced Roy Hamey as general manager] and I found out that I wasn't going to have as much of a say as I had before."

The Phillies opened the 1960 season losing to the Reds in Crosley Field. After that game, Eddie resigned as manager, saying, "I am 49 years old and I want to live to be 50."

"Frankly, I thought I would be better off and that somebody else could do it better than I could," mused Sawyer. "I didn't know whether I wanted to go through another losing season or not, so I just said, 'Thank you, but I have had enough.'

"I stayed with the Phillies, scouting for them through 1966. Then I left and joined the Kansas City Royals and scouted for them. On Jan. 1, 1974, I retired from baseball."

By then, though, Sawyer had earned a place as one of the greatest managers in Phillies history.

Forty

Curt Schilling

A Modern Pitching Marvel

by Jeff Moeller

The Phillies had their backs to the wall in a World Series no one ever truly dreamed they would be in.

Nevertheless, the magical mystery tour of the 1993 season that was fueled by swashbuckling manager Jim Fregosi and his band of "Macho Row" misfits wasn't about to quit.

They had just come off a stunning 15-14 defeat at the hands of the Toronto Blue Jays, and many fans believed they had already fired their best shots.

But then there was Curt Schilling. The fireballing right-hander was the team's workhorse during the season, fashioning a 16-7 record and seven complete games. He had set a career high in innings pitched during the regular season with 235 and had gone over the 200-inning mark for the second consecutive season, as he began to become fully recognized as one of the game's stalwarts.

Schilling's bulldog approach that season served as a catalyst for the Phillies. "Quit" was never found in his and his teammates' vocabulary.

He started Game 1 of the National League Championship Series against Atlanta and set a record by striking out the first five batters he faced. Schilling gained a no-decision in a 4-3 Phillies' 10th-inning victory, and he fell into a similar situation in Game 5.

Still, despite going winless, he was named the Most Valuable Player of the NLCS, as he recorded 19 strikeouts over 16 innings and a stingy 1.69 ERA.

Schilling got the call in the World Series opener in Toronto, but he couldn't extend the magnificent showing he had made in the NLCS.

He ran into trouble in the second inning when he issued four hits and two runs. Unfortunately, it didn't get any better. Schilling couldn't find his groove and later gave up solo homers to Devon White and John Olerud.

In the seventh, Schilling was knocked out, the victim of seven runs (six earned). He recorded just three strikeouts in his official 6 1/3-inning stint.

"I think Schilling had enough good stuff to win," Fregosi said after the game in his usual bland, frank style. "He just didn't make enough good pitches when he had to."

So Fregosi and Phillies fans across the country took a deep breath when Schilling took to the mound in a must-win situation on a chilly Philadelphia night in Game 5.

Before the game, Fregosi informed his players that there would be a workout on their day off at Toronto's Skydome the Friday before Game 6.

Schilling fed off his manager's optimism and delivered his own state of the situation message.

"I wanted the ball," Schilling said. "I wanted the responsibility. If you don't want the ball in these situations, why show up?"

Schilling certainly did, and he sealed any unleft speculation that he was his team's ace and one of the top hurlers in the game.

He handcuffed the Blue Jays by moving his pitches around the entire plate and his fastball blazed in the mid- to high 90s. No Blue Jay reached second base until the sixth inning.

In the eighth inning, the first two Blue Jays hit safely. With runners on first and third, Rickey Henderson hit a smash that Schilling knocked down near the mound. His throw to catcher Darren Daulton trapped pinch runner Willie Canate in a rundown and helped preserve the Phillies' 2-0 lead.

After that, Schilling retired the next five Toronto batters in a row.

"I started to run out of gas in the seventh," Schilling recalled. "I knew when Daulton told me that we would be using mirrors to get these guys out, I'm starting to lose it."

"In the eighth, I looked in the bullpen, and there was nobody up. It pumped me up. I knew this team would go to Toronto based on what I did. If I had to point to one inning in my career where I gave everything I had for one inning, it was that inning."

Schilling finished the complete game with five hits allowed and six strikeouts and he became the first Phillie to hurl a complete game in a World Series since Robin Roberts accomplished the feat in the second game of the 1950 World Series.

Yet, his 1993 heroics have taken a backseat to his arm ailments.

Schilling started off the 1994 season with an 0-7 mark. He sprained a ligament in his right foot in late April and underwent surgery in late May for a bone spur. Schilling later suffered a freak knee injury and didn't win his first game until late July.

After missing the first month and a half of the 1996 season, Schilling managed to post a 9-10 mark, the second-lowest win total of his Phillies career.

He rebounded, though, to become only the fifth pitcher in major league history to record two consecutive 300-plus strikeout seasons (319 and 300). His 391 strikeouts in 1997 broke J.R. Richard's National League record for most whiffs by a right-hander (314).

Over the last three years, heading into the 2000 season, Schilling has an overall record of 47-31. Since being acquired from Houston for little-known Jason Grimsley in 1992, Schilling has an overall mark with the Phillies of 95-72. His 95 wins are seventh overall on the club's all-time victory list.

But it was on a cold October 1993 night that Schilling made Phillies fans and the rest of the baseball world finally take notice.

Curt Schilling's Phillies Statistics

Year	W	L	SV	G	GS	CG	SH	IP	H	BB	SO	ERA
1992	14	11	2	42	26	10	4	226.1	165	59	147	2.35
1993	16	7	0	34	34	7	2	235.1	234	57	186	4.02
1994	2	8	0	13	13	1	0	82.1	87	28	58	4.48
1995	7	5	0	17	17	1	0	116.0	96	26	114	1.29
1996	9	1	0	0	26	8	2	183.1	149	50	182	3.19
1997	17	11	0	35	35	7	2	254.1	208	58	319	2.97
1998	15	14	0	35	35	15	2	268.2	236	61	300	3.25
1999	15	6	0	24	24	8	1	180.1	159	44	152	3.31
Totals	**95**	**63**	**2**	**200**	**210**	**57**	**13**	**1544.8**	**1,334**	**383**	**1458**	**3.10**

Forty-one

Mike Schmidt

Baseball's Greatest Third Baseman

by Jeff Moeller

The story of Mike Schmidt is one with many subtitles.

He is considered by many the greatest Phillie of all time. After all, he remains the club's top career home run hitter and, overwhelmingly, its best-fielding third baseman.

Schmidt was a man for all seasons and a man of many moods. His quietness was often interpreted as a sign of arrogance, introversion, or a combination of both. His robotic-like personality at times on the field caused many fans to view Schmidt as a player lacking in leadership qualities.

But Schmidt put the fans and many of his own ghosts to sleep when he almost single-handedly carried the ball club during the final month of the regular season in 1980. Schmidt hit .304, drove in 27 runs, and had a .688 slugging percentage.

He clouted 13 homers during the month of September, including one in each of the last four regular-season games. His 11th-inning shot on Oct. 4 against Montreal gave the Phils the division title.

His 48-homer, 121-RBI regular season easily won him the league MVP honor, as he became the first player since Orlando Cepeda of St. Louis in 1967 to be chosen first on all 24 ballots. He would later add a World Series MVP with a two-homer, seven-RBI, .381 showing.

In the strike-shortened 1981 season, Schmidt again led his club to the postseason and became only the fourth National League player to win consecutive MVP awards, with 31 homers and a career-high .316 average.

Schmidt helped bring his club back to the World Series two years later when he smashed 40 homers and drove in 109 runs. In the postseason, he hit .467 in the National League Championship Series, but he struggled with just one hit in 20 at-bats in the World Series.

"Michael Jack" also picked up his share of hardware for his fielding, as he won 10 Gold Gloves and posted a lifetime fielding average of .955, including .980 in 1986.

He would later win his third MVP award in 1986, becoming only the seventh player in major league history to capture the honor. Less than three years later, Schmidt retired 42 games into the 1989 season.

One of the proudest moments for Schmidt and the Phillies' fans occurred on April 18, 1987, when he took a major step in eventually becoming the seventh-best home run hitter in the game and securing a spot on the game's All-Century team.

The Phillies had a 5-2 lead heading into the bottom of the eighth inning in Pittsburgh, and manager John Felske replaced starter Don Carman with Steve Bedrosian.

The usually reliable "Bedrock" was rocked for four runs to give the Pirates a 6-5 lead, and they put the game in the hands of closer Don Robinson.

The Phillies' Milt Thompson rapped a one-out single, but he was forced at second by Juan Samuel, who stole second and moved to third on a wild pitch. Von Hayes followed with a walk.

Schmidt stepped to the plate—a victim of Robinson's 50 of the 57 previous times the big right-hander had faced him. But Schmidt had hit four homers off him.

Robinson served up three balls to Schmidt. His fourth pitch was right over the lower part of the plate and Schmidt swung. There was little doubt that it would be his 500th homer, as the ball sailed over the fence and landed against the backdrop.

Schmidt vaulted out of the batter's box, did a little dance, then hurried to first. He clapped his hands between first and second base and clapped again between second and third.

Schmidt was mobbed by his teammates at the plate, and bullpen coach Mike Ryan retrieved the ball and presented it to him. He thus became only the 14th player in baseball history to hit his 500th the day after his 499th.

Before his career was over, Schmidt would hit 48 more homers.

"It was the greatest thrill of my lifetime," Schmidt said after the game. "The situation being what it was, it was, without question, the most exciting moment of my career, right on a par with 1980."

He also admitted that he was swinging for the fences his three previous times up, but he could only hit "weak pop-ups."

Mike Schmidt played in more games (2,404) than any other player in Phillies history. He is still tops in the club's record books with 548 home runs; 1,506 runs scored; 2,234 hits; 4,404 total bases; 1,015 base-hits; and 1,507 walks.

He hit four consecutive homers twice, four in one game at Wrigley Field in a 10-inning, 18-16 Phillies win. Later, he hit four straight against San Francisco in July 1979 over two games. Schmidt holds the record for major league third basemen for most homers in a career with 509 and tied the NL record for the most consecutive seasons with 30 or more homers with nine. He also set the NL record for the most years leading the league in homers with eight.

In 1995, his first year of eligibility, Mike Schmidt was voted into the Hall of Fame with 444 votes.

Since his retirement, Schmidt has been an active golfer and barely missed the cut for a U.S. Senior Tour event.

During the past 10 years, Schmidt has often been mentioned as someone who might join the Phillies in a front-office capacity. But his apparent reluctance to work his way through the team's farm system has been a stumbing block.

Mike Schmidt Phillies Statistics

Year	G	AB	R	H	2B	3B	HR	RBI	AVG	OBP	SLGP
1972	13	34	2	7	0	0	1	3	.206	.325	.294
1973	132	367	43	72	11	0	18	52	.196	.324	.373
1974	162	568	108	160	28	7	36	116	.282	.395	.546
1975	158	562	93	140	34	3	38	95	.249	.367	.523
1976	160	584	112	153	31	4	38	107	.262	.376	.524
1977	154	544	114	149	27	11	38	101	.274	.393	.574
1978	145	513	93	129	27	2	21	78	.251	.364	.435
1979	160	541	109	137	25	4	45	114	.253	.386	.564
1980	150	548	104	157	25	8	48	121	.286	.380	.624
1981	102	354	78	112	19	2	31	91	.316	.435	.644
1982	148	514	108	144	26	3	35	87	.280	.403	.547
1983	154	534	104	136	16	4	40	109	.255	.399	.524
1984	151	528	93	146	23	3	36	106	.277	.383	.536
1985	158	549	89	152	31	5	33	93	.277	.375	.532
1986	160	552	97	160	29	1	37	119	.290	.390	.547
1987	147	522	88	153	28	0	35	113	.293	.388	.548
1988	108	390	52	97	21	2	12	62	.249	.337	.405
1989	42	148	19	30	7	0	6	28	.203	.297	.372
Totals	2,404	8,352	1,506	2,234	408	59	548	1,595	.267	.380	.527

Forty-two

Andy Seminick

One of the Phillies' Top Catchers

by Skip Clayton

O f all the players who have caught for the Phillies, only a few would qualify as the club's all-time greats at that position.

Ranking right up there at the top is Andy Seminick, a rock-ribbed strongman who was one of the steadiest, most solid backstops ever to pull on Phillies livery.

Seminick came out of the hills of Western Pennsylvania (He was born in West Virginia) and gave the Phillies topflight receiving for parts of 12 seasons. In all, he played 15 years in the majors. While he was usually not among the league's top-hitting catchers, he had few equals as a handler of pitchers and as a guardian of the plate.

Andy was best known for being the solid veteran of the Whiz Kids. In 1950, when the Phillies won the pennant, he had his finest season, hitting .288 with 24 home runs.

Now a resident of Melbourne, Fla., Seminick still does some instructing at Phillies training camps for minor leaguers in Clearwater. After retiring in 1957, he served as a coach with the Phillies, a minor league manager, an instructor, and a scout.

He originally joined the club in September of 1943, a raw rookie who could play the infield, the outfield, and could also catch. Although he would become not only one of the Phillies' finest catchers, but also one of the most popular players in the team's history, the first of the Whiz Kids to join the Phillies would have a tough time in his early years in the majors.

"It was hard to convert to catcher," recalled Seminick. "I wasn't a full-time catcher until I got to the big leagues. I did catch some games in the minors."

After a rocky beginning, Andy divided the 1944 season between the Phillies and Buffalo of the International League, but in 1945, he returned to Philadelphia to stay, splitting the catching job that year with Gus Mancuso.

Toward the end of the year, Ben Chapman took over as manager. He not only made Andy the first-string catcher, but he also brought in two new coaches who could help the youngster. Andy had some problems behind the plate for three years, but in 1945, all that started to change.

"Benny Bengough and Cy Perkins worked with me an awful lot," said Seminick. "Ben Chapman kept encouraging me about being a catcher, but Cy and Benny were the big people that helped."

In 1946, Andy hit .264 and knocked out 12 home runs. He followed up in 1947 with a .252 average and 13 homers.

During the 1948 season, Seminick hit 13 home runs but his average dropped to .225. But Andy led National League catchers in putouts and assists.

On June 2, 1949, against the Cincinnati Reds, the Phillies hit five home runs in the eighth inning, tying the National League record for the most home runs in one inning. Seminick hit two of those homers, tying the record for the most homers in one inning. He also hit a third homer earlier in the game.

"One of the highlights of my career was those two homers in one inning," said Seminick, whose blasts were joined by ones by Del Ennis, Willie Jones, and School-boy Rowe.

"As for the club," Andy added, "we could see it coming together during the last six weeks of the season when we moved up to third. Eddie Sawyer saw the club coming on a lot sooner than most of us. He had many of the younger players in the minor leagues and knew what most of them could do."

Seminick was voted the starting catcher on the All-Star team that year. He finished the season with only a .243 average, but he hit 24 home runs.

In 1950, the Phillies were considered a team that would finish in the first division. A pennant, however, still seemed a year or two away. But the team captured its first pennant since 1915 on the last day of the season.

"The thing that stuck out about 1950 was, we were a young team and a close team," Seminick said. "When you had two starters like Robin Roberts and Curt Simmons, you were pretty sure of coming out with two wins when you went into a town for a three- or four-game series. Jim Konstanty had a great year coming out of the bullpen. We had a real good club and everyone had confidence in one another."

On July 25, behind the shutout pitching of Church and Roberts, the Whiz Kids took two from the Cubs at Shibe Park and moved into first place to stay. By the middle of August, the Phillies' lead was at five games when the Giants moved into Philadelphia for a four-game series. The two teams split the first two, then an explosion erupted that turned into one of the biggest brawls in Phillies history.

"It started the night before, when Eddie Stanky began jumping up and down and waving his arms at second base," Seminick said. "When he first did it, I stepped back and said to the umpire, 'What in the world is going on here?' He said he couldn't do anything about it. I got back in the box and got hit by the pitch.

"The following day, in my first time up, the bat flew out of my hands and landed on the mound. I went out and got it. Then I singled and went to third on a ball hit to left. Hank Thompson was playing third base for the Giants. As he took the throw from the left fielder, I slid into him and knocked him down. The ball got away, and I scored. They took Thompson out of the game because he was hurt.

"The next time I came up, Stanky started jumping up and down again. This time he got thrown out of the game. I guess the umpires got word from Ford Frick [National League president] to stop that stuff. I got on base again, and now Bill Rigney was playing second. I slid into him, and we got into a fight. Then everybody started fighting."

When peace was restored, Andy and Rigney were tossed out of the game. Seminick had been in only a few fights in his career, but he never lost one, including this bout. The Phillies went on to win the game, while New York sent out an SOS to Jersey City for some reserve infielders.

Late in September, the Phillies made a final trip to New York, which proved disastrous for Andy and the team. Andy got hurt at home plate and he was not the same the rest of the year.

"Monte Irvin ran into me," Seminick said. "I got a bone separation in the ankle on the play, but I didn't know about it at the time. I caught a doubleheader the next day and the final two games of the season at Brooklyn. My ankle was hurting bad."

Andy played in the World Series, but before each game, he had to have his ankle shot full of novocaine to mask the pain. After the season ended, his ankle was put in a cast.

Andy finished the season with 24 homers, 68 RBIs, and a career-high .288 batting average. In the World Series, he hit only .182 with two hits in 11 at-bats.

The Phillies dropped to fifth in 1951. Andy was hurt in the early part of May. "I don't know if the team's downfall began with my injury," he said. "I got beaned and I never recovered. But Del Wilbur was our backup catcher. He did a real good job when they put him in."

Playing in 101 games, Andy hit only .227 with 11 homers and 37 RBIs. At the end of the year, he and Dick Sisler were traded to Cincinnati as part of a seven-player deal that brought the Phillies Smoky Burgess.

After spending a little more than three years with the Reds, Seminick was traded back to the Phillies in early 1955 in a six-player deal that returned Burgess to Cincinnati. Andy took over as the No. 1 catcher, but the following year, Stan Lopata took over as the regular catcher. Andy usually caught if a left-hander pitched, and Lopata then played first base.

Seminick retired after the 1956 season. He finished with 123 homers, which rank 11th on the all-time Phillies' list. His final homer came off Warren Spahn at Connie Mack Stadium. He hit it on the roof, a feat he had performed several times in his career.

Overall, Seminick had 164 home runs, 556 RBIs, and a lifetime average of .243.

Before the year was over, "Andy Seminick Night" was held at Connie Mack Stadium between games of a twi-night doubleheader with Cincinnati. "It was a very memorable night for me, my wife and family," said Seminick. "I was choked up and couldn't say much when it was my time to speak. It was a real happy evening, especially after we took two from the Reds."

Mayo Smith added Andy as one of his coaches in 1957. By Sept. 1, injuries had kayoed the catching corps. So Seminick went back on the roster for the rest of the season.

He remained with the club in 1958 as a coach, then managed in the Phillies' farm system for eight years. Seminick rejoined the parent club in 1967 as a coach for three years. He returned to the minors to manage for three more years; then in 1973, he became a scout for the Phillies.

Andy's final year of managing was at Eugene in the Pacific Coast League. His club captured the PCL's West Division title with a lot of the players who later played for the Phillies, including Bob Boone, who was converted from an infielder to a catcher.

"I was very lucky to have been sent to Eugene to play every day under Andy," Boone said. "It was a valuable experience."

"I give Andy all the credit for the development of Bob Boone," added Paul Owens.

Seminick was easily one of the most popular players ever to play for the Phillies and one of the best catchers they ever had.

Andy Seminick Phillies Statistics

Year	G	AB	R	H	2B	3B	HR	RBI	AVG	OBP	SLGP
1943	22	72	9	13	2	0	2	5	.181	.253	.292
1944	22	63	9	14	2	1	0	4	.222	.300	.286
1945	80	188	18	45	7	2	6	26	.239	.313	.394
1946	124	406	55	107	15	5	12	52	.264	.334	.414
1947	111	337	48	85	16	2	13	50	.252	.370	.427
1948	125	391	49	88	11	3	13	44	.225	.328	.368
1949	109	334	52	81	11	2	24	68	.243	.380	.503
1950	130	393	55	113	15	3	24	68	.288	.400	.524
1951	101	291	42	66	8	1	11	37	.227	.370	.375
1955	93	289	32	71	12	1	11	34	.246	.333	.408
1956	60	161	16	32	3	1	7	23	.199	.332	.360
1957	8	11	0	1	0	0	0	0	.091	.167	.091
Totals	985	2,936	385	716	102	21	123	411	.244	.351	.419

Forty-three

Chris Short

One of the Phillies' Greatest Left-Handed Pitchers

by Skip Clayton

I n the Phillies' 117-year history, the club has had three great left-handed pitchers. Ironically, they all pitched within 40 years of each other and in consecutive order.

First, there was Curt Simmons, who came up at the end of the 1947 season. Steve Carlton took over the role in 1972. In between, there was Chris Short.

Until Carlton came along, Short was generally regarded as the greatest southpaw in Phillies history. He was voted that honor in 1969, by which time he had built a reputation as one of the toughest lefties in the National League.

The 6-4, 205-pounder from Milford, Del., was a two-time member of the National League All-Star team, and he had seasons in which he won 20, 19, 18, and 17 games for the Phillies.

In his 15-year major league career, 14 years of which were spent with the Phillies, Short posted a 135-132 record with a 3.43 earned run average. Pitching in 2,325 innings in 501 games, he gave up 2,215 hits, struck out 1,629, and walked 806.

Hurling for the Phillies from 1959 to 1972, Short was 132-127 in 459 games. At the peak of his career, his ERA was under 3.00 in five of six consecutive seasons.

On the Phillies' all-time career pitching list, Short ranks second in walks; third in strikeouts, runs, earned runs, and losses; and fourth in wins, games played, shutouts, innings pitched, and hits.

Short holds two unusual distinctions. He was the winning pitcher in the first game ever played in the Astrodome, beating Houston, 2-0, on a four-hitter on April 12, 1965. And he was also the winning pitcher in the last game ever played at the Polo Grounds, beating the New York Mets, 5-1, on Sept. 18, 1963.

"It meant a lot to win the first game in the Astrodome," recalled Short. "But when I beat the Mets in the last game at the Polo Grounds, that meant even more."

Probably Short's greatest game came in the second game of a doubleheader on Oct. 2, 1965, when he set a club record by striking out 18 Mets at Shea Stadium. Short worked 15 innings, giving up nine hits and walking three. The game was called after 18 innings of a scoreless tie because of a 1 a.m. curfew.

"It was frustrating not to win that game because I pitched so well," Short said. "But you had to give the Mets and their pitchers a lot of credit because they held us scoreless, too."

At the time, Short, nicknamed "Styles" because of his unflattering attire as a young player, was in the midst of the finest part of his career.

The son of a distinguished judge in Delaware, Short was signed in 1957, after attending the University of Delaware.

After two years in the minors, Short started the 1959 season with the Phillies and pitched his first game on April 19 against the Cincinnati Reds in Crosley Field, in relief.

"I remember my first game well," Short said. "The first batter I faced was Gus Bell with the bases loaded. He hit a line drive to Wally Post for an out. The next time he came up, he hit another shot back at me for another out. He wasn't too happy, going 0-for-2 against me, even though he hit a liner and a hard grounder."

A week later, Short got his first start against Pittsburgh, but got a no-decision. Soon afterward, he was sent to Buffalo for more seasoning.

In 1960, Chris was back with the Phillies and got his first win, in relief, over Cincinnati at Connie Mack Stadium. Short went back to the minors and pitched three games at Indianapolis, then came back to win his first complete game on June 11 over the Chicago Cubs at Wrigley Field.

"Ernie Banks hit a homer off me, but we won the game, 7-1," Short said. "I always wanted to play major league baseball, and when I completed that game, I was on top of the world."

Short was 6-9 in 1960 and 6-12 in 1961 as the Phillies finished last both years. The 1961 season was especially tough, as the club was only 47-107, which included a 23-game losing streak.

"That 23-game losing streak wasn't too nice to go through," remembered Short. "I lost the 23rd game, which was the first game of a doubleheader at Milwaukee. John Buzhardt won the second game, 7-4. Sometimes you have to go through things like that, but it molded us into a better ball club."

In 1962, the Phillies moved up to seventh place in the new 10-team league, posting an 81-80 record. Short improved his record to 11-9, at one point beating Warren Spahn twice in five days.

"I had good luck against Spahn," he said. "The first time I beat him, I also had four hits. He was all over me. 'How can you go four for four?' he yelled. The four hits I got off him were ground balls that just found holes.

"Four days later, I beat Spahn again, 2-1, when Johnny Callison hit a homer off the foul pole in the 11th inning.

The Phillies moved up to fourth in 1963, capturing 87 games, although Short's record dropped to 9-12.

By the time the 1964 season arrived, many thought the Phillies had a shot at the pennant.

"We played well together, and we didn't have any key injuries, or for that matter, any injuries at all," Short explained. "Everything just fell into place. Then, all of a sudden, everything started falling apart. Frank Thomas, who we had gotten in a trade with the Mets, and who was hitting home runs to win games, got hurt. Then Danny Cater got hurt. We had some pitchers who had some problems with their arms. After 150 games, we were six and a half games in front and we hadn't lost four in a row—then came the 10-game losing streak."

After the Phillies snapped their 10-game losing streak, they won their last two to finish in a tie for second place with Cincinnati as the Cardinals captured the pennant by one game.

Short finished the season with a solid 17-9 record and an earned run average of 2.20, third lowest in the National League. He also made the All-Star team.

In 1965, the Phillies dropped to sixth with an 85-76 mark, but Short had an 18-11 record. The Phillies moved up to fourth place in 1966.

"I won my 20th on the last day of the season in the first game of a double-header," Short recalled. "If Los Angeles had won the first game, they would have won the pennant. Gene Mauch brought me in to relieve in the eighth inning when we were losing, 3-2. We scored two in the bottom of the inning and won. I pitched the eighth and ninth. It was some kind of feeling to get that third out for your 20th win. It was a great feeling.

"In the clubhouse, I thanked Gene Mauch for giving me the chance to win 20. He said I didn't have to thank him, that I did the job myself. But I still thanked him."

The Phillies dropped to fifth in 1967 with an 82-80 record. Short missed about 12 starts due to back and knee injuries.

"The injury to my knee was a freak accident. It happened before a game," Short said. "I was running in the outfield. Doug Clemens was taking flies and we ran into each other. The injury didn't come when we hit, but when I fell, I turned my leg under me and popped some ligaments."

Chris pitched in 29 games and posted a 9-11 record, but his earned run average of 2.40 was third best in the league. Short made the All-Star team and pitched two scoreless innings.

Short came back strong in 1968 with a 19-13 record.

The 1969 season had to be the most dismal of Short's career. He hurled four innings on opening day against the Cubs in Chicago. A week after that, he went six against the Mets. Short never pitched the rest of the season. In June, Chris had a two-hour operation for the removal of a herniated disc below the last lumbar vertebra.

The Phillies opened their season at home on April 7, 1970, for the last time at Connie Mack Stadium. Short earned the start and blanked the Cubs, 2-0. It was the third time that he had pitched a 2-0 shutout on opening day.

"I knew I wasn't throwing as hard as I had before," Short recalled, "A couple of the Cubs players said to me the next day, 'What happened to your fastball?' Probably there was four to five miles an hour off my fastball, which doesn't sound like a lot. But it is when you are in the big leagues.

Short finished the season with a 9-16 record. In 1971, he was 7-14. Short appeared in only 19 games in 1972, all in relief, and posted a 1-1 record. On Oct. 26, the Phillies released him.

He joined the Milwaukee Brewers in 1973 and posted a 3-5 record, pitching mostly in relief. After the season, he retired.

In 1988, Short was felled by a brain aneurysm and lapsed into a coma. He suffered serious brain damage, heart attacks, and strokes. He had no hope of recovery and died on Aug. 1, 1991.

Short is still regarded as one of the top pitchers in Phillies history.

Chris Short Phillies Statistics

Year	W	L	SV	PCT	G	GS	CG	SH	IP	H	BB	SO	ERA
1959	0	0	0	.000	3	2	0	0	14.1	19	10	8	8.18
1960	6	9	3	.400	42	10	2	0	107.1	101	52	54	3.94
1961	6	12	1	.333	39	16	1	0	127.1	157	71	80	5.94
1962	11	9	3	.550	47	12	4	0	142.0	149	56	91	3.42
1963	9	12	0	.429	38	27	6	3	198.0	185	69	160	2.95
1964	17	9	2	.654	42	31	12	4	220.2	174	51	181	2.20
1965	18	11	2	.621	47	40	15	5	297.1	260	89	237	2.82
1966	20	10	0	.667	42	39	19	4	272.0	257	68	177	3.54
1967	9	11	1	.450	29	26	8	2	199.1	163	74	142	2.39
1968	19	13	1	.594	42	36	9	2	269.2	236	81	202	2.94
1969	0	0	0	.000	2	2	0	0	10.0	11	4	5	7.20
1970	9	16	1	.360	36	34	7	2	199.0	211	66	133	4.30
1971	7	14	1	.333	31	26	5	2	173.0	182	63	95	3.85
1972	1	1	1	.500	19	0	0	0	23.0	24	8	20	3.91
Totals	132	127	16	.514	459	301	88	24	2,253.0	2,129	762	1,585	3.38

Forty-four

Curt Simmons

Ace Lefty of the 1950s

by Skip Clayton

After World War II, the Phillies, under new owner Bob Carpenter and general manager Herb Pennock, signed as many new players as possible. Money wasn't a factor. Whatever it took, the Phillies spent, eventually laying out $2 million for players during a period in the mid-1940s.

One of the players they signed in 1947 was a 17-year-old left-handed pitcher named Curt Simmons. A native of Egypt, Pa., near Allentown, Simmons would enjoy a 20-year major league career and post a 193-183 record (115-110 with the Phillies).

Signing Curt was no easy task. Most of the other big-league clubs were after him. The main contenders, though, were the Phillies, the Boston Red Sox, and the Detroit Tigers.

Simmons was a high school phenom. Pitching for Whitehall, he averaged 15 strikeouts per game while leading his team to three Lehigh Valley championships. He also hurled his American Legion club to two Pennsylvania titles.

Scouts galore were on his trail, including the Phillies' Cy Morgan. In an attempt to get ahead of the competition, Morgan persuaded Carpenter to send the Phillies to Egypt to play a midsummer game against Curt's hometown team—the game the Phillies hoped would help them win the favor of the Simmons family.

"My father lined up the game, and it was a real gamble," Simmons recalled. "I could have gotten knocked around, and that could have sent my value down. But he had confidence in me, being the proud father he was. He felt I could do the job."

Curt did just that. He struck out 11 Phils and allowed only five hits. His team should have won the game, but two outfielders collided going after a fly ball that would've ended the game. The mishap allowed a run to score and gave the Phillies a 4-4 tie.

A few days after the game, following his graduation from high school, Simmons was signed to a Phillies contract. He received a $65,000 bonus.

After Simmons signed with the Phillies, they farmed him out to Wilmington, where he went 13-5, posted an earned run average of 2.69, and struck out 197 batters in 147 innings. The Phillies called up Curt at the end of the season, and he pitched the final game against the New York Giants at Shibe Park.

The Giants had set a record in 1947 for most homers in a season (221). Johnny Mize had 51 and was trying to break a tie with Ralph Kiner for the home run crown. The Giants put Mize in the leadoff spot, but to no avail, as he went one for five. Simmons beat the Giants, 3-1, striking out nine and allowing only five hits.

"I was nervous, but I was also a kid, and I just wanted to get the ball over against New York," said Simmons. "I felt I had good enough stuff. I didn't feel I was overmatched at that point."

The 1948 and 1949 seasons were not good ones for Curt. The Phillies, having given Curt a bonus and put him in the minors in 1947, were forced by the rules to keep him in the major leagues. He posted records of 7-10 and 4-10 and had serious control problems.

In 1950, Simmons got straightened out and became one of the best pitchers in the league.

"When you are young, you pitch mostly mechanically," explained Simmons. "You just let it go naturally. At first, I was thinking about a lot of things, but finally, I just relaxed and did it my own way and my pitching started to come around. It's mostly confidence. I was never that wild in high school."

Simmons hurled superbly during the season, and the Phillies were in the thick of the pennant race. "We had good personnel in the key areas and they were bear-down kinds of players," Curt said. "Our pitching was good and Jim Konstanty came in and was tremendous. Robbie was our kingpin. Most series, he pitched first, and then I pitched the second game."

But on July 27, with his record 14-5, Curt had to report for two weeks of National Guard duty at Indiantown Gap. Except for one start when he got a pass to come home, Curt didn't start again until Aug. 11. By then, though, he had learned that the 28th Division of the National Guard, of which he was a member, was going to be called to active duty because of the Korean War. Curt left the team on Sept. 10. His record was 17-8, and his winning percentage of .680 was third best in the league. His 146 strikeouts tied for fourth, but his average of 6.12 strikeouts per nine innings was second best in the league.

Had Simmons been with the Phillies until the end of the 1950 season, the Whiz Kids would have won the pennant a lot sooner instead of having to clinch on the final day of the season.

But Curt did not pitch again in 1950. There was some talk that he would be added to the roster for the World Series, but—even with a 10-day furlough—his only role was that of spectator. "I had been in the Army for a month and hadn't worked out except on Sundays behind the barracks," said Simmons.

Curt finally rejoined the Phillies in 1952. "I didn't have any spring training at all," he said. "I came back from Germany on opening day. I had worked out in an air hangar. Two and a half weeks after I came back, I got my first start. I was young and willing, and I pitched the whole game against the Cubs in Wrigley Field. We won, 8-2. The next day, I couldn't get out of bed. I was so stiff.

"I pitched my next game with four days' rest and got beat. It was difficult for me not to have spring training, but I thought I did a pretty good job, coming right back and pitching."

Curt had a 7-2 record at mid-season. He was the starting pitcher for the National League in the All-Star Game at Shibe Park and Simmons hurled three scoreless innings. Simmons finished the 1952 season with a 14-8 record and tied for the league lead in shutouts with six. He also was second in strikeouts per nine innings with an average of 6.30 per game.

In 1953, Curt pitched his greatest game, a one-hitter. It was the Phillies' first game in Milwaukee following the Braves' move from Boston. Billy Bruton got a leadoff single for Milwaukee. After that, Curt retired 27 straight batters.

One month later, Simmons was at home cutting the grass when he sliced off the tip of his toe with a power mower. "More than anything, it scared the heck out of me," said Simmons. "Pitching-wise, I don't think it hurt me that much. I won 16 games that year and I was out for only a month. Whether it changed my delivery is questionable. I don't think the accident bothered me."

That year, Curt tied for third in complete games with 19. He pitched two scoreless innings in the All-Star Game, which the National League won in Cincinnati, 5-1.

The next year, Simmons came up with a bad arm. "I thought it was a coincidence," he said, referring to the suggestion the lawn mower accident had something to do with it. "The toe thing was exaggerated. It didn't bother me that much. What probably caused the arm trouble was that I was a herky-jerky pitcher, wild at times, and I threw a lot of pitches. I beat the heck out of my body when I pitched."

Curt dropped to a 14-15 record in 1954, but posted the third-best earned run average (2.81) in the league. The arm problems returned in 1955, and Curt finished at 8-8. He came back in 1956 with a 15-10 record, then was 12-11 in 1957 and started the All-Star Game for the National League. In those days, Curt was one of only a few left-handed pitchers to have a winning record against the Brooklyn Dodgers in Ebbets Field, although it was almost impossible for a left-hander to pitch there.

In 1958, Curt's record dropped to 7-14 and he spent part of the following season in the minors with Williamsport after having an elbow operation. He pitched four games with the Phillies in 1960, then was released.

Simmons was then signed by the Cardinals. Over the next six years, he was 18-4 against his former club, including 4-0 in 1964.

"When I went to St. Louis, I started throwing slow curves and put a little turn on the fastball," said Simmons. "I had better control and was a more consistent pitcher with the Cardinals than I was with the Phillies."

In Curt's fifth year with St. Louis, he helped the Cardinals to the pennant in 1964 as the Phillies collapsed. Had Simmons still been with the Phillies, they might not have collapsed.

"We were fortunate because we thought the Phillies were in," Curt said. "We were just trying to finish second. We were playing good ball, but the Phillies had a lead of six and a half games with 12 to go. We just happened to slide in because the Phillies messed up."

During the 1966 season, Simmons was sold to the Chicago Cubs. Then in 1967, he was sold to the California Angels. At the end of the year, Curt retired.

Today, Curt is the general manager and part owner of the Limekiln Golf Course in Horsham Township. Robin Roberts is also a part owner.

Curt was the last of the Whiz Kids to retire from baseball. "I have no regrets, looking back over my career," he said. "Certainly there are things I would have done differently—get someone to cut the grass in my yard maybe—but I did the best I could. I tried hard and worked at it. I would have loved to have won more games. I was happy to have been up so long, but it probably wasn't as good as I hoped I would have done."

Based on their Phillies production, Simmons and Roberts are the seventh-winningest left-handed/right-handed pitching combination in baseball. Had Curt had fewer injuries and better luck, he might have won more than 250 games.

Curt Simmons Phillies Statistics

Year	W	L	SV	PCT	G	GS	CG	SH	IP	H	BB	SO	ERA
1947	1	0	0	1.000	1	1	1	0	9.0	5	6	9	1.00
1948	7	13	0	.350	31	22	7	0	170.0	169	108	86	4.87
1949	4	10	1	.286	38	14	2	0	131.1	133	55	83	4.59
1950	17	8	1	.680	31	27	11	2	214.2	178	88	146	3.40
1952	14	8	0	.636	28	28	15	6	201.1	170	70	141	2.82
1953	16	13	0	.552	32	30	19	4	238.0	211	82	138	3.21
1954	14	15	1	.483	34	33	21	3	253.0	226	98	125	2.81
1955	8	8	0	.500	25	22	3	0	130.0	148	50	58	4.92
1956	15	10	0	.600	33	27	14	0	198.0	186	65	88	3.36
1957	12	11	0	.522	32	29	9	2	212.0	214	50	92	3.44
1958	7	14	1	.333	29	27	7	1	168.1	196	40	78	4.39
1959	0	0	0	.000	7	0	0	0	10.0	16	0	4	4.50
1960	0	0	0	.000	4	2	0	0	4.0	13	6	4	18.00
Totals	115	110	4	.511	325	262	112	18	1,939.2	1,865	718	1,052	3.66

Forty-five

Dick Sisler

Home Run Hero in 1950 Pennant Race

by Skip Clayton

The date was Oct. 1, 1950, and Gene Kelly was broadcasting the Phillies-Brooklyn Dodgers game from Ebbets Field. Nearly everyone in and around Philadelphia was tuned in, hoping that the Whiz Kids could win this game and wrap up the National League pennant on the last day of the season.

Dick Sisler was at bat. Here are Kelly's words: "Count 1-and-2 on Dick Sisler . . . Score tied 1-1, top of the 10th, men at first and second . . . Now Newcombe decides to call time, a real tough moment for this big right-hander. Of course, Roberts had one, too, in that last of the ninth . . . One ball, two strikes, now Newcombe set, in the stretch, delivering, swinging. A fly ball, very, very deep to left field. Moving back, Abrams, way, way back. He can't get it—it's a home run. . . . Wow. A home run for Dick Sisler. The Phillies lead, 4-1. One out and Sisler gets a left-field home run, his 13th of the season. It just cleared the barrier in left field, 350 feet from home plate. Pandemonium breaks loose at Ebbets Field."

In the bottom of the 10th, Roberts set the Dodgers down in order and the Phillies won their first pennant in 35 years.

"I already had three hits in the game," he said. "I also had a slightly sprained wrist. I wasn't thinking about a home run at the time. I was just trying to hit the ball hard somewhere.

"Newcombe had almost struck me out on the pitch before because it was a bad ball and I almost swung at it. But he came back with almost the same pitch, and he got it in high over the plate. I just swung as hard as I could swing, hoping to make contact. Thank God the ball went out of the park.

"I had hit one like that earlier in the game, but the ball didn't go all the way to the wall and was caught. So I didn't know this ball was going to go in. I was hustling around the bases when I saw it drop in."

The home run is generally regarded as the most memorable hit in Phillies history. It touched off pandemonium in the streets of Philadelphia and launched the pennant-starved Phillies into the World Series against the New York Yankees.

For Sisler, it was obviously his greatest moment in baseball. Dick had an eight-year career in the major leagues, hitting .276 over that span with 55 home runs, 360 RBIs, and 302 runs. He had 720 total hits.

Sisler played four years in a Phillies uniform. He had come to the club in 1948 after serving nearly nine years in the St. Louis Cardinals organization.

Originally signed after attending Colgate University for one year, Sisler soon found himself in a delicate position after inking a Cardinals' pact in 1939. His father, George, had been one of the greatest players in baseball history. He had a career batting average of .340, and twice he batted over .400. The older Sisler was voted into the Hall of Fame in 1939.

"There was pressure on me because of my father," said Dick, whose brother Dave also played in the major leagues as a pitcher for seven years. "When I came up in the minor leagues and I would strike out, I would hear boos. I also heard, 'Your dad wouldn't have done that,' but I overcame that.

"When I got to the major leagues, it was a big honor, especially in my hometown. St. Louis was also where my dad played, although he was with the Browns. It was tough. I had to bear down all the time. As soon as the game started, I tried to forget the name of George Sisler. But there was always a lot of pressure."

By the time he reached St. Louis, Sisler had already spent four years in the minors and three more in the military. He hit .260 in 1946—his rookie year with the Cards.

The Cardinals not only won the pennant that year, but also captured the World Series in seven games. In the Series, Dick went hitless in two trips to the plate as a pinch-hitter.

In 1947, Sisler's average dropped to .203, as he played in only 46 games. Two weeks before the 1948 season got under way, he was traded to the Phillies for infielder Ralph LaPointe.

"I had told the Cardinals that I wanted to be traded because I wasn't playing in St. Louis," said Sisler. "I told them to trade me anywhere but Philadelphia. As it turned out, coming to Philadelphia was the greatest break I ever had."

Sisler came to the Phillies as a first baseman, although at the time, he could also play the outfield. The Phillies used him exclusively at first in 1948.

Dick had a good season, hitting .274 with 11 home runs and 56 RBIs.

Before the 1949 season began, the Phillies made a trade with the Chicago Cubs, acquiring first baseman Eddie Waitkus. He was a .300 hitter and easily the best fielder in the league at this position. Initially, Dick was relegated to a pinch-hitting role.

On June 15, Waitkus was shot by Ruth Ann Steinhagen in the Edgewater Beach Hotel in Chicago. Sisler went back to first, hit .289 for the season, and helped the Phillies move up to third place.

The following year, though, Waitkus pulled through, and when the Whiz Kids opened the 1950 season, Eddie was back at first. Sisler was moved to left field.

"I didn't feel any pressure on myself going back to first when Eddie got shot," said Sisler. "I did the best I could. When I moved to the outfield in 1950, it wasn't much of an adjustment."

Sisler batted .296, drove in 83 runs, and hit 13 homers. It was his best year in the majors.

When Sisler hit the homer against Brooklyn, his father was working for the Dodgers as a scout and was in the stands for the game. "I am sure he had mixed emotions because his son hit a homer against his ball club," Sisler said. "But I know he was awfully happy for me."

Nobody was happier, however, than the youthful Whiz Kids themselves.

"The Whiz Kids all got along together," Sisler continued. "We had good years together, perhaps our best years. The closeness of the ball club certainly helped us as a team. I think Eddie Sawyer contributed to that. Bob Carpenter had a lot to do with it, too."

After winning the pennant, the Phillies lost the World Series in four straight to the Yankees. As a team, the Phillies hit .203. The Yankees didn't exactly tear the cover off the ball with their .222 average.

"The World Series was anticlimactic," said Sisler, who managed one hit in 17 at-bats for a .059 average. "It just didn't work out. We enjoyed being in the series, but we were shot. All four games were close. Had we been healthier, we might have scored some runs."

The Phillies had a team earned run average of 2.27. But the Yankees' pitching staff was outstanding, with an earned run average of 0.73. The Phillies were not only tired and had pitching problems, but Andy Seminick was playing on a broken ankle, Bill Nicholson was in the hospital with diabetes, and Sisler had hurt his wrist in September.

Sisler batted .287 in 1951, but hit only eight home runs and drove in only 52 runs.

After the season, Dick was traded, along with Seminick, Niles Jordan, and Eddie Pellagrini, to the Cincinnati Reds for Smoky Burgess, Howie Fox, and Connie Ryan. Then one month into the 1952 season, Sisler was traded back to the Cardinals. That year, Dick hit only .256.

In 1953, Sisler played in only 32 games before being sent back to the minors with Columbus of the International League. He never returned to the majors as a player. But after spending three years in the Pacific Coast League with San Diego, he became a player-manager at Nashville in 1957 and 1958. After retiring as a player, he managed Nashville in 1959 and Seattle in 1960.

Dick joined Cincinnati as a coach under Fred Hutchinson in 1961. That season, the Reds captured their first pennant in 21 years.

Tragedy struck the Reds in 1964 when Hutchinson had to leave the team after it was discovered that he had lung cancer. Dick took over, but the Reds lost the pennant by one game, finishing in a tie for second with the Phillies. St. Louis won it on the last day of the season.

"That was the toughest job I ever had because I had to watch a good friend slowly die," recalled Sisler. "I had to take over his club, and we almost won it for him."

Hutchinson died on Nov. 12. Shortly afterward, Sisler was named the regular manager. The Reds finished fourth in 1965, behind Los Angeles, San Francisco, and Pittsburgh. At the end of the year, the Reds let Sisler go. His two-year record was 121-94.

Later he was a coach with St. Louis, San Diego, and the New York Mets. Then he joined the Yankees as a minor league hitting coach.

"It was a pleasure to be in baseball all these years in some capacity," Sisler said. "I loved the work, and I don't know what else I would do if I didn't do it."

If he hadn't hit that home run in 1950, there's no telling what the Phillies would have done either.

Dick Sisler died of pneumonia at the age of 78 in a nursing home in Nashville on Nov. 20, 1998.

Dick Sisler Phillies Statistics

Year	G	AB	R	H	2B	3B	HR	RBI	AVG	OBP	SLGP
1948	121	446	60	122	21	3	11	56	.274	.344	408
1949	121	412	62	119	19	6	7	50	.289	.333	.415
1950	141	523	79	155	29	4	13	83	.296	.373	.442
1951	125	428	42	123	20	5	8	52	.287	.351	.414
Totals	508	1,809	227	519	89	18	39	241	.287	.352	.421

Forty-six

Tony Taylor

One of the Phillies' Finest Infielders

by Skip Clayton

In the Phillies' 117-year history, few players have been as popular as Tony Taylor, the hustling Cuban infielder of the 1960s and 1970s.

Although he came to the club in a controversial trade that, at the time, drew the wrath of local fans, Taylor became a Philadelphia favorite during a career that lasted nearly 15 seasons with the Phillies.

He also became one of the finest second basemen in club history, and was so well liked by the organization that he stayed with it after his retirement as a player.

Taylor's career extended for 19 years altogether, including stints with the Chicago Cubs at the start and the Detroit Tigers near the end. He finished with a lifetime batting average of .261 with 2,007 hits, 1,005 runs, 598 RBIs, and 75 home runs.

With the Phillies, for whom he also hit .261, Taylor played more games (1,669) than anyone in club history except Mike Schmidt, Richie Ashburn, and Larry Bowa. Tony also ranks sixth in at-bats and 10th in hits on the team's all-time lists.

Taylor played all four infield positions and left field (18 games) for the Phillies. But his main position was second base. He is the Phils' all-time leader in games played at that position with 1,003.

Taylor's 53 pinch hits rank second on the Phils' all-time list, and his six steals of home are the most by a Phillies player since 1946.

A solid and dependable hitter, Taylor was also a fine fielder who led National League second basemen in fielding in 1963. In fact, it was a defensive play by Tony that was his most memorable play as a Philly.

It came in the fifth inning of Jim Bunning's perfect game in 1964. The New York Mets' Jesse Gonder lined a ball between first and second.

"The ball was going toward the hole," Taylor recalled. "I dove for it and dropped it, but kept it in front of me. Then I threw to first while on my knees. Gonder was a slow runner, and I got him by two steps."

The play saved Bunning's masterpiece. It also accomplished just what the pitcher had instructed his fielders to do.

"We were all keeping quiet about the game," Taylor said. "But I knew what he was doing. He said, 'All I want you guys to do is catch the ball, because I am pitching a perfect game.'"

In the beginning, Taylor wasn't that popular with the local fans. In fact, they were irate when the Phillies got him early in the 1960 season in a trade with the Chicago Cubs. The Phillies sent two well-liked players, first baseman Ed Bouchee and pitcher Don Cardwell, to the Cubs for Taylor and reserve catcher Cal Neeman.

Making the deal even more unpopular, Cardwell pitched a no-hitter against the St. Louis Cardinals two days after the trade.

The trade made sense, though, because the Phillies had two first basemen—Bouchee and Pancho Herrera—and, in an effort to keep both their bats in the lineup, the club was playing Herrera at second. The trade stabilized the Phillies' lineup, although it didn't make Tony too happy at first.

"I almost quit when I was traded to the Phillies," Taylor recalled. "The Cubs were the first team that I played for in the major leagues, and Ernie Banks treated me like I was his own son."

It didn't take long for Tony to win the hearts of local fans. Combining solid talent with a dashing style of play, Taylor hit .287 for the Phillies, stole 24 bases, and was named to the All-Star team. He stole home twice that year.

"Gene Mauch told me that whenever I could get a good jump, I had the green light," recalled Taylor. "I even had the green light to steal home. The pitchers didn't pay any attention to me."

Following his banner year with the Phillies, Taylor—who broke in with the Cubs in 1958—slipped the next two years at the plate to .250 and .259. The Phillies, meanwhile, finished last in 1961 for the fourth straight year, in the process, setting a major league record with 23 losses in a row.

Then, after climbing out of the basement in 1962, the Phillies seemed ready to become National League contenders.

"John Quinn made some trades in 1960, getting Johnny Callison, Tony Gonzalez, and myself, and we struggled for two years," said Taylor. "We had a young team, and we started to improve in 1963, winning 87 games and moving up to fourth. When we went to spring training in 1964, everybody knew we were going to win a lot of games."

Unfortunately, the Phillies, after leading the league most of the summer, blew a 6 1/2-game lead with 12 games left to play, losing 10 straight games and finally finishing tied for second.

"We never thought something like that could happen to us," Taylor said. "We played great, we had a lot of fun, and the team was a family.

"The game that hurt us the most," he added, "was the first of 10 in a row that we lost. Chico Ruiz stole home off Art Mahaffey, and we lost, 1-0. Everything seemed to go wrong afterward. It took a lot out of us.

"A lot of people said that Gene Mauch used Bunning and Short too often," Taylor said. "He knew that we had to win one game and I think he used them because he knew they could win. But looking back, I think we as a team lost the pennant. We made errors. People blame Gene for the loss of the 1964 pennant, but in my mind, we lost the pennant."

After having raised his average to .281 in 1963, Taylor fell back to .251 in 1964, then had five straight years in which his highest mark was .262 (1969). Along the way, the Phillies began using him at other positions, primarily third base.

"It wasn't a big adjustment to me, playing other positions," Taylor said. "I used to come to spring training every year, catch ground balls at first, second, short, and third. I would go to the outfield and catch flies. I was preparing myself in case something happened.

In 1970, Taylor started the season in left field. That was the Phillies' last year in Connie Mack Stadium. It was the only year that Taylor hit above .300 for the Phillies (.301). Tony also hit the last grand slam at the old ballpark.

"I remember it well," Taylor said. "Mike Davison was pitching for the Giants. I swung and missed the first pitch he threw to me. I never used to hit that many homers.

"I told the catcher, Dick Dietz, that I missed my pitch. He asked me if I would like to have it back. I told him, 'Yes.' He told me to be ready. You figure you aren't getting it back, but he threw the same pitch that I had missed before, a slider, and I hit it out. That was a great thrill."

It was the ultimate grand slam, as Tony hit it to win the game in the bottom of the 9th with the Phillies trailing by three runs.

In 1971, the Phillies traded Taylor to the Tigers for minor league pitchers Mike Fremuth and Carl Cavanaugh.

"That was a sad day because I played here so long," remembered Taylor. "I never thought they would trade me."

Taylor played two and a half seasons in Detroit, hitting .303 in 1972 and helping the Tigers win their division title. But he was released after the 1973 campaign.

"When I left the Phillies, Bob Carpenter had said that I could come back," Taylor added. "After the 1973 season, I asked the Phillies if they wanted me back. They said, 'Yes.' I was always thankful to the Carpenter family because they said, 'You will always have a job here.'"

Taylor spent three more seasons with the Phillies, mostly as a pinch hitter. Near the end of the 1975 season, he got his 2,000th career hit.

Toward the end of the 1976 season, as he neared 41, Taylor was made a coach. He stayed a coach with the Phillies through 1979. He then became a minor league instructor for three years (1980, 1981, 1984) and a minor league manager (1982-83, 1985-87).

Taylor had developed an excellent reputation as a teacher of young players and had helped many in the Phillies' system.

Taylor returned to the Phillies in 1988 as a coach and stayed for two years.

From 1990 to 1992, Taylor worked for the San Francisco Giants in their minor league organization as a hitting and infield instructor before joining the Florida Marlins. For six years, he was the club's minor league infield coordinator before becoming the Marlins' infield coach in 1999.

Having Tony in your organization, whether it was as a player, a coach, or an instructor in the farm system, was a big plus.

Tony Taylor Phillies Statistics

Year	G	AB	R	H	2B	3B	HR	RBI	AVG	OBP	SLGP
1960	127	505	66	145	22	4	4	35	.287	.330	.370
1961	106	400	47	100	17	3	2	26	.250	.304	.322
1962	152	625	87	162	21	5	7	43	.259	.336	.342
1963	157	640	102	180	20	10	5	49	.281	.330	.367
1964	154	570	62	143	13	6	4	46	.251	.320	.316
1965	106	323	41	74	14	3	3	27	.229	.302	.319
1966	125	434	47	105	14	8	5	40	.242	.294	.346
1967	132	462	55	110	16	6	2	34	.238	.308	.312
1968	145	547	59	137	20	2	3	38	.250	.302	.311
1969	138	557	68	146	24	5	3	30	.262	.317	.339
1970	124	439	74	132	26	9	9	55	.301	.374	.462
1971	36	107	9	25	2	1	1	5	.234	.291	.299
1974	62	64	5	21	4	0	2	13	.328	.389	.484
1975	79	103	13	25	5	1	1	17	.243	.350	.340
1976	26	23	2	6	1	0	0	3	.261	.320	.304
Totals	1,669	5,799	737	1,511	219	63	51	461	.261	.322	.346

Forty-seven

Eddie Waitkus

The Slick-Fielding First Baseman
Who Came Back from a Shooting Incident

by Skip Clayton

Baseball being the hazardous occupation it is, injuries will happen. Sprained ankles, broken legs, torn rotator cuffs, and many other blows to the body keep players out of action for weeks or months. Sometimes they find their careers in jeopardy.

Off-field accidents also happen. What befell Phillies first baseman Eddie Waitkus in 1949 threatened not just his career but his life. The miracle was that Waitkus recovered and continued a fine big-league career.

In one long stay with the Phils and a brief stint later, Waitkus played in 613 games. He batted .281. He also played with the Chicago Cubs and the Baltimore Orioles. His lifetime batting average was .285 with 24 home runs and 373 RBIs. In 4,254 trips to the plate, he struck out only 204 times. His on-base percentage was .344.

Waitkus arrived in Philadelphia after the 1948 season when the Phillies traded pitchers Dutch Leonard and Monk Dubiel to the Cubs for pitcher Hank Borowy and Waitkus.

On June 12, 1949, the Phils were 28-25 and only 4 1/2 games out of first. Waitkus was hitting .307 when the club took off on its second western trip of the season.

First stop was Chicago, where the Phillies beat the Cubs, 9-2, in the opener as Waitkus picked up a hit in four at-bats. His average was .306. Nobody knew then that he had played his final game of 1949.

The Phillies were staying at the Edgewater Beach Hotel. That evening, Waitkus got a note from a 19-year-old stenographer named Ruth Ann Steinhagen saying that she had to see him in her room.

Steinhagen turned out to be a crazed woman who had a crush on Waitkus since he first played ball in Chicago. She pulled a .22 rifle out of a closet and shot him.

The bullet passed through a lung and stopped in the heavy muscular part of Waitkus' back near his spine. (The book *The Natural*, which later became a movie, was based on the incident.)

"It was shocking and we were stunned," said Richie Ashburn, then the club's starting center fielder. "We went out to dinner that night, all of us. They told us as a group, and the Chicago police were involved. They thought somebody might want to wipe us all out."

To pull Waitkus through, Phillies owner Bob Carpenter called for the best doctors. It took five operations.

Two months after the shooting, Waitkus was honored with a night at Shibe Park. He was also selected to the 1949 National League All-Star team.

Waitkus spent the winter of 1949-50 with trainer Frank Wiechec in Clearwater, getting back in shape. He had weighed 179 but dropped to 145, his low point after the shooting. Yet, when 1950 rolled around, Waitkus was in uniform.

Dick Sisler finished out the 1949 season at first base, but on opening day in 1950, Waitkus was at first base and Sisler was in left field. In the season opener against the Dodgers, Eddie had three hits in five at-bats as the Phillies beat Brooklyn, 9-1.

Waitkus came back strong in 1950. He hit .284 and led the league with 143 singles. He also led all first basemen in putouts with 1,387 and set a club record for most double plays at first base (142). He played 154 of the club's 157 games, missing three when he injured his finger in May. In only four games did he go less than the distance.

"As a fielder, he was a magician with the glove," said Ashburn. "He always picked the ball clean."

"With a good-fielding first baseman like Eddie," said Granny Hamner, "you very seldom threw the ball away, because you weren't trying to keep it out of the dirt. We didn't have to worry too much about throwing the ball into the dirt, and with the young infield that we had, especially the club that won the pennant in 1950, this was quite important.

"Sometimes we would hurry too much and make a mistake that young players would make. But as long as we didn't throw it too high, Eddie would come up with it. This was a great asset to an infielder, believe me."

On the last day of the 1950 season, the Phillies captured the pennant. They beat Brooklyn in 10 innings, 4-1, at Ebbets Field on Dick Sisler's three-run homer. Winning pitcher Robin Roberts led off the 10th with a single, and Waitkus followed with a single, sending Robbie to second.

Ashburn, who had saved the game in the ninth when he threw out Cal Abrams at the plate, bunted into a force at third. Sisler homered, scoring Waitkus with what turned out to be the winning run. Roberts got the first two batters in the 10th. Then Tommy Brown hit a foul ball on the first-base side. Waitkus camped under it. "I'll always remember that last out," Waitkus said. "When the ball was coming down, I said to myself, 'If I drop this, I'm going to bury myself right here in a hole by first base.'"

The World Series was a different story. The Phillies lost four straight to the Yankees, three by one run. Waitkus played in all four games and hit .267.

With Curt Simmons in the National Guard for all of 1951 (he had also missed one month of 1950), the Phillies dropped to fifth. Waitkus hit only .257.

At Shibe Park on the last day of the 1951 season, Waitkus almost prevented the Dodgers from tying the New York Giants for first place. With the bases loaded and two outs in the 12th, Waitkus hit a shot back through the middle. Jackie

Robinson leaped for it and then fell to the ground, holding onto the ball. Brooklyn won it in the 14th when Robinson homered, setting up a best-of-three playoff with the Giants that New York won on Bobby Thomson's homer in the bottom of the ninth in the third game, giving the Giants the pennant.

In 1952, Waitkus batted .289 and the Phillies finished fourth with an 87-67 record.

Before the 1953 season began, the Phillies acquired Earl Torgeson in a trade. Torgeson took over at first and Waitkus went to the bench, where he did mostly pinch-hitting. When Torgeson got hurt toward the end of June, Waitkus went back to first for six weeks. Over most of the final six weeks, the two took turns playing first. For the year—the last in Waitkus' first stretch with the Phils—Eddie batted .291.

Waitkus was born on Sept. 4, 1919, in Cambridge, Mass. After graduating from high school, Waitkus signed with the Cubs when he was 18. He also spent a year at Boston College and spoke three foreign languages.

Waitkus spent the 1939 and 1940 seasons in the minors. Chicago brought him up in 1941, but he hit only .179 in 12 games. He went to Tulsa, where he hit .293. The 1942 season was his best in the minors. He batted .336 in Los Angeles in the Pacific Coast League.

For the next three years, Waitkus served in the Army. He manned a machine gun on several beachheads in the Pacific, earning several battle stars and returning home without having been wounded.

In 1946, Waitkus rejoined the Cubs. He took over first base for the next three years. Waitkus hit .304 in 1946 and followed up the next two years with averages of .292 and .295. Then came the trade to the Phillies and his five-year tenure, ending in 1954.

On March 16, during spring training that year, the Phillies sold Waitkus to Baltimore. Torgeson would be the Phillies' first baseman in 1954. Waitkus became the Orioles' first baseman and hit .283.

During the 1955 season, he returned to the Phillies for the final two months. In 33 games at first, he hit .280. He retired at the end of the year. Waitkus died on Sept. 15, 1972, at age 53.

"For a number of years," said Sawyer, "Eddie was probably the greatest-fielding first baseman in the National League. He was the greatest at taking the ball off the runner, and very seldom did you see him make a bad throw. He made it look so easy. He could handle a glove better than anybody I ever had play for me."

When the Phillies' all-time team was selected in 1969, Waitkus was picked as the best first baseman.

Eddie Waitkus Phillies Statistics

Year	G	AB	R	H	2B	3B	HR	RBI	AVG	OBP	SLGP
1949	54	209	41	64	16	3	1	28	.306	.403	.426
1950	154	641	102	182	32	5	2	44	.284	.341	.359
1951	145	610	65	157	27	4	1	46	.257	.317	.320
1952	146	499	51	144	29	4	2	49	.289	.371	.375
1953	81	247	24	72	9	2	1	16	.291	.330	.330
1955	33	107	10	30	5	0	2	14	.280	.379	.383
Totals	**613**	**2,313**	**293**	**649**	**118**	**18**	**9**	**197**	**.281**	**.348**	**.361**

Forty-eight

Bill White

Phillies' Only First-Base Gold Glove Winner

by Skip Clayton

Over the years, the Phillies have been blessed with an abundance of outstanding first basemen who could field their position as well as anybody who played the game.

There was Mike McCormick, who set a National League record in 1946 for highest fielding percentage (.999) by a first baseman and most consecutive games (131) without an error.

Later, Eddie Waitkus, Marv Blaylock, Tommy Hutton, Willie Montanez, Pete Rose, and now Rico Brogna gave and are still giving the Phillies outstanding defense at first.

Since *The Sporting News* began awarding Gold Gloves in 1957, only one Phillies first baseman has captured the award. The honor went to Bill White in 1966.

White played for the Phillies for three seasons, arriving in Philadelphia in 1966. Although hampered by injuries after that season, White is still remembered for his fluid style and grace around the sack.

Bill could also hit. In 13 big-league seasons, beginning in 1956 and ending after the 1969 campaign, the smooth left-hander had a .286 lifetime batting average with 1,706 hits, 202 home runs, and 870 RBIs.

White's best years were with the St. Louis Cardinals. He played on the World Series-champion Redbird team in 1964. A member of five All-Star teams, White had his best year in 1962, when he hit .324.

Before joining the Phillies, White won Gold Gloves for six consecutive years, from 1960 to 1965. The Lakewood, Fla., native, who holds a degree in general science from Hiram (Ohio) College, had his best year with the Phillies the first season he was with the club. That year, he hit .276 with 22 homers and 103 RBIs.

White broke into the majors with the New York Giants. After the Giants signed him in 1953, he spent a little over three seasons in the minors playing at Danville, Sioux City, Dallas, and Minneapolis.

Bill was playing for Minneapolis of the American Association in 1956, but three weeks into the season, the Giants called him up to take over at first in place of the slumping Gail Harris. At the time, New York was playing the Cardinals in St. Louis.

"I remember my first time at bat in the majors very well," said White. "The count was two-and-two. Ben Flowers threw a pitch that I thought was a third strike. I started walking back to the dugout, but the umpire called it a ball. On the next pitch, I hit a homer."

On Bill's second trip to the plate, he missed hitting another homer by just two feet. He had to settle for a double, which drove in two runs.

White finished his rookie season with a .256 average, driving in 59 runs and hitting 22 homers. He spent the 1957 season in the service, then returned to the Giants late in 1958 after the club had moved to San Francisco. By that time, the Giants had installed another youngster, Orlando Cepeda, at first base. Before the next season, White was traded to the Cardinals with infielder Ray Jablonski for pitchers Don Choate and Sam Jones. White played in St. Louis for seven years. His two biggest days with the Cardinals came on July 17-18, 1961, when in a pair of twin bills, he had 14 hits in 18 trips to the plate, tying a record set by Ty Cobb in 1912.

The year the Cards won the pennant was the year the Phillies blew a 6 1/2-game lead with 12 games to play.

"I didn't think we had a chance with two weeks to go," said White. "But the Phillies had been playing over their heads. Gene Mauch did a good job managing, moving people around. But it is hard to win with the people that they had. We had gotten Lou Brock that year, and we wouldn't have won if we hadn't gotten him."

The Cards went on to win the World Series against the Yankees. But White was gone after the 1965 season. St. Louis traded him to the Phillies, along with Dick Groat and Bob Uecker, for Art Mahaffey, Alex Johnson, and Pat Corrales.

The Phillies knew when they picked up White that they were receiving a topflight first baseman. But White wasn't so happy.

"I didn't like the trade to the Phillies," he said. "I didn't want to come to Philadelphia. Connie Mack Stadium was an old ballpark, and it wasn't a good park. The fans were tough, and I didn't want to go through that. But if you hustled, they didn't bother you. As it turned out, I don't believe I was ever booed in this town. If you give the fans their money's worth, they appreciate it."

White learned to like Philadelphia so well that he moved to the area in 1968 and still makes his home in Bucks County. "The town has been good to me," he said.

After coming close in 1964, the Phillies dropped to sixth place in 1965. With a stronger club, bolstered by a number of veteran players, the Phillies were contenders for the flag in 1966. They moved up to fourth with an 87-75 record.

"I felt we should have won with that club," White said. "We had an All-Star at almost every position. It was a good ball club. I felt it was the best ball club I ever played on. If Richie Allen hadn't gotten hurt and been out a month, and if Johnny Callison had a Callison year, I think we would have won the pennant. Allen and I drove in more than 100 runs. Callison had been driving in 100, but he drove in only 55."

On the final day of the season, the Dodgers were battling for the flag with the Giants, who trailed Los Angeles by one game.

"We beat the Dodgers and [Don] Drysdale in the first game Sunday," said White. "They had to start Sandy Koufax in the second game and they beat us, 6-3, and won the pennant. We got three runs in the ninth, but they were already six runs ahead. Koufax was tough. You could see the ball, but you couldn't hit him."

Koufax's win turned out to be his last regular-season game. White was the last player to get a hit off the future Hall of Famer in a regular-season game, when he hit a double in the ninth off the right-field wall. The hit drove in two runs.

"Bob Gibson, who had been my roommate at St. Louis before I came to the Phillies, was also tough," added White. "The first time I ever faced him, after I came to the Phillies, he hit me. He just wanted to let me know who was the boss.

"Don Newcombe did the same thing to me in my rookie year. He would knock me down. Then, after the game, he would invite me over for dinner.

"One of my favorite stories occurred when I first faced Newcombe. I was digging in," continued White. "Roy Campanella said, 'What are you doing?' Sure enough, the first pitch Newcombe threw knocked me down. All Campy said was, 'Big Newk don't like it when you dig in.'"

Before the 1967 season, Bill got hurt. "I hurt my Achilles tendon in December playing racquetball," he remembered. "I had played for 10 years and it kept me in shape. When I snapped the Achilles tendon, I should have gone into broadcasting permanently.

"But John Quinn talked me into playing one more year with the Phillies. It turned into two, then I returned to play with the Cardinals in 1969.

"I couldn't play anymore. I hadn't wanted to play much past 35. Before I got hurt, I was looking for something to do, and broadcasting came along. Before I left Philadelphia, I was doing the pregame show on television before the Phillies games."

Bill played in only 110 games in 1967 as the Phillies dropped to fifth. He hit .250 with eight homers and drove in just 33 runs in 308 times at bat.

The 1968 season wasn't any better. White's average fell to .239 with nine homers and 40 RBIs. Right before the beginning of the 1969 season, the Phillies traded White back to the Cardinals for Jerry Buchek and Jim Hutto. He played that year, then retired. Afterward, he returned to broadcasting, this time on a full-time basis.

In 1971, White joined the New York Yankees as a broadcaster. He held that job through the 1988 season and became the President of the National League on April 1, 1989, succeeding Bart Giamatti, who became the Commissioner of Baseball.

Bill, in addition to broadcasting Yankee games, had worked for ABC radio network covering the Winter Olympics. He had also done weekend sports for ABC in the off-season.

Today, Bill is retired. He stepped down as NL president on March 1, 1994. His last act was to present the Phillies with their 1993 National League championship rings.

White became a member of the Veterans Committee in 1994 that meets once a year to select new Hall of Famers. Whether it was as a player, a broadcaster, or an executive, Bill always did an outstanding job.

Bill White Phillies Statistics

Year	G	AB	R	H	2B	3B	HR	RBI	AVG	OBP	SLGP
1966	159	577	85	159	23	6	22	103	.276	.352	.451
1967	110	308	29	77	6	2	8	33	.250	.359	.360
1968	127	385	34	92	16	2	9	40	.239	.309	.361
Totals	396	1,270	148	328	45	10	39	176	.258	.341	.402

Forty-nine

Pinky Whitney

One of the Phillies' Finest Third Basemen

by Skip Clayton

Since the first All-Star game was played in 1933, the Phillies have had four starting third basemen on the National League team.

Willie Jones, Dick Allen, and Mike Schmidt have carried the Phillies banner from 1949 to 1989, but the first one to do it was Arthur "Pinky" Whitney, a good-hitting, good-fielding third sacker who played 10 seasons with the Phillies.

The 5-10, 165-pound Whitney is easily one of the top third basemen in Phillies history. His league's All-Star third baseman in 1936, the San Antonio, Tex., native was the captain and one of the mainstays of the Phillies during two stints with the team.

Playing with the Phillies in 1928-33 and 1936-39, Whitney batted .307, ninth best in the club's history, and drove in 734 runs, 10th best on the Phils' all-time list. He played more games at third base (1,076) than anyone except Schmidt and Jones, and his .982 fielding average in 1937 ranks as the best in the team's hot-corner history.

During his 12-year career, in which he also played for the Boston Bees, Whitney posted a lifetime batting average of .295 with 93 home runs, 927 RBIs, and 696 runs. He had 1,701 hits, including 303 doubles in 1,539 games.

Whitney drove in more than 100 runs four times while he was with the Phillies. He hit over .300 four times, too, including a high of .342 in 1930.

"After I retired from baseball, I had a bowling alley for 12 years," Whitney said. "Then I left that and went to work for the Lone Star Brewing Co. When I became semiretired, I worked for the San Antonio Spurs of the NBA and the San Antonio Dodgers of the Texas League. I took care of the entrance for the media."

If he took care of the press gate as effectively as he handled third base for the Phillies, there weren't any gate crashers in San Antonio.

While he was with the Phillies, Whitney was a member of one of the heaviest-hitting outfits in the majors. Along with Chuck Klein, Don Hurst, Lefty O'Doul, and others, Whitney and the Phils regularly peppered enemy pitching, once compiling a team batting average of .315, which is still a club record.

"Chuck Klein was a great player," Whitney recalled. "I roomed with him for eight years. He could run, throw, and hit.

"In batting practice, Chuck was Babe Ruth. He would put them over the right-field fence out on Broad Street, and some of them went down into the Reading Station [across Broad Street]."

Klein and Whitney joined the Phillies the same year (1928).

"I was originally signed by the Cleveland Indians," Whitney recalled. "They gave me $2,500 to sign a contract. I played the 1925 and the 1926 seasons in

Decatur, Ill. The following year, I went to New Orleans in the Southern League. Cleveland had me there. After the 1927 season, Philadelphia drafted me."

Pinky hit .301 in his rookie year with the Phillies in 1928 with 10 homers and 103 RBIs, still the club record for a rookie. He also tied the rookie record, at the time, for the most doubles in a season (35).

The 1929 Phillies set a team record with 153 home runs, and their team batting average was a league-leading .309. Pinky hit .327 with eight homers and 115 RBIs. He also established the club record for third basemen for most doubles in a season with 43—which held up until Scott Rolen hit 45 in 1998—and most triples with 14.

Whitney had 200 hits. That year, the Phillies set the National League record for most players on a team with 200 or more hits in a season. Lefty O'Doul led the league with a record-setting 254, followed by Chuck Klein with 219, and Fresco Thompson with 202.

On defense, Pinky set the club record for the most assists in a season by a third baseman with 333. The mark held up until Mike Schmidt registered 404 assists while setting the National League record in 1974.

In Whitney's era, the City Series between the Phillies and the A's was a major event. And in 1930, although the A's had won the 1929 World Series, the Phillies stunned baseball fans by capturing the City Series, three games to two. The Phillies also won the City Series in 1931 and 1932, and each time, the A's had won the pennant the preceding year and the World Series in 1930.

"There was a lot of competition between the two clubs," recalled Whitney. "We used to have that City Series every spring before the regular season began. It was played at both parks, and both teams kept the regular ball club in the games."

The 1930 Phillies set all kinds of club records: highest team batting average (.315), most runs scored (944), most hits (1,873), and most total bases (2,594). Despite such records, the Phillies fell to last place. The team earned run average was 6.71, and hitters' battles at Baker Bowl were the rule rather than the exception.

"We didn't have any pitching that year," said Whitney. "We got Grover Alexander back that year, but he was past his prime."

Whitney set the club record that year for highest batting average in a season by a third baseman, batting .342 with 207 hits. For the third straight year, he went over the century mark in runs batted in with 117.

"We had some great hitters," Whitney said. "Lefty O'Doul was a great hitter. Don Hurst could hit. Tommy Thevenow wasn't a bad hitter. Our catcher, Spud Davis, was a good hitter. Denny Sothern, who hit .300 and played center, was overshadowed by O'Doul and Klein.

"That was also the last year that Cy Williams played here," Whitney added. "Cy could pull the ball. He was a good player. When he batted, the shortstop played second and they would pull the infield around to the first-base side. The third baseman would play shortstop every time that Cy came to bat. Cy wouldn't bunt down third. If he did, he could have walked to first base. He tried to hit the ball through them. They had the shift on him way before Ted Williams. Sometimes they would pull a shift on Klein, but one not quite as extreme as the one they pulled on Cy Williams. He was mostly a right-field hitter, but he could hit the ball to left-center."

In 1931, Pinky's average dropped to .287 and his runs batted in dropped to 74 as the Phillies moved up to sixth.

The Phillies finished fourth in 1932, their highest finish since they placed second in 1917.

Whitney hit .298, and his 124 runs batted in are still the most by a Phillies third baseman in a season. He also led the league in fielding.

On June 17, the following year, Pinky, who was hitting .264, was traded to the Boston Bees along with outfielder Hal Lee. In return, the Phillies got outfielder Wes Schulmerich, infielder Fritz Knothe, and cash. Pinky would be traded back early in the 1936 season for Mickey Haslin.

"I got to play with Babe Ruth in Boston," Whitney said. "I hit in back of him in the lineup. In batting practice, he would hit 10 or 12 balls out of the park. He certainly brought people into the park."

Whitney checked in with a .284 mark and a spot on the All-Star team the year he returned to the Phillies.

"That year was the first time that the National League beat the American League," Whitney reminded. "We beat them in Braves Field, 4-3."

Whitney went 1-for-3 and drove in a run for the Nationals. He also broke his thumb in the game. "But I was very happy to make the team. It was quite an honor," he said.

In 1937, a year in which Whitney led the National League in fielding, he also established the club record for highest fielding percentage by a third baseman that year.

At the plate, Whitney had his second-highest batting average of his career, hitting a lusty .341.

Whitney hit .277 in 1938, but that was to be his last year as a regular. In 1939, Pinky May took over at third and Whitney got into only 34 games. His average fell to .187, and he retired at the end of the season.

Whitney had many other fond memories as he looked back on his outstanding career.

"I enjoyed my years in Philadelphia," he said. "In fact, when I was traded back to the Phillies, I was very happy. The fans always treated me good in Philadelphia."

Pinky Whitney died Sept. 1, 1987, at the age of 82. He certainly was one of the best third basemen in Phillies history.

Pinky Whitney Phillies Statistics

Year	G	AB	R	H	2B	3B	HR	RBI	AVG	OBP	SLGP
1928	151	585	73	176	35	4	10	103	.301	.342	.426
1929	154	612	89	200	43	14	8	115	.327	.390	.482
1930	149	606	87	207	41	5	8	117	.342	.383	.465
1931	130	501	64	144	36	5	9	74	.287	.331	.443
1932	154	624	93	186	33	11	13	124	.298	.335	.449
1933	31	121	12	32	4	0	3	19	.264	.310	.372
1936	114	411	44	121	17	3	6	59	.294	.354	.394
1937	138	487	56	166	19	4	8	79	.341	.395	.446
1938	102	300	27	83	9	1	3	38	.277	.336	.443
1939	34	75	9	14	0	1	1	6	.187	.263	.253
Totals	**1,157**	**4,322**	**554**	**1,329**	**237**	**48**	**69**	**734**	**.307**	**.357**	**.432**

Fifty

Rick Wise

Young Hurler Had Phillies' No-Hit Game

by Skip Clayton

E verybody remembers the first game of a doubleheader in 1964 in which Jim Bunning pitched a perfect game for the Phillies against the New York Mets. But only the most trivia-minded fans recall who hurled the second game.

The record shows that it was an 18-year-old rookie by the name of Rick Wise. And not only did Wise pitch six innings and allow just three hits, he got the win—the first in his career—as the Phillies triumphed, 8-2.

Wise went on to win a total of 188 major league games (losing 181) during a 17-year career. He also tossed a no-hitter of his own in 1971.

Rick was an outstanding moundsman who spent all or parts of seven seasons with the Phillies. During that time, he posted a 75-76 record. From a local stand-point, though, he may be best remembered as the guy the club gave up to get Steve Carlton from the St. Louis Cardinals.

A hard-throwing, 6-2 right-hander, Wise a native of Jackson, Mich., broke into organized baseball in 1963 with Bakersfield of the California League. He posted a 6-3 record with a 2.63 ERA in 12 games.

Despite his inexperience, Wise had signed a big bonus and was required to stay with the Phillies in 1964 (because of the bonus rule then in effect). Thus, the young hurler came to be on the Shea Stadium mound on that June 21 day, after Bunning had pitched his perfect game. He remembers it well.

"I was more involved in Jim's game than I was worrying about my own game," recalled Wise. "I was in the clubhouse when Bunning was pitching. It was Father's Day.

"After the game, all of the players and writers swarmed into the clubhouse. I had a tough time finding a ball and getting somebody to warm me up.

"I didn't feel any pressure. I was nervous, as I normally was before a game. But I wanted to do well.

"A funny thing happened about the fourth inning or so. They hadn't had a hit off me, when I walked a guy. The Mets fans went really wild. All of a sudden, the whole crowd got up and started roaring. That was the first Mets runner of the day."

Being an 18-year-old pitcher in the big leagues was not easy for Wise. "There were problems," he said. "First, I had to be there because of the bonus rule. Also, being a long way from home and not knowing anyone made problems at the time. The previous year, I was in high school and the minors, and then all of a sudden, I was with the Phillies. I had confidence in my ability, and I tried to do the best I could when I got the chance.

"I was playing for one of the really smart managers, Gene Mauch, and I learned a lot about strategy. Of course, there are some people who say that he wasn't so smart at the end of 1964. I was just so caught up with being in a pennant race that I tried to help the club any way I could. It was such a fun year because we weren't picked to win. It was a great year until that collapse in the final two weeks."

In 1964, Rick got into 25 games and posted a 5-3 record.

Wise went back to the minors in 1965. In 1966, Wise was in the service and missed most of spring training. Then, he was sent to San Diego, the Phillies' Triple-A farm team.

He was recalled on June 1, 1966, and went on to post a 5-6 record.

Wise started the 1967 season in the bullpen, but was back in the starting rotation after two months. His record was only 2-6 on July 1, but he went 9-5 the rest of the way to finish at 11-11.

"It's a two-way street when you get sent to the bullpen," Wise said. "If you get where you can correct your mistakes and the problems you are having, great. But if you go to the bullpen and sit and sit, you get rusty, you lose your confidence, and it's hard to look good. Every time out, you feel you have to look good so the manager will put you back in the rotation."

With the Phillies dropping from fifth in 1967 to a tie for seventh in 1968, Wise's record slipped to 9-15. Because of military obligations, Wise missed several starts and found it difficult to get rolling.

"The veteran players always helped me in my career," said Wise. "Larry Jackson helped me a lot, and so did the everyday players—Cookie Rojas, Tony Taylor, and Bobby Wine.

"You learn a little bit every year. It is a learning process until you retire. And the more you retain, the quicker you put someone else's knowledge and your own ability to good use, the longer you stay around. If you don't do that, you are not going to stay around too long."

In 1969, Rick posted a 15-13 record, although the Phillies were 63-99. The following season, Wise was 13-14 as the Phillies finished their last season in Connie Mack Stadium.

When the Phillies moved into Veterans Stadium in 1971, Wise had his best year. His record was 17-14 with a 2.88 ERA. He hit .237 with six homers, which set a Phillies record for most homers in a season by a pitcher. (His 11 career homers with the Phillies set a club record for pitchers, since tied by Larry Christenson.)

On June 23, Wise hurled a no-hitter against the Cincinnati Reds in Riverfront Stadium. Rick walked only one and struck out three, while becoming the first pitcher to hurl a no-hitter and at the same time hit two home runs in the same game. Wise retired Pete Rose for the final out in the ninth.

"In retrospect, that really makes the no-hitter something special, now that Pete has the all-time hit record," he said. "I have always respected him.

"The thing I remember most about the no-hitter was, I didn't feel good that day. It was extremely humid and about 95 or 96 degrees at game time. We weren't exactly knocking the baseball world on its collective ear. We were struggling. Although I was having a good year, we were losing two out of three. Cincinnati was a formidable opponent.

"I didn't feel good warming up. I was wild, and I had doubts, but after I crossed the line and took my position on the mound and the game started rolling along, there was kind of a snowball effect. I got stronger and better. There were some nice plays early in the game, but going into the eighth and ninth innings, I knew I had a shot at a no-hitter. I felt strong and I was going to go for it; there was no doubt about that."

Wise lost his bid for a perfect game in the sixth inning when he walked Dave Concepcion. Eventually, he threw 95 pitches. The Phillies picked up one run in the second, then Rick hit a two-run homer off Ross Grimsley in the fifth and a solo homer in the eighth off Clay Carroll.

"I took a lot of pride in my hitting, and it helped the club win a lot of games," Wise recalled. "It kept me in games longer than some of the other pitchers who couldn't hit as well because they would be lifted for pinch hitters. All it meant to me was that it put more runs on the scoreboard for the Phillies."

Rick hit two homers in another game in 1971. One was a grand slam. The Phillies beat the Giants at Veterans Stadium, 7-3.

"I hit the grand-slam homer off a tough competitor, Don McMahon," recalled Wise. "The game was tied, 3-3, when I hit it. I fouled off a couple of high sliders, then got a high slider and drove it out."

Wise had another outstanding pitching and batting performance that year. It came against the Chicago Cubs at the Vet. He won, 4-3, in 12 innings, driving in the winning run with a single. At one point during the game, Rick retired 32 in a row, second best in National League history to Harvey Haddix, who retired 36 straight with the Pirates against the Milwaukee Braves in 1959.

On Feb. 25, 1972, Wise was traded to the Cardinals for Carlton. "I was shocked at the trade to St. Louis," recalled Wise.

"I finally had come into my own and was the ace of the staff. I worked hard to earn those credentials, but I had a contract hassle at the time.

"There were no agents, no trade clauses. It was me against John Quinn. I was only making $30,000 a year after seven years in the big leagues. I wanted more money, and, to be quite frank, I think I deserved it. I guess Steve had the same problem in St. Louis with August Busch.

"The darnedest thing happened. We got traded, and we both got what we wanted from our new clubs. It was within a couple of thousand dollars of what each of us wanted."

Rick went on to pitch with St. Louis for two years, then played for the Boston Red Sox, Cleveland Indians, and San Diego Padres before retiring in 1982. His biggest year was 1975, when he was 19-12 with the Red Sox. He was the winning pitcher in the sixth game of the World Series when Carlton Fisk hit his dramatic homer to win it for the Red Sox, 4-3, in 12 innings.

Rick has stayed in the game as a minor league pitching coach and is currently working for the Anaheim Angels' Triple-A farm team in Edmonton.

Rick Wise Phillies Statistics

Year	W	L	SV	PCT	G	GS	CG	SH	IP	H	BB	SO	ERA
1964	5	3	0	.625	25	8	0	0	69.0	78	25	39	4.04
1966	5	6	0	.455	22	13	3	0	99.1	100	24	58	3.72
1967	11	11	0	.500	36	25	6	3	181.1	177	45	111	3.28
1968	9	15	0	.375	30	30	7	1	182.0	210	37	97	4.55
1969	15	13	0	.536	33	31	14	4	220.0	215	61	144	3.23
1970	13	14	0	.481	35	34	5	1	220.1	253	65	113	4.17
1971	17	14	0	.548	38	37	17	4	272.1	261	70	155	2.88
Total	**75**	**76**	**0**	**.497**	**219**	**178**	**52**	**13**	**1,244.1**	**1,294**	**327**	**717**	**3.60**

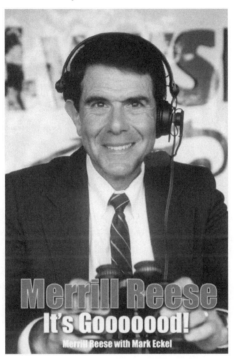